D0971519

69

DATE DUE

ILL 4/2</18			
GAYLORD			PRINTED IN U.S.A

STRONG WOMEN, DEEP CLOSETS

Lesbians and Homophobia in Sport

Pat Griffin, EdD

University of Massachusetts

Human Kinetics

Library of Congress Cataloging-in-Publication Data

Griffin, Pat.
  Strong women, deep closets : lesbians and homophobia in sport /
Pat Griffin.
    p.   cm.
  Includes bibliographical references (p.   ) and index.
  ISBN 0-88011-729-X
  1. Lesbian athletes.   2. Homophobia in sports.   I. Title.
GV708.8.G75   1998
796'.086'643--dc21   97-32363
                                                                CIP

ISBN: 0-88011-729-X

Copyright © 1998 by Pat Griffin

Acquisitions Editor: Becky Lane; **Developmental Editor:** Kristine Enderle; **Assistant Editor:** Laura Hambly; **Copyeditor:** Karen Bojda; **Proofreader:** Jennifer Stallard; **Indexer:** Joan Griffitts; **Graphic Designer:** Robert Reuther; **Graphic Artist:** Denise Lowry; **Photo Editor:** Boyd LaFoon; **Cover Designer:** Jack Davis; **Photographer (cover):** The Stock Market/Michael Kevin Daly; **Printer:** United Graphics

Printed in the United States of America   10 9 8 7 6 5 4 3 2

Human Kinetics
Web site: http://www.humankinetics.com/

United States: Human Kinetics, P.O. Box 5076, Champaign, IL 61825-5076
1-800-747-4457
e-mail: humank@hkusa.com

Canada: Human Kinetics, 475 Devonshire Road, Unit 100, Windsor, ON N8Y 2L5
1-800-465-7301 (in Canada only)
e-mail: humank@hkcanada.com

Europe: Human Kinetics, P.O. Box IW14, Leeds LS16 6TR, United Kingdom
(44) 1132 781708
e-mail: humank@hkeurope.com

Australia: Human Kinetics, 57A Price Avenue, Lower Mitcham, South Australia 5062
(088) 277 1555
e-mail: humank@hkaustralia.com

New Zealand: Human Kinetics, P.O. Box 105-231, Auckland 1
(09) 523 3462
e-mail: humank@hknewz.com

For my mother, Augusta Scott Griffin,
who gave me roots and wings and taught me how to love.

Contents

Foreword

We know that any statement that imparts a specific characteristic to a group as a whole is false. Stereotypes are the product of ignorance and discriminatory bias. All of us should question the motive and intelligence of those who falsely generalize individual characteristics to large and diverse groups of people. There is no truth in:

- all football players are dumb;
- all African-Americans have rhythm;
- all white men can't jump;
- all Jews are wealthy but frugal; and
- all female athletes are lesbians.

It is unfortunate that there are those who still focus on defining the differences between groups of people rather than celebrating our commonality and the vast diversity among individuals. The use of stereotypes is most common among people who are unfamiliar with the groups they attempt to describe and, in many cases, fearful of that which they do not know. Those who use stereotypes seek to define a group in negative terms so they can declare themselves "better than." There is power in promulgating negative opinions about unfamiliar groups. Ultimately, the negative description is offered as proof that they are not worthy of displacing those in power.

Everyday, many coaches, athletic directors, athletes, and parents use their fears of homosexuality (homophobia) and unfair stereotyping of female athletes to keep young women from participating in sports or choosing to play for certain coaches and schools. Many people think that all women who play on varsity teams are lesbians. Parents might discourage their daughters from playing softball or basketball because they are "lesbian sports." Coaches might label another coach or a player as a lesbian. Or they might say that a certain school "allows" lesbians. Parents think they are "protecting" their daughters from lesbians. Coaches and athletic directors use such scare tactics in hopes of deterring athletes from rival schools, refusing to acknowledge that negative recruiting is unfair and ruthless. Some coaches believe this is just the extra "edge" they need and greedily build up their own recruit pool.

Other coaches, athletic directors, or school administrators feel threatened by Title IX and oppose this federal law guarantying women equal opportunity in sports. They may threaten to expose a woman coach as a lesbian or attach the lesbian stigma to her players. They may ask a candidate for an open coaching position if she is married. And if she is single, they assume she is a lesbian.

Whatever the reason, using sophomoric tactics like directly calling a woman athlete a lesbian or implying that women who play sports or those who play at a particular school are lesbians is unethical and hurtful. In addition, homophobia contributes to continuing, institutionalized sexism in society and blatant discrimination and prejudice against women athletes.

Strong Women, Deep Closets: Lesbians and Homophobia in Sport explores just that. It is a hip and spirited book exposing the ugly head of homophobia, discrimination, and sexism in sport and the diverse, real life perspectives of lesbians in sport. A combination of interviews, research findings, and historical accounts as well as personal narrative, brings such experiences in athletics to life.

The Women's Sports Foundation is also concerned with homophobia. Sports are too important to the physical, psychological, and sociological well-being of our daughters, sisters, and mothers for such tactics to be used to deter participation. Girls and women who play sports have more confidence, stronger self-images, and lower levels of depression. High school girls who play sports are less likely to be involved in unwanted pregnancies and more likely to earn higher grades and graduate from high school. As little as two hours of exercise a week reduces a teenage girl's risk of breast cancer, a disease that afflicts one out of every eight American women. Women who play sports also reduce their risks of heart disease. We need only look at generations of women who were denied the opportunity to play sports and discouraged from engaging in lifestyles where they were active and strong — our mothers and grandmothers — to see what happens when women are discouraged from participating in sports. One out of every two women over the age of 60 are suffering from osteoporosis. The combination of adequate calcium intake and weight-bearing exercise lays down bone mass that can prevent this condition.

We must all work against homophobia. We cannot allow others to use homophobia as a tool to scare women away from participating in sports. We cannot tolerate individuals or the media instilling unwarranted fears in parents and their daughters. Read *Strong Women, Deep Closets: Lesbians and Homophobia in Sport.* Work to ensure that women will play sports and benefit from all the positive and healthy experiences associated with athletic endeavors. We must not deny women their athleticism and physical strength. We must support our daughters', sisters', and mothers' quests for excellence on the court, in the arena, and in every facet of their lives.

Donna A. Lopiano, PhD
Executive Director
Women's Sports Foundation

Preface

Sports and lesbians have always gone together. If not overt, this association roils beneath the surface as a subtext of all discussions about women athletes and their appearance, prowess, and acceptability. Until recently, concerns about lesbian athletes and coaches simmered under a lid of silence or were camouflaged as concern about the femininity of women athletes. Articles about a woman athlete often devoted as much space describing her appearance as they did discussing her athleticism. Since the early 1980s, the association between lesbians and sport has become more openly discussed in the mainstream media. Every few years since then a news story about lesbians in sport captures public attention for a while and then fades away: Billie Jean King's acknowledgment of a seven-year lesbian relationship, Martina Navratilova's highly public legal battle with former partner Judy Nelson, Penn State women's basketball coach Rene Portland's "no lesbian" policy, and CBS sportscaster Ben Wright's comments about lesbians on the LPGA tour, for example. The mainstream press reports and analyzes these stories for a few days or weeks. Insiders in women's sports make a few dismissive comments in an attempt to clean the mess on the stove and put the lid securely back on the pot. Eventually the incident is forgotten until the next occurrence boils over into the press.

For the most part, women's sports organizations and women athletes and coaches choose to avoid public discussion of lesbians in sport. When they do address these issues, it is with reluctance and great concern for how focusing attention on what they perceive to be a highly controversial topic will affect public relations, corporate sponsorship, recruitment of athletes, and the image of women's sport. Incidents of discrimination against lesbians and gay men in sport are overlooked, condoned, or addressed in private to avoid attracting public attention.

The lingering association of women's sports with lesbianism makes many women in sport defensive about their athleticism and insistent on being perceived as heterosexual. This sensitivity to the negative connotations of the "lesbian label" and the association of women's sports with lesbians create a hostile athletic climate in which many lesbian athletes and coaches hide their identities to protect their access to sports.

This book is an exploration of these and other issues related to lesbian participation in sport. The title, *Strong Women, Deep Closets*, attempts to capture the apparent contradiction of physically strong and competent women who feel compelled to hide their deepest personal commitments, families, and love relationships in order to be members of the women's sports world. The closets in sport are deep because so many women are hiding there. These deep closets are full of not only lesbians, but also heterosexual women who fear that women's sport is always one lesbian scandal away from ruin. These strong women coach and compete in the shadow of a demonized stereotype so reviled that all women in sport are held hostage by the threat of being called a lesbian.

The purpose of this book is to initiate a long-overdue discussion about the experiences of lesbians in sport, the effects of homophobia and heterosexism on all women in sport, and the connections between homophobia, heterosexism, and sexism in sport. *Strong Women, Deep Closets* challenges the hypocrisy of championing equality for women's sports yet tolerating discrimination and prejudice against lesbian athletes and coaches. The point of view presented in this book will challenge some readers, affirm others, and outrage still others. I hope the perspective I present can be a catalyst for spirited discussion, reflection, and, of course, action toward creating a sports world where all women are openly welcomed and protected from discrimination.

Though I value theoretical discussions, this book is not intended primarily for a theoretical audience. Instead, I hope this book will be of interest to a broad audience of women and men who care about women's sport. I think this book also can be useful in high school or college courses on women's studies, women's sports, or coaching women's sports.

Coaches, athletes, and athletic directors will find food for thought and ideas for making sport a safer and more welcoming place for all women. Parents of women athletes will be invited to listen to the stories of the struggles of young lesbians who fear rejection and to understand the ways that parents' fears and judgments can affect coaches and athletes. Fans will learn more about what happens when the final buzzer sounds and the gym lights are dimmed, and how lesbian athletes protect themselves from coaches or teammates who resent their presence in the team family. In addition to these stories of tragedy and bigotry, other stories of courage and idealism are included. As women reach across their differences to join in a collective joy and passion for sport, they develop friendship bonds that can overcome a lifetime of silence and lies about what it means to be a lesbian athlete or to have a lesbian teammate or coach. I hope that all readers will find this book useful in better understanding the nature of discrimination against lesbians in sport and the human cost of this injustice. I hope to make the experiences of lesbians in sport visible and, in the process, discredit the corrosive stereotypes of lesbians that haunt all women in sport.

For lesbians in sport, *Strong Women, Deep Closets* is an affirmation, a breaking of silence, and a collective act of coming out that challenge the despised sexual predator image that has forced too many of us into the shadows of the closet out of fear: fear of losing our jobs, our place on the team roster, our families, our friends, and our credibility. *Strong Women, Deep Closets* provides a way for young lesbian and bisexual athletes in particular to understand their experiences and learn to challenge the self-hatred and fear that live inside so many of them.

I hope this can be an illuminating book for heterosexual women in sport as well as lesbian and bisexual women. The only way we can successfully address heterosexism and homophobia is for heterosexual women to understand how their lives are affected by these social injustices. It is in the interests of heterosexual women to stand with their lesbian and bisexual teammates and colleagues to challenge antilesbian discrimination. In doing so, they also free themselves to achieve their potential as athletes, coaches, and women in the world without the tyranny of compulsory femininity, heterosexuality, and fear of being called a lesbian.

Strong Women, Deep Closets begins with a description of my own story as a lesbian athlete and coach and how these experiences influenced my desire to speak out about lesbians in sport. Chapter 2 describes the larger cultural significance of sport in the United States in reinforcing traditional gender roles and sexism. Chapter 3 provides a historical overview of how women have been discouraged from sport participation by threats to their sense of themselves as "normal" women, and how these threats have become focused on the image of lesbians as gender and sexual deviants. This stereotypical image of lesbians in sport and how it is used to justify discrimination against lesbians are explored in chapter 4. Chapter 5 describes the ways that women and men attempt to protect women's sport from association with lesbians. Different climates in athletics for lesbians are the focus of chapter 6. Chapter 7 explores the effects of evangelical Christian sport ministries on the experiences of lesbian athletes and coaches. In chapter 8, I describe ways that lesbian athletes, coaches, and athletic administrators protect their identities in sport. Lesbian athletes and coaches who choose to be open about their identity within their athletic teams or schools are the focus of chapter 9. Chapter 10 discusses the development of community among lesbians in sport as well as the double standards applied to lesbian and heterosexual relationships in sport. Chapter 11 identifies 10 "unplayable lies" that must be addressed if we are to make sport more open and accepting of women of all sexual identities. This chapter also identifies strategies for change.

I believe Audre Lorde (1984) was right when she said that our silence will not protect us. *Strong Women, Deep Closets* is, I hope, a strong, clear voice speaking out against the corrosive silence surrounding lesbians in sport, for honesty and integrity in how we respond to the differences among us, and toward a common bond of love of sport and ourselves as sportswomen.

Acknowledgments

I have so many people to thank for help and inspiration. Let me start by acknowledging some of the women upon whose shoulders I stand. Bonnie Beck, Bobbie Bennett, Pearl Berlin, Jan Felshin, Lennie Gerber, Ann Hall, Betty Hicks, and Carole Oglesby are all women whose courage and outspokenness have inspired me. Without their bright lights to follow, I would never have had the confidence to speak out myself.

Thanks also to several earlier inspirations: my seventh grade gym teacher, Betty Bray, for inspiring me to teach and coach; my high school coach, Mary Boswell, who modeled the joy of play and competition; my college coach, Dottie McKnight, who taught me how to coach, how to win, and how to control my temper on the court—a painful lesson; Joan Nessler, who gave me an appreciation for the joy of teaching sport skills to others; Esther Wallace, whose scientific approach to teaching swimming made me a much better coach than I ever would have been on my own.

Though I never knew either one, Babe Didrikson, the greatest athlete of the 20th century, and Joanie Weston, the queen of roller derby, were the only women athlete role models I had in the 1950s. I needed to know they were there.

I thank Mariah Burton Nelson (Spiderwoman) and Mary Jo Kane (Batgirl), my sport feminist sisters, for nurturance, support, and encouragement during this project when I periodically lost confidence in my voice and faith that what I have to say matters.

I am so grateful for friends who read early drafts of some or all of the book and provided me with suggestions, critiques, and encouragement: Lee Bell, Paulette Dalpes, Patt Dodds, Betty Hicks, Mary Jo Kane, Mary McClintock, Mariah Burton Nelson, Sue Rankin, Linda Scott, Pat Sullivan, and Linda Zwiren.

Thanks to Mary McClintock and "Better Me Than You" for library search and research assistance as well as editing and general encouragement and faith.

Thanks to Reeny Groden and Kathy Neal for their careful proofreading.

Without the willingness of lesbian athletes, coaches, and administrators to talk with me about their experiences, this book would never have been written. I hope I have done justice to the courage and inspiration I heard in your stories.

I owe so much to Becky Lane and Human Kinetics for believing in this project from the very beginning. And to my editor, Kristine Enderle, thank you for such careful attention to this project and helping me through the publishing process. To my copyeditor, Karen Bojda, thank you for your personal touch and gentleness with my technophobia.

The best gift that came from writing this book was meeting the love of my life, Kathy Neal. Thanks to Gayle Hutchinson, our fairy Godmother, for setting up that interview! Thank you, Kathy, for enduring all those hours while I sat in front of the computer and for believing absolutely in me and loving me. You are the wind beneath my wings.

Thanks to Maryann Jennings for love and support, for being a member of my family of choice. It goes too deep to put into words.

Thanks to my heterosexual allies who over the years have co-led homophobia in sport workshops with me and have provided so much clear thinking and support: Don Sabo, Tom Schiff, Cooper Thompson, and Charmaine Wijeyesinghe. I especially want to acknowledge my friends and colleagues Jim and Jean Genasci for their love and support and the wonderful work they have done and continue to do through Parents, Families and Friends of Lesbians and Gays.

To Bobbie Harro, with whom I co-led my first homophobia workshop in 1980: My dear friend and colleague, we have been through so much together.

To Warren Blumenfeld, thank you for your constant support and insight.

To Martina Navratilova, for your grace, strength, and courage; you have inspired so many of us. Thank you.

Thank you to the thousands of invisible lesbian coaches and athletes whose dedication to women's sports has persisted despite the threats and the discrimination.

And last, but certainly not least, thanks to my long-time family of choice, the Common Womon team, for 20 summers of feminist softball, a little dyke drama, and lots of pizza and beer. You will always be players on the ballfield of my heart.

Introduction

Heterosexism is a system of dominance in which heterosexuality is privileged as the only normal and acceptable form of sexual expression. In this system of dominance, heterosexual identity is valued and rewarded, while homosexual and bisexual identity are stigmatized and punished. Heterosexism operates on multiple levels (individual, institutional, and cultural). As a result, not only are lesbians, gay men, and bisexual people subjected to individual fear, prejudice, and violence, we are also discriminated against in institutional policy and practices that do not protect our civil rights or recognize the legitimacy of our love and family relationships. For example, the institutions that organize our lives (education, law, religion, and medicine, to name a few) support basic privileges of heterosexuality, such as the right to marry, and deny these rights to lesbians and gay men. The right to have children or legal protection from harassment and discrimination in the workplace are also denied to most lesbians and gay men in the United States. Cultural norms about what constitutes a family or even the names we have available to identify intimate sexual partners do not include the family and love relationships of lesbian, gay, or bisexual people.

Homophobia, meaning irrational fear or intolerance of lesbians, gay men, and bisexual people, has become a part of our national vocabulary. Fifteen years ago few people outside the lesbian and gay rights movement knew what homophobia was. In the early 1980s I remember telling a colleague that I was conducting a workshop on homophobia. She asked if homophobia meant "fear of one's home." It is difficult to imagine this exchange happening now. Some writers have pointed out the limitations of using *homophobia,* a psychological term, to describe a systematic societal form of oppression such as heterosexism (Blumenfeld 1992; Kitzinger 1996). The oppression of lesbians, gay men, and bisexual people is based on much more than irrational personal fear, and the use of a psychological term to describe this system of injustice is inadequate. While some people do fear, hate, or are intolerant of lesbians and gay men, these personal reactions are based on pervasive cultural and institutional beliefs and practices that support and reinforce them. Far from being irrational, fear, hatred, and intolerance of lesbians and gay men are the logical consequences of living in a culture that severely stigmatizes anyone who steps out of traditional boundaries of gender and sexual expression. Some writers prefer *homonegativity* to describe this reaction (Krane 1996a). While I agree with the purpose of removing *phobia* from this description, homophobia is at least recognizable now by many North Americans, and I am reluctant to introduce yet another awkward descriptor to the discussion.

I also believe the use of the term homophobia has a place in the discussion of the systematic oppression of lesbians, gay men, and bisexual people because it does describe a personal reaction some people have. However, it is important to differentiate personal reactions from the overarching institutional and cultural policies and norms that support individual fear, prejudice, hatred, or intolerance. Though I also have reservations about the awkward term *heterosexism,* I consider it to be the equivalent of other forms of social injustice such as racism, sexism, or anti-Semitism. To address this dilemma of language use, I have chosen to use heterosexism and homophobia together when I am referring to the oppression of lesbians and gay men.

The information I will discuss in this book comes from four sources: (1) my own experiences as a lesbian coach and athlete; (2) my experiences leading discussions and workshops about heterosexism and homophobia in sport over the last 15 years, during which I have been privileged to listen to the stories of hundreds of lesbians in sport all over the United States; (3) research, professional writing, and articles in the popular press; and (4) interviews with lesbian athletes, coaches, and sport administrators that I conducted specifically for this book. Though I have talked with professional athletes and high school coaches in preparing to write this book, most of the women I talked with are college athletes, coaches, and athletic administrators. For this reason I focus on college athletics and the experiences of lesbian college coaches and athletes.

For the interviews, I accepted each woman's self-definition as a lesbian. No matter how she named herself—"gay," "queer," "lesbian," or if she avoided labels altogether—I was interested in her sport experiences as long as her primary sexual and emotional bonds were with other women. I interviewed 48 women (38 were white and 10 were women of color). These women constituted a mix of college athletes and coaches with a smaller number of high school coaches and professional or Olympic athletes and coaches. Their ages ranged from 18 to 74, with most between the ages of 20 and 40. These women represent a broad cross section of different social classes and regions of the United States with a small number of participants from Canada. I contacted about half of the participants through personal networks and interviewed them in person. The other half I contacted through computer bulletin board lists focused on women's sports and interviewed them by phone.

Lesbian athletes' and coaches' primary survival strategies are secrecy and invisibility. Thus, it is not surprising that, though many lesbians were willing to talk with me about their experiences, few felt safe enough to have their identities revealed publicly. This need for protection is an important piece of the story about lesbians in sport. That stories about lesbians in sport must be told primarily from the closet speaks, in part, to the internalized homophobia of some of the women I interviewed, but it also illustrates the genuinely dangerous atmosphere in women's athletics for many lesbians and other women thought to be lesbians.

I made a purposeful choice to focus on lesbians rather than lesbians and gay men in sport. I chose this focus partly because that is where my passion and experience lie. Also, I believe that, though gay men and lesbians share some similarities of discrimination and stigmatization in sport, there are also significant differences in their experiences related to sexism, gender role expectations, and the relationship of athletics and sport to societal roles for men and women. Explorations of these issues for both women and men have important contributions to make in helping to deconstruct the dehumanizing effects of sexism and heterosexism in the United States. This book is one step in this exploration. Other excellent sources of information about gay men and sport are available (Galindo 1997; Louganis and Marcus 1995; Pronger 1990; Waddell and Schaap 1996; Woog 1998; Young 1994).

Before we begin an exploration of lesbians and homophobia in sport, I want to tell you a little about how I became interested in this topic. My own experiences in sport as a coach and an athlete deeply influence my perspective and provide a backdrop for understanding the stories of the other women presented in this book. Thus, my journey will be the focus of the first chapter of *Strong Women, Deep Closets*.

1

My Journey Home

I am not a dispassionate outsider exploring homophobia and heterosexism in sport solely out of academic curiosity. I deeply care about homophobia and heterosexism in sport because they had a tremendous impact on my life. I am a lesbian. I am an athlete and a former coach. Being an athlete and being a lesbian have profoundly shaped who I am. Home for me is finally being able to embrace both proudly. I remember the deception, the fear, and the shame I felt as a closeted lesbian athlete and coach. I know the psychological toll the closet exacts from its inhabitants. The vigilance and protectiveness I learned in the closet are still second nature to me even now.

I am also white, Protestant, and middle class. My journey reflects the privileges of growing up in a predominantly white, middle-class Maryland suburb in the 1950s and 60s. My family could have been the model for such 50s and 60s TV shows as "Leave It to Beaver," "Ozzie and Harriet," or "The Donna Reed Show." My parents loved each other and created a comfortable, loving home for my younger brother and me.

I knew early in my life that I was an athlete. I understood this about myself on some primal level. Sport wasn't just something I did; being an athlete was who I was. Sport and physical challenge were my passion. As a child, I loved the feel of my body running and the wind in my face while hurdling down hills on my bike. I savored the thwack of a baseball in my glove, the crack of the bat on a well-hit ball, the smell of the neat's-foot oil I lovingly rubbed into my baseball glove every spring. I pitched entire fantasy games against the side of my house with a tennis ball. I played baseball with neighborhood boys for hours every day during the summer. I fervently threw myself into every physical challenge, eager to excel. On the playing field I was completely me. I felt a comfort and confidence there that eluded me in other settings. In elementary school I was tall and shy, and I hated the dresses I had to wear to school because at recess I could not play baseball in them. I saw no point in playing with dolls and, unlike many other girls in school, I didn't want to kiss boys or have a boyfriend. I wanted to play baseball and football with them instead. This passion for sport and love of myself as an athlete has sustained me, driven me, and nurtured me throughout my life.

When I was 12 years old, I heard the word *lesbian* for the first time. When I understood that it meant women who loved other women, I knew immediately that's who I was. I recognized this in the same primal way that I knew I was an athlete. This recognition explained the feelings I had for girlfriends and helped me understand the crushes I had on my women physical education teachers and Girl Scout camp counselors.

But instead of feeling proud and special, as I had felt about being an athlete, I felt shame and terror. I believed that being a lesbian was such a sick and terrible thing that I must never reveal my secret to anyone. And so I entered my teenage years with a profound sense of loneliness and isolation, guarding a secret about myself that I had no way to accept or understand. I stuffed a part of my soul and spirit deep within me and tried to pretend it wasn't there.

Thursday in my junior high school was designated by students as "Queer's Day." Anyone who wore anything green or yellow on Thursday was teased mercilessly by other students about being a queer. This was one of the worst things any of us could imagine at a time in our lives when fitting into prevailing junior high school norms of heterosexual conformity reigned supreme. Of course, few of us had ever met a "queer," but we still knew what it meant and the mysterious aura surrounding the topic of homosexuality both titillated and repelled us. I was always careful about my wardrobe selections on Thursday. It wasn't just a game to me. I was queer and didn't want anyone else to know.

I felt good about myself in the gym and on the playing field. I sought out every opportunity to play any sport available. The gym was a haven in school where heterosexual interest and popularity were becoming increasingly important to social success and acceptance. Outside the gym I felt like an alien as my girlfriends started going steady with boys, going to "make out" parties, and attending school events with dates instead of a gang of girls.

In high school I threw myself into school activities as I tried to prove to myself that I was "normal." I was elected junior class treasurer, acted in school plays, and of course, played on every sports team available for girls. My senior year I was voted "Most Athletic Girl" in my class. I was very proud of this recognition. I planned to be a high school physical education teacher and looked forward to coaching my own teams. I also won the "Best Thespian" award for my acting in school plays. I felt uneasy about this award because *thespian* was too close to *lesbian,* and I worried that somehow winning this award might reveal my secret. When friends teased me about being the "best lesbian," I cringed inside, panicked that they had guessed the truth.

I dated boys who asked me out and went steady in the 10th grade, but only because it was a way to feel popular. As hard as I tried to enjoy dating, I could never muster more than a lukewarm response to the boys with whom I went out. I liked them; I just didn't feel anything special for them. I dreaded the end of the evening and the expected goodnight kiss.

I had a series of crushes on women coaches and girlfriends in junior high and high school but was too terrified to reveal my feelings to anyone. I remember the jealousy and pain I felt when one of my best friends, whom I was in love with, began dating a boy. I listened in silent agony as she rattled on about how much she loved him and how cute he was. I survived on a rich fantasy life, unable to imagine what an adult lesbian life might look like. I knew no lesbians that I was aware of. Instead, I threw myself into sports and avoided thinking too deeply about what might lie ahead for me.

As a high school and college lesbian athlete, I was caught in a web of silence. I was afraid that if people knew about my lesbian identity, I would lose friends, credibility, and perhaps my place on the team. Later, as a coach, I worried about losing my job. I was not prepared to face the scandal that I was sure would follow if people knew I was a lesbian. I could not accept myself without shame or fear, so how could I stand up to the projections that others would place on me once they knew my secret? I could not bear rejection by my teammates and coaches and, later, by the athletes I coached and their parents. I was also afraid of school administrators' power to fire me or make my life miserable.

My lack of inner resources was matched by a lack of external support. In the 1960s when I was a high school and college athlete and in the 1970s when I was a high school and college coach, there were no nondiscrimination policies or laws to protect me or help me address the onslaught of prejudice I anticipated. There were no lesbian or gay groups at the University of Maryland where I attended undergraduate school. When I was a high school coach in suburban Maryland in the late 1960s, the emerging gay liberation movement did not touch me.

During my freshman year I fell in love with a teammate on my college basketball team. After much agonizing (and many late night heart-to-heart talks) and trying to resist our feelings for each other, we finally gave in to the overwhelming desire to kiss each other. This first kiss with a woman sent me to my own bed trembling with an intensity of feelings I had never experienced kissing a boy. These feelings were mixed with shame and terror because I believed something was wrong with me. Nonetheless, we became each other's first lovers. We kept our relationship secret, primarily at my insistence.

As far as I knew, my lover and I were the only lesbians on campus (or in the world, for that matter). I did not understand the strong societal association between being an athlete and being a lesbian, but then I started to hear the innuendos about athletic women. We worried about the rumors that began to circulate in the dorm because we spent so much time together, so we dated men with the explicit intention of camouflaging our relationship. I learned to lie. I carefully studied our friends to detect whether or not any of them suspected anything about us. I lived in dread that someone would find out about us: friends, my coach, my parents. We had a pact with each other that if either of us met a man we cared about, the other would "step aside."

Just because we tried to hide our relationship, however, did not mean my first lover and I were entirely invisible. We began to receive invitations to parties held in the apartments of older teammates and women physical education majors. Though nothing was ever explicit, they saw through our camouflage and invited us into their community. No one ever talked about being lesbians, and I don't even remember any overt expressions of affection between women at these parties. We danced (fast dances), we drank (a lot), we smoked, we laughed. We talked about sports. I remember feeling excited by our inclusion in this circle of older women and enjoyed this expansion, however circumspect, in the social network my partner and I could share.

My lover played softball in a summer recreation league. I went to her games and spent as much time checking out the women who came to watch the games as I did the action on the field. I was alternately repelled, frightened, and fascinated by many of the women players and spectators. I maintained the self-delusion that we, my lover and I, were somehow different and better than these women. For a long time, this socioeconomic class and antigay prejudice kept me from accepting myself or claiming membership in the small lesbian community I had available. As a consequence, I secretly suffered breaking up and silently celebrated falling in love a couple of times during the next few years.

I spent my years as a college athlete and a high school teacher and coach in this secret and silent world. I lived a double life, censoring what I revealed about myself. On the outside I was a popular and successful student athlete and coach. On the inside I was haunted by shame and the fear of disappointing and losing the respect of my parents, my coaches, my high school athletes, and their parents.

While teaching high school, I dated the wrestling coach. We went to school events together, and I felt relieved to be able to pretend to be heterosexual. As in high school, dating men was a way to try to fit in. It was also a way to camouflage my identity. When I returned home from dates, my lover would be waiting for me in the apartment we shared.

I watched painfully from the closet, unable to reach out to young high school women I assumed might be lesbians struggling with their own self-acceptance. I feel sad now when I think of these young women. If they suspected I was a lesbian, it must have confused them to see me dating this man. I taught them that using secrecy and deception were how lesbian teachers and coaches survived.

I remember a teacher evaluation meeting I had with the principal of the high school where I taught and coached. He complimented me because I "presented such a good image for physical education, not like some of the other women P.E. teachers and coaches in the county." Though he never explicitly mentioned being a lesbian, I knew exactly what he meant and cowered further back in my closet.

In 1969 I was reading a newspaper in an airport on the way to my summer job as a camp counselor in the Adirondack Mountains. One article described riots in Greenwich Village in which homosexuals were fighting police who had raided a gay bar called Stonewall. I remember looking around the airport to make sure no one was sitting near me as I read the story. I was afraid they might guess I was a lesbian because I was reading about the riots.

I could not imagine any other way to live. Coming out was unthinkable. I assumed that coming out would risk my place in the athletic world that had always been my home. Like many athletic women, I loved coaching and teaching. I loved playing sports. I enjoyed the feeling of exhaustion after a hard practice. I reveled in the strength and grace of my body. I lived for the camaraderie with my teammates and the buzz I got from competition. As a coach, I loved working with young women who shared my love of sport, and I enjoyed the bond our teams developed as we worked together for a common goal.

It wasn't until I became a college coach that I began to associate openly with other lesbian coaches. I moved to Massachusetts and found a community of lesbians who were open with each other about their identities and relationships. I was influenced in particular by Lennie Gerber, Pearl Berlin, and Jan Felshin, all lesbians in physical education, whose openness both amazed and inspired me. I began to question my assumption that something was wrong with me. Through my friendships with other lesbians, I began to understand that the sickness was not in me, but in a society that insisted that I conform to gender and sexuality expectations that did not fit. I gradually learned to love and be proud of who I am and to believe that I deserve respect and equal treatment. I became less and less comfortable hiding my identity and my relationships.

As a swimming coach at the University of Massachusetts in the 1970s, I was influenced by the burgeoning feminist and gay rights movements to envision a different way to be a lesbian in sport. I began to intentionally infuse feminist principles into my coaching. I came out to a few of my lesbian swimmers. In particular, I was affected by the campaign in Dade County, Florida, to recall a gay rights ordinance in 1977. The spokesperson for this antigay campaign was singer Anita Bryant. The first political act I ever took was to buy a T-shirt in Provincetown that said, "May the great seagull of P-Town shit on Anita." I was too scared to wear it in public, but it sat neatly folded in my T-shirt drawer, a symbol of my desire to take more public action.

Lesbian athletes from my own and other teams began seeking me out as someone who would talk with them about some of the issues they faced as young lesbians: fears, heartbreaks, questions, joys. They came to my office, and we talked about coming out, falling in love, breaking up. We laughed and we cried together. I helped some who were struggling with their identities to get counseling, for others I was just an older lesbian willing to talk about their lives and mine. I loved being available for them. I was able to provide the support I never received in college. I was sad that they were still struggling with the same issues of shame and secrecy that I faced as a college athlete. I became more and more frustrated about how denial and secrecy shrivels the spirit and limits dreams. I was angry about the injustice of prejudice and discrimination against lesbians in sport and our own silent collusion with it.

Another important turning point came for me in 1979 when I attended the first March on Washington for Lesbian and Gay Rights. It was an incredible experience to be among the 100,000 people in the march. I remember how my friends and I took turns sitting on each other's shoulders to look around at the huge crowd gathered for the rally on the Washington Monument grounds. I had never seen so many lesbian and gay people. This experience made me want to come out more publicly and take an active role in educating others about homophobia and heterosexism. Not long after the march I began leading workshops on homophobia for educators, guidance counselors, and other community-based groups. I joined a lesbian, gay, and bisexual speakers' bureau and became more active in the Northampton lesbian, bisexual, and gay community.

With this experience, I wanted to do something to change what it was like to be a lesbian in sport. I wanted to be part of ensuring that the next generation of lesbian athletes and coaches would not face the same internal and external barriers that I had. Though I had been coming out and speaking against homophobia and heterosexism in other areas, I was not speaking out against homophobia and heterosexism in athletics. Athletics was where my spirit had always thrived. I was afraid that if I spoke out in athletics, I might not be welcomed anymore in a place I called home. I think I was waiting for a time when I would not be afraid anymore. That changed after I attended a workshop led by an African-American lesbian educator and activist, Angela Bowen. Angela paraphrased an Audre Lorde quote that made me realize that I would have to act in spite of my fear, rather than let it keep me silent. She paraphrased Audre Lorde's words, "If we wait until we are not afraid, we will be speaking from our graves." Like a splash of cold, refreshing water, Audre Lorde's quote gave me the courage I needed to begin.

I had my first opportunity to speak about homophobia and heterosexism in athletics in 1983 during the planning of the first New Agenda for Women in Sport in Washington, DC. In the brochure announcing the conference, an assistant to the conference director had, without the approval of conference organizers, included "lesbianism" as one of the topics the conference would address. When the Women's Sports Foundation (WSF) realized that the "L-word" was in the brochure, there

Author Pat Griffin (left) and Deb Edelman finish
the Gay Pride Run on New York Pride Day.

Courtesy of Pat Griffin

was immediate panic among the executive board and fear that corporate and other sponsors of the conference, such as the U.S. Olympic Committee and AT&T, would object and withdraw their sponsorship. My friend and former colleague at the University of Massachusetts, Carole Oglesby, who was on the WSF executive board, asked me to do a homophobia workshop for the board. My friend Bobbie Harro and I conducted this workshop in New York City in the summer of 1983.

Despite our efforts, the word *lesbian* was removed in subsequent conference descriptions. The executive board made the decision not to initiate discussion of this topic and to leave it to conference participants to bring it up. This way they could claim they were not responsible for raising the issue. I promptly decided that I would bring it up at the conference. I had been assigned to a conference panel discussion of the question, "How can women athletes disarm and deflect threats to our sense of femininity?" I wrote a speech that attacked the question itself. During the panel I presented the case that this question was a smoke screen while the real issue that women in sport faced was whether they looked like, acted like, or actually were lesbians. I did not come out as a lesbian during my speech (though I am sure now it would not have been a surprise to most in attendance). I was not yet ready for that, but I had taken my first step toward opening the closet door. I made two recommendations for resolutions that focused on addressing homophobia in women's sport and discrimination based on sexual orientation in athletics.

The topic of lesbians in sport was discussed in my panel session as well as another session. There was a great deal of controversy about whether or not the word *lesbian* should appear in the wording of any resolutions sent forward to the conference organizers. In an informal caucus meeting of women who attended both sessions, a conservative faction, of which I was a member, argued that the conference planners would flip if the word *lesbian* was used and that we needed to take one step at a time. In this spirit I thought we should use the word *homophobia,* a safer, less threatening word that was more likely to be accepted by nervous conference organizers. The other faction insisted on the importance of using the word *lesbian* and said they were sick and tired of being invisible. I found myself torn between the righteousness of their argument and the knowledge that the conference organizers were not ready for this. The conference was receiving huge media coverage, and the organizers thought the lesbian issue was too hot to handle. The faction in favor of using *lesbian* instead of *homophobia* in our resolutions eventually won, and we sent our recommendations forward, L-word and all.

That evening word was passed around during the banquet that there would be a "lesbian" meeting after the banquet because the conference organizers wanted us to reconsider the inclusion of the word *lesbian* in our resolution. Billie Jean King was a part of the executive board. She was smarting over her public outing by an ex-lover and the loss of her commercial endorsements as a result. At this divisive and painful midnight meeting, we lesbians fought among ourselves about how to respond to the organizers' rejection of the L-word. Some women insisted that *lesbian* be included in the resolution as we had originally decided and threatened to call a news conference the next day if it wasn't. Some of us were afraid that we had overstepped the bounds of what the conservative organizers could handle and that this controversy would set us back in our quest to have these issues addressed in sport. Finally, the more radical faction angrily walked out of the meeting. Those of us who remained decided to use *homophobia* instead of *lesbian.* I felt sad and sick at the compromise I was endorsing. The resolution read before the

Former professional tennis player Billie Jean King was the first prominent sportswoman to publicly acknowledge a lesbian relationship in 1981 when a former lover filed a "palimony" suit against King.

entire plenary the next day was a watered-down, ambivalent statement that I took no pride in and said so in a statement during our final plenary session.

I had intended to take a courageous step out of the closet by speaking out against homophobia in women's sport at the New Agenda Conference and found that I still lacked the courage to stand up completely for lesbians. My fear was still holding me back. I needed to be able to come out myself before I could speak effectively against homophobia and heterosexism.

I was asked to be on a panel again the next summer at a follow-up regional New Agenda meeting in New York. I playfully constructed a list of the "Twenty Warning Signals of Homophobia in Women's Sports," parodying the American Cancer Society's "Ten Warning Signals of Cancer." (Griffin 1988). The other panelists and the audience sat politely and uncomfortably as I delivered my speech with as much élan as I could muster. The world of women's sports was still not ready to address this topic, and I was not ready to come out to help us do it.

In 1987 I proposed a program for the American Alliance for Health, Physical Education, Recreation and Dance (AAHPERD) annual conference entitled, "Doing Research on Controversial Topics: Homosexuality and Homophobia in Physical Education and Sport." I asked Jim Genasci from Springfield College, Don Sabo from D'Youville College, and Sherry Woods, one of my doctoral students, to do the program with me. Jim is now a retired physical education professor and, as the father of a gay son, an active leader in Parents, Families and Friends of Lesbians and Gays. Don is a profeminist sport sociologist who I had come out to seven years before when he was speaking at the University of Massachusetts. I knew both Don and Jim were staunch heterosexual allies. Sherry was completing her doctoral dissertation research with me at the University of Massachusetts on lesbian physical education teachers. I believe it was the first time the words *lesbian, gay, homophobia,* and *homosexuality* had ever appeared in the AAHPERD program. Sherry and I decided ahead of time that we were both going to come out as part of our presentations. We agonized over just how and when in our speeches we would do this. But we were both sure that we could not address this topic from the closet and maintain our integrity.

When we arrived at the conference in Las Vegas, we were disappointed to discover that our session was scheduled for the last session of the final day, a typically poorly attended time slot in most conference programs. All during the conference, people kept coming up to us expressing their regret that they would not be able to attend our session because of early flights back home. The night before the session, Jim, Don, Sherry, Sherry's partner Gayle, and I had dinner together. We convinced ourselves that even if only a few people attended our session, at least we were on the conference program and this was an important first step.

The next afternoon we arrived in our assigned presentation room nervous and excited. The elevated speakers' platform and podium looked out over a huge room with chairs set up for at least 300 people. I anticipated my disappointment if only a few people came to our session. As the time for our presentation approached, people started coming into the room. There was an incredible buzz of excitement as people kept coming and coming. Soon all the chairs were filled, and people were standing in the back of the room. The audience was mostly women and, if I had to guess, mostly closeted lesbians. I looked out at them and fought back tears. I knew the next 90 minutes would change my professional life forever, and I hoped they would begin to change the lives of lesbians in sport and physical education too. The presentation went well. Sherry and I came out. Lightning did not strike. The building did not collapse. People kept coming up afterwards to congratulate and thank us. I felt liberated from all the silence and fear I had lived with all of my playing and coaching days. I hadn't felt as free since I came out to my mother several years before. As we basked in our success, I noticed one of my male colleagues from the University of Massachusetts approaching me. Because I perceived him to be fairly conservative, I was surprised to see him and a little apprehensive about his reaction to the presentation. As I was talking to someone else, he put a slip of paper in my jacket pocket and, without speaking, walked away. It said, "You and Sherry make me proud to be associated with you and the University of Massachusetts." It taught me not to make assumptions about how people will respond to discussing lesbians and gays in sport and my coming out. I keep that slip of paper in my study at home as a reminder.

This presentation launched me into 10 years of workshops, seminars, research, and writing about homophobia and heterosexism in sport. I've worked with colleges, coaches' associations, and teachers' conferences. I have written in professional journals and been interviewed for newspaper and magazine articles. I've helped create a video and resource materials for coaches and teachers. I've been on national TV and have spoken on a panel about homophobia in sport with Martina Navratilova.

In 1990 I competed in my first Gay Games in Vancouver, British Columbia. I used my training for the triathlon to get myself back into shape. I was six months out of cancer surgery and grateful to be alive and healthy when I splashed into the waters of English Bay to start the swim. The race itself—a mile swim, 20-mile bike race, and 7-mile run—took on a spiritual dimension I was unprepared for. I felt blessed to be alive, to feel the burn in my chest and thighs and taste the salt of my sweat. I felt so connected to all my lesbian and gay sisters and brothers in the race. Every one of us had a survival story about the courage and joy of confronting our own fears and societal prejudice to be in that race competing as out and proud lesbians and gay men. I realized how much it meant to me to be competing as a lesbian athlete. Not just a lesbian or just an athlete, but a lesbian athlete. It felt so good to integrate these two core parts of who I am after the long journey to get there.

In 1992 I was asked to conduct a homophobia workshop for the Penn State athletic department. This request came from the Penn State administration in response to the public outcry about the women's basketball coach Rene Portland's policy of not allowing lesbians on her teams. I was concerned about the workshop for a number of reasons. The university administration had required the athletic department to participate in a homophobia workshop. Under these circumstances I questioned the athletic administration's commitment to seriously addressing the issues. All coaches were required to attend the workshop, and many were tired of the attention and uproar surrounding the controversy. Moreover, some of the approximately 70 coaches supported Portland and her policy. To make matters worse, the athletic department was willing to schedule only an hour and a half for the workshop.

Courtesy of Pat Griffin

Author Pat Griffin competes in the women's triathlon
at Wellesley College, Massachusetts.

Despite these drawbacks I decided to do the workshop in hopes that we
might be able to schedule some follow-up sessions. I asked a good friend
and colleague, Cooper Thompson, a heterosexual man with whom I had
co-led other workshops on lesbian and gay issues, to work with me at
Penn State. We planned what we hoped would be a good introduction to
the topic. In preparation, I wrote Rene Portland, whom I had never met,
a letter introducing myself, explaining that I hoped we could make the
workshop a useful learning experience, and stating my intention not to
place her on the spot. I asked if we could meet and talk one on one
because I wanted to understand her perspective and share mine with
her. I never got an answer to my letter.

Rene Portland sat next to Joe Paterno in the workshop, surrounded
by a group of older white men. Anger and discomfort were the predomi-
nant feelings in the room. Though some coaches were supportive, it
was risky for them to speak in this gathering. Toward the end of the
session the group finally began what I thought was a useful discussion
of the topic and how to address the needs of lesbian, gay, and bisexual

athletes. Sue Rankin, then the softball coach at Penn State and an out-spoken lesbian coach, took some courageous risks in speaking up, as did a few other coaches. Some of the quiet coaches began to ask good questions and express some heartfelt concerns. Unfortunately, one of the athletic administrators chose this time to literally jump up and abruptly end the session without allowing Cooper and me to bring the workshop to a close ourselves. There were so many conflicting issues and feelings and so little time to address them that I left the session feeling drained, naive, and used.

I don't think I have ever felt as exposed, vulnerable, or ineffective as I did during the Penn State workshop. I always identify myself as a lesbian when I do this work because I can then speak from my own experience and from my heart as well as from the position of "expert." That night I felt naked, stripped bare of my usually tough defenses. The hostility and fear in the room went right into my heart. That night at Penn State I saw how far we had to go and how difficult the journey could be.

Fortunately, not all workshops are so frustrating. I am also encouraged by the willingness of many coaches and athletes to grapple with what they see as a difficult and confusing topic. In this work I have been privileged to meet many courageous women and men, straight and gay, who share my passion for social justice in sport. Some are lesbian and gay teachers and coaches who fight injustice every day they come to work, most in the closet, some out. I have met a heterosexual male athletic director with a lesbian daughter and young, queer-identified athletes who shave their heads and wear freedom rings to practice. I have witnessed lesbians coming out to teammates and colleagues. I have talked with heterosexual coaches and teachers whose commitment to social justice provides a safe haven for lesbian, gay, and bisexual athletes and colleagues. I worked with the Mills College basketball team, who were so proud of themselves for addressing their homophobia and welcoming all women on their team—lesbian, bisexual, and straight.

I am not coaching now. I am a tenured professor in a progressive university in a state that has a law protecting me against discrimination on the basis of my sexual orientation. I am no longer living in the hostile athletic world where many lesbians coach and compete. This privileged position gives me an opportunity to speak out, and I feel a responsibility to do so. I want to do what I can to end the legacy of fear, shame, deception, and discrimination that defines so many lesbians' experience in sport. I share the stories in this book, not as a disinterested observer, but as a witness and a participant. Each of the stories in this book is a part of my journey too.

The next chapter places the discussion about lesbians and homophobia in sport in a broader cultural context that examines the role sport plays in supporting traditional gender roles and sexism in the United States.

2

Sport:

Where Men Are Men and Women Are Trespassers

At first it might seem odd to discuss men and sport in a book about lesbians in sport. However, an understanding of the larger cultural role sport plays in men's lives forms a foundation for understanding the sport experiences of all women, and lesbians in particular (Birrell and Coles 1994; M.A. Hall 1987, 1996). Sport is more than games. As an institution, sport serves important social functions in supporting conventional social values. In particular, sport is a training ground where boys learn what it means to be men. Masculinity does not come naturally; it must be carefully taught. Specific rewards and punishments provide clear messages about acceptable and unacceptable behavior for boys. Boys who show an interest in "girl" activities, such as playing with dolls, dancing, or cooking, are teased by peers. Young boys learn at an early age that participation in athletics is an important, if not required, part of developing a masculine identity and gaining acceptance among peers.

Every Saturday morning in the fall little boys stagger up and down fields under the weight of full football drag, imitating the swagger and ritual they see in their professional sports heroes. Many fathers worry if their sons do not exhibit an interest in sports. They teach their sons to throw, catch, swing bats, shoot hoops. Adults comment on the size of young boys by predicting in which sports they will excel. Participation on school athletic teams, especially the big four (football, basketball, baseball, and ice hockey) ensure popularity and prestige among classmates and in the larger community. Young boys idolize professional and college team-sport athletes and coaches because of their physical size, strength, toughness, and competitiveness. Young boys and adult men wear caps, T-shirts, and jackets with their favorite professional or collegiate team mascot and colors.

Men's athletic events, especially the big four team sports, draw huge numbers of spectators. Men of all colors and social classes study team statistics and participate in intense postcontest analyses of strategy and performance. Cities spend millions of dollars building sports arenas with tax subsidies to woo men's professional teams to town or prevent them from moving to another city. The athletic equipment and clothing industries are multibillion-dollar enterprises that depend on the large number of boys and men who buy their increasingly sophisticated and specialized products.

The importance of sport in socializing men into traditional masculine gender roles also defines the sport experience for women (Sabo and Messner 1990). Because sport is identified with men and masculinity, women in sport become trespassers on male territory (Bryson 1990), and their access is limited or blocked entirely. Despite huge increases in women's sport participation, there is still tremendous resistance to an equitable distribution of resources between men's and women's athletics. *USA Today* reported that on the 25th anniversary of the passage of Title IX, the federal law prohibiting sex discrimination in education, 80 percent of college and university athletic programs in the United States are still not in compliance with the law (Brady 1997).

Sometimes resistance to women's sport participation is more personal. In the spring of 1997 Melissa Raglin, 12, was the starting catcher for a Boca Raton Babe Ruth baseball team. During a game the plate umpire asked Melissa if she was wearing a protective cup. Melissa removed her helmet and catcher's mask and told him she was a girl. However, the Babe Ruth rules state that all players (assumed to be male) must wear a cup to protect their genitals. When Melissa, who had been playing in the Babe Ruth league for over two seasons, refused to comply with the rule, she was prohibited from playing catcher. She was allowed play again only when she ordered a special cup designed for women, even though most doctors agree that there is no medical reason why a girl should wear a protective cup. This example shows the absurd lengths to which some men will go to try to humiliate a young girl to make sure she knows that she is trespassing on male turf. Male league officials' insistence that Melissa wear a cup, even at the risk of ridicule in news stories, demonstrates the seriousness and importance of protecting sport from female encroachment.

Women's presence in sport as serious participants dilutes the importance and exclusivity of sport as a training ground for learning about and accepting traditional male gender roles and the privileges that their adoption confers on (white, heterosexual) men. As a result, women's sport performance is trivialized and marginalized as an inferior version of the "real thing." These arguments ignore the overlap in sport performances among men and women in all sports and the growing interest among young girls in sport participation.

Sexism as a system of male privilege and female subordination is based on the acceptance of particular definitions of gender (what constitutes a man or a woman) and gender roles (what qualities, talents, and characteristics women and men are supposed to have). Women's serious participation in sport brings into question the "natural" and mutually exclusive nature of gender and gender roles. If women in sport can be tough minded, competitive, and muscular too, then sport loses its special place in the development of masculinity for men. If women can so easily develop these so-called masculine qualities, then what are the meanings of femininity and masculinity? What does it mean to be a man or a woman? These challenges threaten an acceptance of the traditional gender order in which men are privileged and women are subordinate.

Kathy Neal was a member of the Connecticut Falcons, the first Women's Professional Softball League, from 1976-79.

Thus, they account for much of the strong resistance to gender equity in sport and the need to marginalize and control the growth of women's athletics.

THE POWER OF THE LESBIAN LABEL

One of the most effective means of controlling women in sport is to challenge the femininity and heterosexuality of women athletes. When a woman is called "masculine," "unfeminine," or "dyke," she knows she has crossed a gender boundary or challenged male privilege (Peper 1994). In this way, homophobia serves as glue that holds traditional

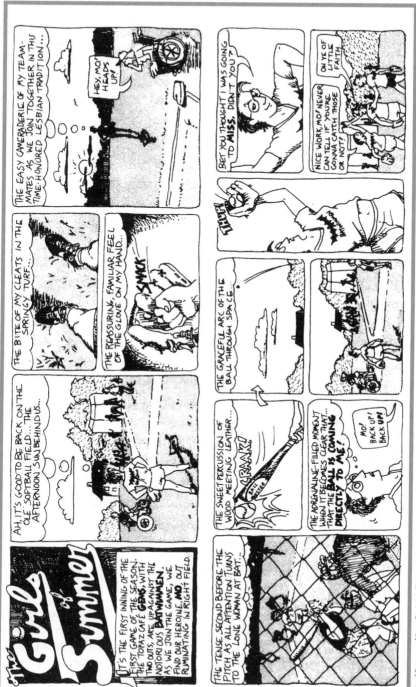

gender role expectations in place. Because most women are afraid to be called lesbian or to have their femininity called into question, their sport experience can be controlled by using the lesbian label to intimidate them (Guthrie 1982). The purpose of calling a woman a lesbian is to limit her sport experience and make her feel defensive about her athleticism.

Though lesbians are the direct targets of these insinuations, antilesbian bias affects the experience of all women (Pharr 1986). Using the lesbian label to discourage the bonding that occurs among women in athletics is an effective way to keep women from discovering their own power. Consequently, stigmatizing lesbian identity serves the interests of those who want to maintain the imbalance of opportunity and power in athletics based on gender. As long as women's sports are associated with lesbians and lesbians are stigmatized as sexual and social deviants, the lesbian label serves an important social-control function in sport, ensuring that only men have access to the benefits of sport participation and the physical and psychological empowerment available in sport.

The preservation of athletics as a male-only activity is essential in maintaining a gender order in which men and women adopt separate and unequal gender roles. The interconnections of sexism, homophobia, and heterosexism are powerful forces that ensure that male privilege and dominance endure.

SPORT AND THE MAINTENANCE OF MASCULINITY

Sport for men serves five social functions that ensure that the gender order supporting presumed male superiority and female subordination is maintained. These functions are (1) defining and reinforcing traditional conceptions of masculinity, (2) providing an acceptable and safe context for male bonding and intimacy, (3) reinforcing male privilege and female subordination, (4) establishing status among other males, and (5) reinforcing heterosexuality.

Defining and Reinforcing Traditional Conceptions of Masculinity

Team sports in particular teach boys masculinity skills (Lenskyj 1990; Messner and Sabo 1994; Messner 1992). They learn to be competitive and tough. They learn to deny feelings of compassion or other feelings that coaches teach them to associate with weakness. Boys learn to value physical strength and size, aggressiveness, and a will to dominate. Young boys learn to accept the necessity of establishing hierarchical relationships among competitors and teammates based on athletic performance. None of these qualities or values are innate, but young boys learn that they are essential and natural components of a masculine identity. Boys who are perceived to be weak or soft or who do not have an interest in developing these traditional masculine qualities are shunned, harassed, and ridiculed by peers. Adult men who were labeled "sissy" in elementary school or "faggot" and "pussy" in later grades can tell painful stories of abuse that attest to the intensity of this socialization process.

Much of this harassment takes place on athletic teams and in physical education classes. Male coaches and physical educators are important teachers of masculinity. Lessons learned on the athletic field reinforce the importance of learning to "be a man." "Proving one's manhood," facing challenge "like a man," and dominating opponents represent a hard strength and stoicism especially prized in team sports.

Not all men in sport can easily meet the standards of masculinity set in athletics. Gay men, men of color, and poor and working-class men represent what Connell (1992) calls *competing masculinities.* Their experiences of masculinity are mediated by their race, sexual identity, and class status. Because their social group memberships deviate from the white, heterosexual, and middle-class norm, these men have less access to privilege even though they might excel in sport. A gay male athlete must hide his identity. An African-American male athlete is stereotyped by racist expectations and disadvantaged by institutional racism. These competing masculinities also enable these men to create a different approach to the development of masculinity, as in the ironic stance of the gay male athlete described by Pronger (1990).

Providing a Context for Acceptable and Safe Male Bonding and Intimacy

Athletics is one of the few social contexts in which men can openly express physical affection and love for other men. Team members spend an enormous amount of time together during the course of a season, practicing and competing, traveling to games, spending nights in hotels, and socializing. The emotional intensity of competition and sharing the highs and lows of winning and losing encourage strong bonds among teammates. Magic Johnson expressed this love of his teammates when he retired from professional basketball, lamenting that what he would miss most was being with "the fellas."

In addition to this emotional bond, athletics involves physical intimacy as well. Participating in team sports in particular requires physical contact with both teammates and opponents. In addition, athletes spend a lot of time together in hotel rooms, locker rooms, showers, and whirlpool baths—all places that suggest a high degree of physical closeness or nudity. During victory celebrations men can, without fear of ridicule, hug and kiss each other. Men can also cry without shame about losing a big game. Fanny slaps and chest bumps are commonplace in men's athletics, especially in team sports. It is not a coincidence that expressions of male-to-male physical affection and love are acceptable in few other contexts. In athletics men can admire other men's bodies and their physical accomplishments openly without arousing suspicions about their heterosexuality. The bond among male teammates is an important lesson in male solidarity around their masculine identities. Athletics provides the setting in which these lessons are learned. These lessons are important not only to establish a bond of solidarity among men, but also to reinforce men's difference from women. For men who are primarily sport spectators, the passion with which they discuss, watch, analyze, and read about sports is testament to the importance of sport in affirming masculine identity and providing a way to connect with other men.

Reinforcing Male Privilege and Female Inferiority

Defining masculinity is as much about rejecting so-called feminine qualities as it is about embracing so-called masculine ones. Male coaches send strong messages about women and about the need for men to avoid being like women when they compare a poor performance by a male athlete to that of a girl (for example, throwing like a girl). Many coaches know they can inspire male athletes to perform better by calling them demeaning names intended for women (pussies) or hybrids like wussy (wimp and pussy). Being called a woman, compared to a woman, or—the worst insult—being beaten by a woman in any sport contest provokes anger and shame in many men and boys.

ESPN2 sport commentator Jim Rome was physically attacked on the air by former New Orleans Saint Jim Everett after Rome repeatedly called Everett "Chris Evert." Apparently Everett had been criticized in the media for avoiding hits. Jim Lampley, an HBO/NBC sports commentator, responded to this incident, "That stuff doesn't belong in our dealings with the athletes. It's one thing to say that he is not a good quarterback, but you don't have to devalue him as a human being." According to Lampley, being called a woman, even an outstanding professional athlete, is reasonable grounds for physical retaliation because it devalues a male athlete *as a human being* to be called a woman.

Some men are obsessed with proving that girls and women are inherently physically inferior to boys and men. In 1990 in Denton, Texas, several male coaches and fathers were barred from attending youth soccer games after questioning the sex of one of the players on a girls' 12-and-under team. The goalie for the winning team, 10-year-old Natasha Den-

UPI/Corbis-Bettmann

1973 match between Billie Jean King and Bobby Riggs.
King won the match, and its $100,000 purse, in straight sets.

nis, was playing well for her undefeated team. According to the newspaper account, two fathers from the losing team demanded "proof" that Natasha was a girl. Natasha's mother said, "They expected her to go to the ladies' restroom and take her clothes off in front of some stranger." After the game Mrs. Dennis took Natasha across the field to introduce her daughter to one of the fathers demanding the "panty check." He looked at Natasha and said, "Nice game, boy" (*Gay Community News* 1990). In this incident the fathers could not accept the fact that their sons were outperformed by a girl. The only explanation for her performance was that she was really a boy. The insistence that outstanding female athletes of any age must undergo a sex check, whether by outraged fathers of little boys or an official Olympic medical board, illustrates the intensity of this conflict.

As Mariah Burton Nelson (1994) points out in her insightful book *The Stronger Women Get, The More Men Love Football,* many men need to establish the "fact" that no matter what gains women make in sport, they could never play football. They believe that football is the epitome of athletic excellence and legitimacy. In New Jersey a female member of a high school football team was physically assaulted by her male teammates who were trying to dissuade her from playing. Elizabeth Balsley was punched, hit with blocking dummies, and spat upon as she walked toward the practice field. Three of her male teammates were charged with assault, suspended from classes for two to four days, and barred from playing in one football game. The father of one of the suspended players protested even this minimal punishment, claiming the incident was "innocent horseplay." As this incident illustrates, young women who dare to challenge the notion that football is too tough for women must be taught a lesson.

This need to establish male superiority extends beyond comparing the performance merits of male and female athletes. Studies of talk in men's locker rooms describe consistent patterns of antiwoman and antigay interactions (Curry 1991). Many men talk about women as sexual possessions or receptacles, not as equals or even as human beings. In this climate male athletes learn to despise qualities within themselves that they perceive to be feminine and to accept female inferiority in sport as fact. They develop a sense of entitlement and superiority in relationship to women on and off the athletic field.

The way *Boston Globe* sports reporter Lisa Olson was treated during and after her sexual harassment by members of the New England Patriots football team in their locker room is symbolic of the resentment and anger directed at women who trespass on sacred male turf. The hatred and contempt, including death threats, directed at Olson by Patriot owner Victor Kiam, players, and male fans reveal the intensity of the resentment directed at women who dare to claim their right to participation in athletics (Kane and Disch 1993).

A study by Crosset, Benedict, and McDonald (1995) indicates that there is a higher incidence of violence against women by male athletes than by other men on college campuses. Athletic team participation in gang rapes or the development of a scoring system to rank sexual conquests are disturbing examples of how bonding among male athletes based on contempt for women can lead to antisocial criminal behaviors. One of the fathers of members of the Spur Posse, a group of California high school male athletes who developed a scoring system to rank and compare their sexual conquests, defended his sons as regular all-American boys who had done nothing wrong.

Establishing Status Among Other Males

Sport is the single most important element of the peer-status system for U.S. adolescent males (Messner 1992). Moreover, athletics is a rehearsal for the status many white, middle-class boys hope to achieve later through work, education, and economic accumulation (T. Chandler and Goldberg 1990). Poor, working-class men of all colors often view success as a professional athlete as the only route, no matter how unrealistic, to economic success and social status. As a result, athletics takes on a special status in the culture of boys and young men (Frank 1993). Messner (1992) describes how boys learn that acceptance by and status with peers, fathers, and coaches is achieved by winning in sports. According to Messner, boys learn that just participating in sports is not enough. To achieve the kind of attention and connections they seek, it is necessary to be better than other boys, to beat them in sports. In high school and college, male athletes, particularly team-sport athletes, are often treated as high-status members of the community by peers, teachers, and other community members. As such, they often receive special treatment and recognition not given to other boys. Messner recounts how eight-year-old boys at a basketball camp were lined up in front of their peers after playing a game. As the coach held his hand over each boy's head, the other boys were to applaud louder or softer according to how well they thought each one had played. He describes the tension and anxiety on each boy's face, other than the few who were confident that they were the best players, as they waited to be judged. Being judged acceptable in this public sport-performance hierarchy is an important ritual in establishing self-worth among boys and young men. Sport for boys is serious business, and girls have no place in it.

Reinforcing Heterosexuality

For many people the male team-sports hero is the epitome of masculinity: strong, tough, handsome, competitive, dating or married to the most desirable woman. An accepted perquisite of professional athletic fame for men is a rich and varied sex life with many willing young female groupies. Many people believe that the terms *gay man* and *athlete* used together are an oxymoron (Pronger 1990; Woog 1998). A gay male athlete violates both the image of male athletes as strong, virile, and heterosexual and the image of gay men as swishy and effeminate. Just as it is important to keep women out of sport or marginalized in sport, it is essential to keep gay men in sport invisible. If gay men can be strong, tough, competitive, and part of a male bonding experience in the locker room with straight men, how can straight men confidently differentiate themselves from gay men? Just as young men in athletics learn that women are inferior, they also learn that gay men are contemptible. Being called a "faggot" or "pansy" is an insult of the highest order to one's sense of masculinity. The incidence of antigay talk in locker rooms and the participation of male athletes in gay bashing reflect this attitude (Curry 1991).

Maintaining the myths that all male athletes are heterosexual and that sexual attraction among male athletes does not occur allow men to enjoy the physical and emotional intimacy of the athletic team experience. They do not need to worry that teammates might think they are gay. These myths also protect male athletes from confronting the possibility that someone else in that locker room might be gay. Many heterosexual men are extremely uncomfortable with the possibility of being the object of another man's sexual interest. By displaying contempt for gays through antigay name-calling, jokes, harassment, or violence, men reassure themselves and teammates that everyone in the locker room is heterosexual in an intimate all-male context (Kane and Disch 1993). If this illusion is threatened by the presence of openly gay men, the complex feelings of love and intimacy, physical contact, and communal nudity could not be enjoyed without fear and suspicion. The fear of being perceived as gay or being the object of gay sexual desire is a powerful social control that keeps men in athletics safely within the bounds of traditional masculinity.

This need to believe that there are no gay men present in the locker room or on the playing field makes the male athletic environment extremely hostile for openly gay athletes and coaches. An openly gay football or hockey player—sports where physical violence is part of the game—risks being targeted by other athletes outraged at the transgression of a gay man on heterosexual male turf. A closeted gay athlete can participate without suspicion, as long as he is willing to keep his identity a secret. Being an athlete is so consistent with traditional masculine and heterosexual expectations for men that gay athletes can pass if they are willing to. While women athletes must constantly prove their heterosexuality, most people assume that male athletes are heterosexual unless they provide evidence that they are not.

THE ROLE OF SPORT IN EMPOWERING WOMEN

Defenders of a sexist and heterosexist status quo are right to fear the potential that sport has for the empowerment of women (Bennett et al. 1987; Bryson 1990; Theberge 1987). Sport can be a catalyst for empowering women to become the center of their own experience, whether demanding equal access to resources; making connections among sexism, racism, and heterosexism; developing and reveling in their own strength and physical competence; or falling in love with a teammate. When women take sport participation seriously, it is, as Mariah Burton Nelson (1994, 30) asserts, a feminist activity: "All of us collectively, are a threat—not to men exactly, but to male privilege and to masculinity as defined through manly sport."

1994 Gay Games in New York City. Women's ice hockey competition.

What women can learn in athletics contradicts societal messages that encourage girls and women to see themselves as powerless and subordinate. Meeting the physical, mental, and emotional challenges in sport is exhilarating. In athletics women develop a sense of physical competence. Training hard and pushing to the edge of physical and mental limits engender an appreciation and pride in one's accomplishments. Women learn to know what their bodies can do and to trust this knowledge in many different situations beyond the athletic context. Women in athletics learn to perform under pressure. They learn the joy of competitive accomplishment and the discipline of training and practice. Being part of an athletic team teaches women how to work together toward a common goal. Women in athletics develop strong relationships with other women as teammates, friends, and lovers; they challenge, comfort, and support each other.

The truth is that women do develop passionate feelings for other women in the sport context, and for some women these feelings are sexual. Even if there were no lesbians in sport, the intimacy and bonding that develop among women athletes are threatening in a society in

Happy Halloween, courtesy of Dianne Reum.

which women learn to seek the approval of men and men learn that their experiences and goals should take priority over those of women.

Understanding how sport helps to teach boys to embrace masculinity and to avoid what is labeled feminine provides a social context for describing the experiences of lesbians in athletics. There are reasons why athletic women are called lesbians and why there is so much fear and silence among lesbians in athletics. There are reasons why there is such resistance to the acceptance of lesbians in athletics. All of these reasons relate to the maintenance of male power and privilege and the fear that is instilled among women about challenging that power.

The social control of women's sport is not a recent development. Various incarnations of stigma attached to athletic women have intimidated many potential sportswomen since the beginning of the 20th century. Though the arguments have shifted as societal values change, concerns about so-called appropriate feminine behavior and sexuality are consistent themes used to control women's sport. The next chapter describes how societal perceptions of women athletes have changed over the course of the 20th century.

3

Damaged Mothers, Muscle Molls, Mannish Lesbians, and Predatory Dykes:

100 Years of Scaring Women Out of Sport

T
hroughout western civilization, sport has been an almost exclu-sively male domain. Only men were allowed to compete in the ancient Greek Olympics. Women were forbidden from witnessing these athletic events. If a woman was caught watching the Games, she was hurled over a cliff to her death. Sport in contemporary western culture developed out of this male-only tradition. In 1896, when Pierre de Coubertin re-vived the Olympics as an international sporting event, only men were allowed to compete, though women were encouraged to spectate and cheer on the male competitors. The United States did not send a women's team to the Olympics until 1920.

This chapter will describe changes in the larger social context, per-ceptions of intimate relationships between women, and sport opportu-nities for women over the course of the 20th century. This historical overview illustrates how antilesbian prejudice in sport is not merely a post-Stonewall or post–Title IX development. The association of sport and lesbianism has a rich tradition rooted in the early 20th century. For a detailed analysis of the history of gender and sexuality in sport be-yond the scope of this chapter, I recommend Susan Cahn's (1994) *Com-ing on Strong: Gender and Sexuality in Twentieth Century Women's Sport,* Mary Jo Festle's (1996) *Playing Nice: Politics and Apologies in Women's Sports,* and Helen Lenskyj's (1986) *Out of Bounds: Women, Sport and Sexu-ality.*

19TH CENTURY ORIGINS

The words *homosexual* and *heterosexual* were coined in the mid-19th cen-tury (Katz 1983, 1995). Before this time, "the sin between women not to be named among Christians" (Katz 1983, 40) was perceived to be an unaccept-able behavior that required punishment or treatment, but there was no conception of people whose identities were homosexual (or heterosexual).

Medical doctors of the late 19th century began to classify homosexual and heterosexual as types of people, rather than descriptions of indi-vidual sexual acts. This classification system conflated gender role, gen-der identity, and sexual orientation, assuming a consistent relationship among these concepts. Consequently, medical doctors believed that les-bians were men trapped in the bodies of women, and so it followed that they would exhibit masculine appearance and behavior, including an interest in women as sexual partners. This classification of heterosexual as normal and homosexual as abnormal reflected the increasing influ-ence of the Eugenics movement (a social movement concerned with the improvement of the human gene pool by controlling the proliferation of "inferior" types: Jews, poor people, blacks, people with disabilities, and homosexuals, for example). Though these classification systems were developed in the late 19th century, the general population would not become aware of them until well into the 20th century. To illustrate this point, the Oberlin College 1920 yearbook identified, without any hint of stigma, a poetry group called the "Oberlin Lesbian Society" in honor of the ancient poet Sappho from the island of Lesbos. The word *lesbian* did not carry widespread negative stigma until after World War I (Faderman 1991; Katz 1995). Nonetheless, this medical construction of homosexuality laid the foundation for the mannish lesbian stereotype that would persist throughout the next 100 years.

EARLY 20TH CENTURY: DAMAGED MOTHERS

At the beginning of the 20th century, Victorian cultural values were still influential for most white, middle- and upper-class Americans. The "cult of true manhood and womanhood" guided relationships between men and women and societal expectations for them as well. According to Victorian tradition, white women were assumed to be sexually passionless and morally superior to white men. In marriage, middle- and upper-class white men and women were not expected to be equals or to share companionship. Marriage was a legal transaction that afforded women, who had no legal rights, safety and protection, and gave men complete authority over their wives. Husband and wife came together for the purpose of procreation and lived largely separate lives otherwise, cultivating same-sex friendships centered around separate, gender-appropriate pursuits. Within these cultural expectations, intense, even passionate, friendships between women were accepted and even encouraged (Faderman 1981). At worst, these relationships were looked at with curiosity; they were not suspect in any sexual way. This acceptance was due, in part, to the prevailing belief that women were not sexual beings. Relationships between women were therefore not a threat to men's sexual access to women or to a male-dominated society.

At the beginning of the 1900s, middle-class women were participating in sports such as golf, tennis, and bicycling in increasing numbers. Women's sport advocates defended this participation as a means to improve women's health. Critics of women's sport participation, however, claimed that women's inherently weak physical and emotional constitution made sport participation a health risk rather than a health gain. Reflecting the influence of the Eugenics movement, medical doctors and social commentators raised fears that strenuous athletic participation interfered with middle- and upper-class white women's ability to perform their "natural" and "patriotic" roles as wives and mothers (Hastings 1918; Parry 1912). Medical experts warned women about damage to reproductive organs, aggravated nervous conditions, and increased masculinization in physical appearance, manner, and dress (Cowan 1919; Engelmann 1900). An article in *Hygeia* (Kidd 1935, 834), an American Medical Association publication, warned, "In some cases, basketball can make too heavy a demand on the organic vitality of a growing girl." Another article in *The Journal of the American Medical Association* cautioned young women about exercising during their menstrual period: "The uterus is physiologically congested and temporarily abnormally heavy and hence, liable to displacement by the inexcusable strenuosity and roughness of this particular game [basketball]" ("Extracts, abstracts and notices . . ." 1925, cited in Gerber et al. 1974, 16).

Critics of sport for women also described women athletes as unattractive, unfeminine, and even unnatural. Dr. Arabella Kenealy (1899) warned that women's "natural delicacy" was being replaced by unnatural assertiveness and increasing masculinization. She warned of a syndrome she called "bicycle face," which she described as excessive muscular tension and strain.

All of these warnings were primarily directed at white middle-class women. Medical doctors, primarily white middle-class men, were not concerned about the effects of exercise on women of color and poor or working-class women who had always engaged in hard physical labor with none of the ill effects predicted for middle- and upper-class white women who engaged in hard physical play.

1920s: MUSCLE MOLLS

Attitudes about women and women's participation in sport underwent a major transformation during the postwar 1920s (Lenskyj 1986). The so-called Flapper Era ushered in a new liberalism in women's roles and relationships between men and women. The growth of women's colleges and women's sports demonstrated that women could withstand the rigors of higher education and physical activity without incurring physical damage to their reproductive organs.

During this time, Freud and other sexologists began to recognize that women had a sexual nature. They approved of this new sexuality as long as it was directed toward men. Expectations for the "new woman," as she was called, included being energetic, active, and assertively heterosexual (Cahn 1994). Well-known women athletes of the day, such as Helen Wills (tennis), Suzanne Lenglen (tennis), and Gertrude Ederle (swimming), embodied this new ideal.

Once women's sexual nature was acknowledged, however, new social

Corbis-Bettmann

Female tennis player in the 1920s.

controls were needed because more-assertive women threatened traditional relationships between men and women and the power men had over women. The first of these controls was a change in marital expectations. The second, which became more prominent in the mid-20th century, was pathologizing close relationships among women.

Rather than the Victorian expectation that men and women would inhabit separate spheres in marriage, the concept of the "companionate" marriage became the ideal (D'Emilio and Freedman 1988). This emerging perspective on marriage was an attempt to adjust to new perceptions of women's sexual and social power. In this new relationship, husbands and wives were expected to be companions and friends. Reflecting this change, medical experts and popular magazines of the day encouraged marriage partners to attend to each other's sexual and emotional fulfillment.

Following World War I the second wave of feminism emerged, and feminists rallied around the demand for women's right to vote. Other changes in the social context also affected the roles of women. Urbanization and the availability of factory and industrial work allowed for increased independence away from families for single, working-class, white women and women of color. Women's colleges provided similar independence for middle- and upper-class white women as well as an opportunity to be with other women away from men. These two changes enabled women, who could now identify themselves as lesbians, to connect with each other in a small and hidden, but developing, subculture.

In this liberalized social context, more women from all social classes participated in sport. Industrial sport teams, community recreation leagues, and college athletics afforded athletic opportunities to women. Critics of women athletes, however, attacked them for violations of gender and sexuality norms. Conservative critics of the changes in women's roles and participation in sport claimed that sportswomen were "mannish" gender anomalies. Other critics, in apparent contradiction, claimed that sport participation by women led to excessive heterosexuality, immorality, and loss of sexual control (Cahn 1994). Some sportswriters called athletic women "muscle molls," implying that they were prostitutes and nymphomaniacs. In response, advocates of women's sport claimed that sport enhanced heterosexual appeal and health, making women better suited for their roles as mothers and wives. These advocates portrayed sportswomen as wholesome girls or beauty queens to counteract the mannish muscle moll image of conservative critics.

Underlying the concerns of critics of women's sport was the fear that changes in gender dynamics and expectations would lead to changes in power relationships between women and men. Sport, as a traditionally male endeavor, would lose meaning, and women would prove themselves to be the equals of men on and off the playing field.

MID-20TH CENTURY: MANNISH LESBIANS

At the same time that doctors and psychologists promoted companionate marriage as the new heterosexual ideal, the popular press warned that the "mannish lesbian" was a threat to feminine heterosexuality (Faderman 1991; Lenskyj 1986). The construction of this image by medical doctors and sexologists began to cast suspicion on close friendships between women that were entirely accepted in the 19th century and early in the 20th century. Pathologizing female friendships, especially between single women, assured men's control over the newly recognized female sexuality.

This cultural nervousness about changes in gender roles and power found a perfect boundary marker in the emerging social consensus that lesbians were pathological threats to normal womanhood. This stigmatized lesbian image constructed by male medical doctors and sexologists could then serve as a powerful social control mechanism for intimidating any woman who challenged traditional norms of femininity and heterosexuality.

After the progressive social changes in women's roles and the increased sport participation by women in the 1920s, the 1930s ushered in a hostile backlash against feminist and independent working women. Economic uncertainty and the depression aborted liberalism on many fronts, including those related to women's freedoms. The image of the mannish lesbian was now firmly established as a threat to "normal" womanhood and companionate marriage (Newton 1989). Medical experts had succeeded in pathologizing close relationships between women. Through articles in the popular press, medical doctors warned the public about "spinster factories," which were all-female settings such as women's colleges, feminist organizations, and athletics (Ballinger 1932).

Babe Didrikson, arguably the greatest athlete of the 20th century, became a national figure in the 1930s, attracting lots of attention from sports reporters and other members of the press. She was great copy because of her outspoken and uncensored talk, but sportswriters often described her as mannish, unfeminine, rude, rough, and unattractive. Early in her career her lack of conformity to feminine appearance or heterosexual interests coupled with her extraordinary athletic talent motivated reporters to portray her as a gender curiosity. Many sports fans and sports reporters treated Babe like a freak and called her a "muscle moll." Questions about her gender and sexual identity placed her outside the boundaries of "normal" womanhood, and she became a lightning rod for social anxiety about women athletes and changing gender norms (Cayleff 1995).

Leaders of women's sport became increasingly sensitive about the growing association between lesbianism and athletic women. Medical doctors, psychologists, and the popular press criticized women athletes as "failed heterosexuals" (Cahn 1994) based on assumed associations between mannishness and lesbians and between masculinity and sport. Based on these assumptions, critics of women's sport now claimed that women athletes were mannish lesbians who were unattractive to men (Cahn 1994). Advocates of women's sport responded by insisting that sport participation increased women's heterosexual appeal. They worked hard to project an image of happy and enthusiastic heterosexuality among women athletes. Women's sport advocates tried to differentiate women's sport from men's sport by attempting to control what they perceived as masculine excess in women's sport. They curtailed varsity competition and preferred play days and sports days where competition was de-emphasized in hopes that these changes would counter attacks on women athletes. As a result, the image of the mannish lesbian athlete marked the border of acceptable women's behavior. Her image, horrific in the public mind, intimidated all women who contemplated crossing the borders of acceptable behavior for women, whether in sport or other arenas.

At the same time that these conflicts were played out in the larger culture, lesbian subcultures were developing in urban areas. Mostly based in small friendship circles or lesbian bars, these emerging, secretive social networks were difficult for most lesbians to find. In addition to bars and friendship circles, athletic teams for women in industrial leagues and colleges provided a way for both working-class and white middle-class lesbians to find each other. Because of the hostile social climate and the persistent associations between lesbians and sport, however, lesbian athletes were extremely secretive. The social climate was so hostile to lesbians that they dared not make themselves visible in any context. As a result, lesbians had no collective voice to counter prevailing negative perspectives and images that were increasingly influential in controlling all women. The invisibility of lesbians enabled the public perception of lesbians as mannish sexual deviants who were not real women to flourish unchallenged.

World War II proved to be an important cultural transition for lesbians in the United States (Berube 1990). The military's heightened sensitivity about homosexual recruits increased the general population's awareness of lesbians and gay men. This awareness increased hostility toward people perceived to be lesbian or gay and, ironically, also made it possible for increasing numbers of lesbians to identify themselves and find other lesbians. The military attracted many lesbians because they could get away from home, achieve some economic independence, and be with other women. For nonmilitary women, the expanded job opportunities at home also provided better paying jobs doing work normally available only to men. Social networks formed around sport, such as softball teams sponsored by bars, private companies, or community recreation leagues.

World War II also prompted the suspension of professional men's baseball as men enlisted in the armed services. Hoping to recover some of the lost revenue from this suspension of play, Philip Wrigley, the owner of the Chicago Cubs, initiated the formation of the All American Girls' Baseball League (AAGBL) in 1943 (Pratt 1993). Wrigley sold his interest in the league to Arthur Meyerhoff, who administered the league from 1944 to 1950. The strict application of a "femininity principle" and the prohibition of black women in the AAGBL, however, reflected Meyerhoff's belief that to sell the league to the public, it was necessary to prove that the women baseball players were normal, wholesome, white, heterosexual girls. As a result, league officials picked players based as much on their feminine appearance as on their baseball skills. They monitored all players for their compliance with required dress, hair, and makeup codes. Players competed in a skirted uniform rather than pants. All play-

An early 1900s women's baseball team, shown in uniform.

ers attended classes where they learned "ladylike" comportment on and off the field. Players who violated these rules were promptly sent packing. Teams also traveled with an older female chaperone to preserve the league's wholesome image. League media guides bragged that "no freaks or amazons" were allowed (Cahn 1994).

Throughout the 1940s and 1950s, school sport opportunities for girls continued to decrease as women physical educators de-emphasized competition and replaced varsity teams with more inclusive and less competitive forms of participation (Festle 1996). Women physical educators distanced themselves from competition as a strategy to protect women's sport from the negative associations between lesbians and athletics and to protect women athletes from the evil influence of men's sports.

In 1948 and 1953 Alfred Kinsey et al. published their studies of male sexuality and female sexuality in the United States. Their findings made the general public aware that homosexuality was more prevalent than they thought and that there was far greater diversity in sexual identity and experience than they had previously believed. This shift in awareness set the stage for the 1950s, in which awareness and condemnation of homosexuality reached an all-time high.

After the end of World War II, the United States returned to conservative traditional values. A media campaign encouraged women who had taken war-time jobs usually reserved for men to give them up for the returning male veterans. White middle-class women were encouraged to go back home and resume their traditional roles as wives and mothers. With this return to domestic conformity and traditional gender roles, it was more difficult for lesbians to hide. As unmarried working women trying to support themselves, they were clearly outside the conservative mainstream.

During this conservative time, the government became more concerned about the threat of communism and other forms of subversion. Any person or group who was outside the mainstream became suspect. The McCarthy hearings in the early 1950s focused on rooting out communists in all aspects of American society. Eventually gay men and lesbians were added to the list of subversives endangering the moral strength of the country (D'Emilio 1983). Newspaper accounts of the search for subversive homosexuals in government and police raids on gay bars and private parties aggravated public fears about lesbians and gay men.

Mental health experts, unanimous in their opinion that lesbians and gay men were sick and could not lead productive and happy lives, focused their attention on curing homosexuals of their "perversion" (D'Emilio 1983). This prevailing medical opinion, combined with national policy aimed at eliminating homosexuals from government and the military, fueled prejudice against homosexuals. As a result, public awareness and disapproval of homosexuality were higher and the social environment more hostile toward lesbians and gay men than ever before. In this oppressive social environment, visibility for lesbians was dangerous. Women who did not conform to traditional expectations of femininity and heterosexuality were perceived to be social misfits. Survival for most lesbians in the 50s required extreme secrecy and vigilance. This legacy of fear created by hostility toward lesbians in the 50s has been difficult to overcome, even in the last 25 years of greater lesbian, gay, and bisexual acceptance and visibility.

In this social climate women athletes were highly visible public representations of the lesbian image: women who defied traditional feminine values and trespassed on male territory. Where suggestions of the association between lesbianism and athletics had been hinted at earlier, the image of the mannish lesbian athlete became a well-known stereotype in the years following World War II. In earlier years concern had focused on the attractiveness of women athletes to men. Now concern focused on the possibility that women athletes were not attracted to men at all (Cahn 1994). As the gulf between perceptions of female athleticism and attractive heterosexuality widened, women's sports advocates maintained their apologetic, defensive position. They continued trying to prove women athletes' femininity, heterosexual appeal, and heterosexual "success," despite the general public's skepticism on all three counts (Cahn 1994; Festle 1996). Even Babe Didrikson, the prototype muscle moll of the 30s and 40s, embarked on a calculated strategy to win mainstream approval and increase her marketability in the conservative 50s by wearing skirts and makeup and marrying a man. She focused her talents on golf, an appropriately feminine and middle-class sport, and even denied her earlier Olympic accomplishments in track and field. The media and public positive response to her "transformation" illustrates the acceptance that women athletes who presented a feminine and heterosexual front could enjoy. Not until the publication of her biography by Susan Cayleff (1995) was Didrikson's intimate relationship with another woman, Betty Dodd, revealed publicly.

In the 1950s, sport provided a place where lesbians and other women who did not fit the feminine and heterosexual ideal could find other women who shared their experience and interests. In sport, many lesbians found community and intimacy as long as they kept their sexual orientation a secret. Despite the association between lesbianism and sport in the public mind, sport competitions such as basketball and softball games were relatively safe social gathering places. In contrast,

Babe Didrikson shown throwing the javelin (early in her career).

Later in her career, Babe Didrikson tried to shed
her "muscle moll" image.

gay bars, and even private homes, were vulnerable to recurring police
raids in which those arrested routinely had their names printed in the
local paper and their employers notified by the police. Lesbians in athletics were insulated by small, closeted circles of lesbian friends and
lovers and were fearful of upsetting this delicate balance. They developed a code of silence that Cahn (1994) describes as "play it, don't say
it" that enabled lesbian athletes to survive and enjoy a circumscribed
social life on athletic teams that was impossible elsewhere. While most
heterosexual women in the 1950s were repelled by the association of
sport with lesbians, lesbians found in sport a place where their so-called
masculine strength and skill were a welcomed advantage. Sport became

a haven where they could meet other lesbians in an atmosphere of relative comfort and safety.

Middle-class lesbian athletes learned to strike a bargain: secrecy in exchange for safety. Working-class lesbian athletes, whose culture often included more butch-femme role playing in which women in relationships adopted variations on traditional masculine and feminine roles, had a more difficult time hiding. They were also more dependent on bar culture and the sports teams sponsored by bars for their social networks. As a result, they were more vulnerable to violence and harassment from the police or thugs and condemnation from the public than were women in college or country club sport circles.

The 1960s climate for lesbian athletes reflected the lingering effects of the McCarthy era. Lesbians were thoroughly discredited as social and sexual deviants, and the association between the mannish lesbian and the woman athlete was firmly established in the popular mind. Consistent with the return to traditional gender roles in the 1950s, women's sports were marginalized and limited and posed no threat to men's domination of sport. The stage was being set, however, for tremendous changes in women's sports and women's roles in general. Several social change movements in the 1960s (black civil rights, feminist, counterculture, and antiwar) challenged the authority and dominance of traditional values accepted in the 1950s. In the shadow of these changes, urban lesbian subcultures continued to grow, and sport remained an arena for the development of hidden lesbian community, identity, and intimacy.

THE LATE 20TH CENTURY: PREDATORY DYKES

In the 1970s, several social movements and a number of social trends had a tremendous impact on women's sport. The feminist movement, reborn during the 1960s, hit its stride during the 1970s. The sexual revolution promised important changes in women's access to sexual freedom, and the legalization of abortion gave women more control over their choice to bear children. The emerging gay and lesbian rights movement changed coming out from a personal declaration to a political statement and sparked the proliferation of a more visible and proud lesbian and gay subculture. Finally, the fitness boom encouraged more women to take their right to sport participation and fitness more seriously than ever before.

Perhaps most significantly, the passage of Title IX in 1972 opened the doors to more school and college sports opportunities for girls and women. Title IX is a federal law prohibiting sex discrimination in educational institutions receiving federal funds. As a result, women's sport participation increased dramatically. Before Title IX, 300,000 women participated in intercollegiate athletics in the United States. In 1997 that figure has increased to approximately 2.25 million participants (President's Council on Physical Fitness and Sports 1997).

In 1972-73, the women-controlled Association of Intercollegiate Athletics for Women (AIAW) organized and began offering national intercollegiate championships for women's athletics. The initiation of the women's professional tennis tour also increased the popularity and visibility of women's sport. In this encouraging atmosphere more women of all ages participated in sport and fitness activities than ever before.

Despite progress in the larger culture toward the greater acceptance and visibility of lesbians and gay men during the early 1970s, the stigma attached to lesbians in sport remained intact. The author of an article about the LPGA tour stated, "Everyone to whom I mentioned my assignment said bluntly, 'Find out if they are dykes.' It is the dearest wish of the golfers' collective heart to put this matter straight, to announce as loudly as possible, they are just as feminine as the next one" (Gornick 1971, 69). A *Newsweek* article on women's sports in 1974 asked, "Who are these women who compete and live together on the closely knit tours?. . . Are they lesbians who hate men or rejected heterosexuals who want to get back at men? . . . Do they sneer at sexiness, glamour, and marriage, or do they secretly covet a 'normal' life?" (Axthelm 1974, 52). A series on women's sports in *Sports Illustrated* suggested that "Behind the myth that participation in sports will masculinize a woman's appearance, there is the even darker insinuation that athletics will masculinize a woman's sexual behavior" (Gilbert and Williamson 1973, 47).

Women athletes responded to these questions with characteristic defensiveness, as illustrated by one pro golfer, "I don't like the implications of so many single women on the tour who are such good friends. I'd like to see a Mrs. in front of every name" (Cuniberti 1978, D8).

In response to these stories Betty Hicks (1979), a founding member of the LPGA, wrote an article entitled "Lesbian Athletes" in which she refuted lesbian athlete stereotypes and provided a strikingly clear political analysis of the functions of antilesbian prejudice in sport. This article was the first written in which homophobia and heterosexism in women's sport, rather than lesbian participation in sport, was identified as the problem.

In the feminist movement internal conflicts about how to address lesbian issues presaged future struggles within women's sport. Heterosexual feminists feared that acknowledging lesbians in the movement, or fighting for lesbian rights would taint and discredit the entire feminist agenda for other women. Similarly, women in sport feared that acknowledging lesbian coaches and athletes would damage the image of women's sport and dampen public support.

Toward the end of the 1970s, conservative political and religious factions, outraged by the cultural changes during the 1960s and 1970s, mounted efforts to reverse some of the earlier legislative victories of the gay, feminist, and black civil rights movements. With the election of Ronald Reagan to the U.S. presidency in 1980, an era of political conservatism swept the country. Consistent with this political climate, several events affected women's sport in general and lesbians in sport in particular.

Once National Collegiate Athletic Association (NCAA) leaders, who controlled men's college sports, realized that Title IX presented a threat to men's control of resources, they began a two-part strategy to control the growth of women's collegiate sport. First, they began offering women's championships, which competed with those offered by the smaller and less powerful AIAW. As a much larger organization with greater financial resources, it took the NCAA only a few years to completely drive the AIAW out of business (Festle 1996). As women's athletics came under the control of male athletic directors and the male-dominated NCAA, and salaries for coaching women's teams improved as a result of Title IX, more men were interested in and hired to coach women's teams. Women were not, however, hired to coach men's teams. As a result, though growth in women's participation in athletics at all levels continued, there was a corresponding decline in women in leadership roles in athletics as women's sports came under the control of men (Acosta and Carpenter 1985).

The second part of the NCAA strategy was to mount a legal challenge to Title IX. In the 1984 Grove City decision, the Supreme Court mandated a much narrower interpretation of Title IX that required each individual program within a school to receive federal funds before Title IX applied. This change made it much more difficult to challenge sex discrimination in athletics. With the narrower interpretation of Title IX, legal challenges to gender inequity in sport became rare. In 1988 the power women had to challenge sex discrimination in sport increased dramatically, however, with the passage of the Civil Rights Restoration Act. This legislation restored the original intent of Title IX and reopened the door for lawsuits charging collegiate and high school athletic programs with sex discrimination.

Social changes in the roles of women, the feminist movement, and the passage and subsequent restoration of Title IX cleared the way for tremendous changes in women's sport and public perceptions of women athletes. Not all women in sport could be seriously dismissed as lesbians because too many women were participating at all levels of sport for this association to be taken as seriously as it had been previously. In response to these changes, perceptions of appropriate sport involvement for women broadened. Instead, the lesbian stigma narrowed to focus, not on all women athletes, but on those women who did not conform to the new heterosexy image of the woman athlete or on women who challenged the power imbalance between men and women in sport.

The emerging cultural attitude toward women athletes was that athletic participation was great for women as long as they could provide evidence that they were not lesbians. Thus, the lesbian stigma could still be used to intimidate and control all women's sport participation because they felt pressured to "prove" their heterosexuality and distance themselves from association with lesbians.

Several changes in women's sports contributed to an increasingly hostile environment for lesbians. First, as more heterosexual women took advantage of sport opportunities, and as being an athlete became more compatible with contemporary women's roles, the focus changed from a generalized concern about all women athletes to a specific concern about lesbians and the sexual threat they posed to heterosexual women in sport. Second, with the passage of Title IX, salaries for coaching women's teams improved, attracting more men in women's sport. Third, with increased professional opportunities and college scholarships, parents of young women athletes took a more active interest in their daughter's sport participation. Fourth, women's college sports came under the control of male-dominated athletic departments and the NCAA. The influx of more heterosexual (and younger) athletes, male coaches and athletic directors, and parents of young women athletes who brought their prejudices about lesbians with them increased the focus on lesbians in sport as sexual predators.

Whereas earlier in the century hostility toward lesbians came primarily from outside of sport, now hostility toward lesbians came from inside sport as well. Based on the belief that lesbians are a sexual threat to other women and that they use their power as older athletes or coaches to entice young, innocent women into unhealthy lesbian sexual relationships, many heterosexual coaches, parents, and athletes openly expressed their desire to exclude or avoid contact with lesbians in sport.

Beginning in the 1980s, a number of highly publicized "lesbian incidents" in women's sport disturbed the still waters of silence and raised the issue of lesbians in sport more directly than ever before. Leaders of women's sports responded to these incidents by attempting to minimize the issue, control damage, and avoid acknowledging the presence of lesbians. This response gave credibility and power to the "dangerous lesbian" image and convinced most lesbian coaches and athletes that they could not count on support from their colleagues in sport or the general public to challenge this destructive image.

The first of these incidents occurred in 1981, when professional tennis player and feminist Billie Jean King held a press conference to reveal that a former lesbian lover was suing her for palimony. With her husband by her side, Billie Jean called her seven-year relationship with Marilyn Barnett a "mistake" (Beach 1981). A subsequent cover story in *People* magazine focused on her relationship with husband Larry and her insistence that she "hated being called homosexual because she does not feel that way" (McCall 1981b, 75). This public revelation opened the discussion of lesbians in sport in a more direct way than ever (Axthelm 1981; Hicks 1981; Kirshenbaum 1981; McCall 1981a; Roberts 1981; Vecsey 1981). Until she admitted her "affair," as Billie Jean called it, no prominent woman in sport had ever acknowledged her lesbianism (B.J. King and Deford 1982). The realization that a popular, attractive, and married woman athlete could also have a lesbian lover shocked the general public. Though Billie Jean's lesbian relationship was well known to other women on the professional tennis tour, it was accepted wisdom that to publicly acknowledge lesbian tennis players would jeopardize the tour's popularity and ability to attract corporate sponsorship. King did lose most of her commercial sponsors, affirming the perspectives that (1) women athletes are accepted as long as they are heterosexual and (2) it is financially ruinous for lesbian professional athletes to publicly identify themselves (Festle 1996). Women's Tennis Association (WTA) officials warned other players that they would not tolerate another player coming out. Rumors circulated that Avon, a major sponsor for the women's tour, was threatening to withdraw its $4 million–a–year sponsorship if anyone spoke about homosexuality on the tour (Zwerman 1995).

In another 1981 incident, an article in the *New York Post* "outed" Martina Navratilova by disclosing her relationship with writer and lesbian activist Rita Mae Brown (Festle 1996; Zwerman 1995). Though this story came as no surprise to most people, the public confirmation of Martina's lesbian relationship caused further consternation among WTA officials, who were already increasingly sensitive about the tour's image.

In 1982, *Sports Illustrated* reported that Pam Parsons, the women's basketball coach at the University of South Carolina, was accused of being sexually involved with a player on her team (Lieber and Kirshenbaum 1982). Given the almost complete invisibility of lesbian coaches and athletes, this article confirmed the fears of many parents and young athletes that lesbians are sexual predators and that young women athletes coached by lesbians or who play on teams with lesbians are at risk of being sexually harassed or coerced into unwilling sexual liaisons. (See chapter 10 for a more detailed discussion of this incident.)

While the broader lesbian and gay movement was placing more political emphasis on pride and coming out, the women's sport establishment was still depending on the strategies used for 50 years to address the issue of lesbians in sport: silence and denial.

The 1990s have ushered in an unprecedented acceptance and visibility of women in sport. The achievements of the women in both individual and team sports in the 1996 Olympics attest to the success of

Title IX in increasing both the number of women in sport and the quality of women's sport performance. Participation in high school and college sport is higher than ever, recreational sport opportunities for women are growing, and sports equipment manufacturers have finally recognized the potential of marketing their products to women. Yet even with all the progress made, women's athletics is still not receiving its fair share of resources. As of spring 1997, only 9 percent of Division 1 schools are in compliance with Title IX, even though women's participation in college athletics has increased fourfold since 1992 (Brady 1997).

Two "lesbian" stories received widespread media attention in 1991. Penn State women's basketball coach Rene Portland came into the media spotlight when former players told a reporter from the *Philadelphia Inquirer* about her policy of not allowing lesbians on her teams (Longman 1991). Portland allegedly told prospective recruits that she did not allow "alcohol, drugs, or lesbians" on her teams. She never publicly acknowledged her policy, claiming that team "training rules" were not public information. However, Portland had been quoted in a *Chicago Sun-Times* article in 1986 saying she would not allow "it" (referring to lesbianism) on her teams (Figel 1986). Much of the media coverage of

Reuters/Corbis-Bettmann

Professional tennis player Martina Navratilova now uses her media attention to gain support for lesbian and gay civil rights.

Portland's policy was critical of her and Penn State (Bull 1991; Lederman 1991; Lipsyte 1991; Solomons 1991). Partly in response to the negative publicity received, Penn State added sexual orientation to the university nondiscrimination policy shortly after Portland's policy became public.

Later that year, like Billie Jean King 10 years earlier, Martina Navratilova was involved in a palimony suit brought by former lover Judy Nelson after the breakup of their eight-year relationship. The media provided the public with extensive coverage of the court proceedings. After this very public and contentious breakup, Martina began to take an active and visible role in several lesbian and gay political causes. She spoke at the 1993 National March on Washington for Lesbian, Gay, and Bisexual Rights, participated in fund-raising for Gay Games IV, and joined a legal challenge of the 1992 Colorado antigay Amendment 2. With these actions, Martina became the first professional athlete to publicly embrace her lesbian identity and take an active political role in the lesbian and gay civil rights movement.

The mainstream press attention paid to lesbians in sport continued in 1995. CBS golf commentator Ben Wright was quoted in a newspaper article saying that lesbians ruin the LPGA tour by "parading it" (meaning lesbianism; Hudson 1995a). The article quoted Wright as saying that lesbians were much more bold and open than they had previously been and that this increased visibility was a liability for the LPGA tour. The media response to Wright's comments filled the sports pages for several weeks following the initial story. Most articles focused on Wright's claim that the reporter had made up the story and his denial of ever making the comments attributed to him. CBS and most of the LPGA players defended Wright until he acknowledged making the comments several months later in a private conversation. Wright was then quietly dropped by the network (Zipay 1996).

In 1996, LPGA player Muffin Spencer-Devlin came out in a *Sports Illustrated* article (Garrity and Nutt 1996). The responses of her corporate sponsors, other players, the media, and the general public to her revelation were different from all of the "lesbian in sport" stories that had come before. Her coming out was almost a non-event. Significantly, Spencer-Devlin controlled her coming out in that there was no controversy associated with her decision to publicly reveal her lesbian identity. Her decision was not in response to a palimony suit, she was not "outed" by a news reporter, and no antilesbian comments were made by TV commentators or other golfers. Whether this response represents an increasing comfort with lesbian athletes remains to be seen, but the public nonresponse to Spencer-Devlin's coming out is in sharp contrast to the earlier, more sensationalized stories about lesbians in sport.

In addition to Spencer-Devlin and Navratilova, professional bike racer Missy Giove is an out lesbian (Browne 1996). Professional tennis players

Professional tennis player Gigi Fernandez competing
at the 1994 U.S. Open in New York.

Gigi Fernandez and Conchita Martinez have not publicly come out, but their relationship was discussed as part of a news story on gays in sport (Wilstein 1996), and Gigi accompanied Martina Navratilova to the 1993 March on Washington for Lesbian, Gay, and Bisexual Rights. For the most part, however, the vast majority of lesbians in sport maintain a veil of secrecy around their identities and are afraid that revealing themselves to the general public would have both financial and professional consequences. The politics of accommodation prevail: The goal is to create a place in sport for women without challenging current dominant perceptions of femininity and heterosexuality.

Several themes become apparent in this brief historical review. Sport has always been a male domain. Women's participation in sport has always been discouraged and controlled. Though the specific means of control have shifted, all focus on accusations and intimidations that challenge women's femininity and heterosexuality. As women's participation in sport has become more acceptable and widespread, norms of femininity have expanded to include athleticism. Lesbians in sport are now more openly targeted within sport and continue to represent the boundary line between acceptable and unacceptable behavior for women. As a result, fear of the lesbian label continues to control women's sport. Fear of the lesbian label ensures that women do not gain control over their sporting experience or develop their physical competence beyond what is acceptable in a sexist culture.

The shadowy image of lesbians in sport, cast against the silence of the closet where most lesbians in athletics reside, denies the diversity, complexity, and individuality of the real lives and experiences of lesbians in sport. The long history of this image as it has evolved over the course of the 20th century underscores its staying power as a boundary marker for women who challenge gender and sexuality norms in and out of sport. The next chapter explores contemporary images of lesbian athletes and coaches that terrify and intimidate parents of young athletes, heterosexual women athletes, and many closeted lesbians alike.

4

Leering, Leching, and Low Down:

Demonizing Lesbians in Sport

There is no such thing as a universal lesbian experience. Lesbian stereotypes ignore the complex and multidimensional nature of lesbian identity and experience (Eliason 1996; Kitzinger 1987; Phelan 1994; Sykes 1996; Wilkinson and Kitzinger 1993). Women who choose to define themselves as lesbians are quite diverse. Many women-loving women in sport reject the lesbian label, preferring to call themselves "gay" or "queer" or refusing to claim a label of any kind. Some women who currently self-identify as gay or lesbian do not rule out having a sexual relationship with a man in the future. Many lesbians have had past sexual relationships with men. Some women continue having sex with men even though they identify as lesbian. Many women believe they have always been lesbians and knew this about themselves from an early age, while others discovered their feelings for women later in life, and this knowledge came as a surprise. For some women, claiming their lesbian identity felt natural and right from the beginning. For others, self-acceptance has

G is for Gretchen, who knew at age seven.

been a long and painful struggle. Some lesbians believe their sexual identity to be a choice, but others believe that they were born lesbians. Some women feel sexually attracted to men and women. These descriptions represent only some of the diversity among women who identify as lesbian, gay, bisexual, or queer.

Lesbian identity is only one of a number of other significant social group memberships that affect how women see themselves and are treated by others. Far from the unidimensional image of lesbians used to intimidate women in sport, the lived experiences of lesbians cut across such boundaries as age, culture, sexuality, gender, race, religion, lifestyle, ability or disability, and class. For example, the sport experiences of a working-class white woman or poor lesbian of color will be different from those of a white middle-class lesbian.

Different regions of the country are more or less hostile to lesbian and gay people, so where a lesbian athlete or coach lives also affects her athletic experience. If she lives in a small rural area in which religious fundamentalism dominates community values, her experience will be different from that of a coach or athlete living in an urban area in which there is more tolerance and acceptance of lesbian and gay people. These and other personal identity and contextual factors make broad generalizations about common lesbian identity and experience difficult to construct.

In sport this multifaceted nature of lived lesbian experience is erased, and instead a stereotypical monolithic image, a lesbian boogeywoman, haunts all women, scaring young women athletes and their parents, discouraging solidarity among women in sport, and keeping women's sport advocates on the defensive. In this atmosphere the lesbian boogeywoman image thrives as a simplistic and inaccurate representation of lesbian identity in women's sport. As a result, lesbian athletes and coaches, despite the diversity of their experiences and self-definitions, are all subjected to social prejudice and discrimination in sport.

IMAGES OF WOMEN IN SPORT

The lesbian boogeywoman is only one of several competing media-created and promoted images of women athletes. Other images include (1) the sexy beauty queen, (2) the wholesome girl next door, (3) the cute little pixie, (4) the bitchy slut, and (5) the wife and mom. In all of these images, women athletes are forced into stereotyped packages for public consumption regardless of their individuality. All gymnasts and most figure skaters, with the exception of Tonya Harding, are portrayed as cute little pixies, beauty queens, or girls next door (Baughman 1995; Brennan 1996; Ryan 1995). Older women athletes are most acceptable if they can be categorized as wife and mom or beauty queen. The LPGA

actively promotes these images for professional golfers. Many professional tennis players are typically described as the girl next door.

The media attention devoted to Tonya Harding and Nancy Kerrigan
in 1994 pitted two of these images against each other: the bitchy "trailer
trash" slut and the wholesome girl next door (Baughman 1995). The long-
time rivalry between Chris Evert and Martina Navratilova had an unspoken subtext of Beauty (Queen) versus Butch (Lesbian). Nancy Lopez is
as well known for being a wife and mother as she is for her golf accomplishments, while Jan Stephenson (beauty queen) was better known for
her cleavage than her club selection. Volleyball player Gabrielle Reece
also is portrayed as a beauty queen. Ironically, in light of Jennifer
Capriati's subsequent problems with drugs, she was adored by the tennis media as the wholesome girl next door. Martina Hingis (tennis),
Rebecca Lobo (basketball), Dot Richardson (softball), and Mia Hamm
(soccer) are also presented as the wholesome girls next door.

Athletes of color do not neatly fit into any of these predominantly
white-associated stereotypes, though the focus on Lisa Leslie's model-
ing career and Flo Jo's glamorous body suits and nails are consistent
with the beauty queen image. Jackie Joyner-Kersee's relationship with
husband-coach Al Joyner receives its share of heterosexualized media
attention. Likewise, Olympic gold medalist and WNBA basketball player
Sheryl Swoopes's picture on the cover of the 1997 premiere issue of
Sports Illustrated Women/Sport highlighted her pregnancy more than her
athletic talent. With the emergence into the media spotlight of athletes
such as tennis player Venus Williams and pro basketball players such as
Cynthia Cooper and Teresa Weatherspoon, how women athletes of color
will be portrayed remains to be seen.

The lesbian boogeywoman image, however, is set apart from the others. While all of these images are limiting and force women athletes to
conform to stereotypes, only the lesbian boogeywoman image is outside the boundaries of acceptable heterosexuality. The lesbian
boogeywoman is cast as a threat not only to "normal" women in sport,
but to the image and acceptance of women's sport altogether. There is
no room for the possibility that the beauty might also be a lesbian or
that a lesbian might be a mother or that the girl next door might be a
dyke. If the lesbian boogeywoman image is to serve the purpose of mark-
ing the boundaries of acceptable (nonthreatening) sport participation,
it must be unambiguously threatening and unacceptable. There is no
room for the complexity of reality. The lesbian label is an effective tool
for social control in women's sport only as long as lesbian identity is
stigmatized and stereotyped. If lesbian identity is accepted as an unre-
markable variation of female sexuality, then lesbian slurs and innuendos lose their power to intimidate women into conforming to traditional
gender roles and sexual expression.

THE LESBIAN BOOGEYWOMAN IN SPORT

Parents, athletes, coaches, and others who express concern about lesbians in athletics typically identify one or more of several beliefs about lesbians that justify their fears: (1) Particular sports are associated with lesbians; (2) participation in athletics promotes lesbianism; (3) lesbians are sexual predators; (4) lesbians are immoral and are therefore poor role models for young women; (5) cliques of powerful lesbians band together to discriminate against heterosexual women and men in sport; (6) lesbians have an unfair advantage over other women in sport because they are not "normal" women.

Lesbians Participate in Particular Sports

Lesbian participation is often associated with team sports, professional sports, sports in which the competitors are older, or sports that are not consistent with traditional feminine expectations of appearance and performance.

Figure skating and gymnastics are individual sports dominated by very young athletes whose appearance and performance conform to traditional feminine expectations. Rarely are female gymnasts or figure skaters suspected of being lesbians. Women's collegiate and professional basketball and softball are team sports, participants are usually older, and the appearance and performance of many of these women do not conform to traditional feminine expectations. Professional tennis players and golfers, though participating in individual sports more associated with "femininity," are often older women and are competing at the highest level and against men for the attention and support of fans and corporate sponsors. Even if there were no lesbian team-sport coaches or athletes or lesbian professional athletes, these sports would probably still be dogged by lesbian baiting because they represent challenges to male supremacy and exclusivity of participation in team sports and professional sports.

If in the past there has been some truth to the belief that lesbians are particularly attracted to team sports or that there are more lesbians in team sports, these differences might be explained in a number of ways. Heterosexual girls might have dropped out of team sports more frequently than lesbians because of the lesbian stigma attached to these sports, though with increasing participation of women in all sports, this might no longer be the case. Some studies indicate that gender nonconformity, though not a cause of homosexuality, is correlated more with young people who identify as lesbian or gay (Bell, Weinberg, and Hammersmith 1981). If this is so, lesbian athletes might be less affected by fears about violating traditional gender expectations in their sport

Same Sex Pairs Ice Dancing Competition
at the 1994 Gay Games in New York City.

participation. However, as gender role expectations have broadened so that being a woman athlete is more acceptable, this explanation seems less likely. Finally, as discussed in chapter 3, team sports have historically provided lesbians with a nontraditional environment in which to explore identity and community (Zipter 1988a). I believe this is still true despite the increasing participation of heterosexual women in sport.

Concerns that lesbians participate in particular sports sometimes lead to fears that there are "too many" lesbians in a particular sport. Collegiate softball and basketball are criticized, as are professional golf and tennis, by those who perceive that many lesbians participate in these sports. These critics claim that the presence of lesbians tarnish a sport's image. This lesbian "taint" is blamed for everything from public image problems to an inability to attract corporate sponsors and spectators. If lesbians are tolerated in sport only when they hide their identity, any assertion of their presence is perceived as "flaunting" and can be used as evidence that there are too many lesbians in that sport.

Participation in Athletics Promotes Lesbianism

Some observers have attributed lesbianism among athletes to such factors as the lack of contact with men, loneliness, or a lack of "social skills" needed for a "normal" life. Several years ago I was part of a conversation with a woman highly respected for her leadership in research on women's sport. We were serving as consultants for a national women's sports advocacy organization at the time. She told me she believed that women's sports teams are an unnatural environment where, if you have some young women who are lonely and possibly lacking in certain social skills, they are vulnerable to unhealthy relationships with teammates or coaches.

To attribute lesbian relationships to loneliness, isolation, or lack of social skills assumes that they are deficient, second-class relationships formed either because men reject women athletes or women athletes are isolating themselves from "normal" heterosexual relationship opportunities. To the contrary, most lesbians do not reject men; they choose women. Loving women, for most lesbians, is a positive commitment that has nothing to do with men.

Similar suspicions about the sexuality of male athletes are rare even though they spend just as much time in all-male environments as women athletes spend in all-female settings. This sex difference reflects that only women in all-female groups engaging in activities that challenge gender roles, sexism, and compulsory heterosexuality need to be controlled and marginalized in this way.

In any environment where emotional intensity and constant togetherness encourage women to respect and love themselves and other women, sexual feelings between women are more available. Some women do identify themselves as lesbians for the first time during their participation in sport. The supportive and close relationships among women in athletics can become sexual. However, those who encourage the idea that sport participation promotes or causes lesbianism are more interested in controlling women's athleticism by threatening them with the stigma of the lesbian boogeywoman than they are interested in the complexities of sexual attraction and identity.

No empirical evidence supports the contention that participation in any activity, sport or otherwise, has any relationship to sexual identity. Though researchers have proposed many different biologically and culturally based theories, how sexual identity occurs is not well understood, and the complexity of gender and sexual identities makes the identification of a simple cause-and-effect relationship unlikely.

Lesbians Are Sexual Predators

This is one of the most enduring, pervasive, and destructive aspects of the lesbian stereotype in sport. Tapping into the deepest fears of parents and heterosexual athletes and coaches, this stereotype encourages much of the prejudice and discrimination against lesbians in sport. According to this stereotype, lesbians coerce innocent, young, weak, and unwilling heterosexual women into unnatural sexual liaisons. In a workshop I was leading, a male coach stated with firm authority that his objection to lesbian athletes was that he had heard about a team where lesbians forced younger teammates to have sex with them in some kind of team initiation rite. When I pressed for more information, it became apparent that he had no specific information about this team. He had heard about it from someone who had heard about it from someone else, who . . . The point is that people are often predisposed to believe the most outrageous stories about the assumed sexual predatory nature of lesbians.

Lesbians supposedly leer at the naked bodies of other women in the locker room with sexual intent. They hit on heterosexual peers and sexually harass them when their advances are rebuffed. Capitalizing on these fears, the tabloid *National Enquirer* published a 1990 front-page "exposé" on lesbian sexual predators on the women's professional tennis tour and how other presumably heterosexual young players like Jennifer Capriati and Gabriella Sabatini were afraid to go into the women's locker rooms unaccompanied because of their fear of older lesbians lurking there (South et al. 1990). The story reported that older lesbian players lured young players to "all girl" hot tub parties and other apparently irresistible enticements to lesbian sex.

In a message on the Women's Sports Foundation homophobia bulletin board, a man wrote that "Ben Wright was right" that the LPGA is "ripe with lesbian activity" and that "the lesbians can't leave the straights alone. The problem is so bad that they have to separate the tee times for the dykes and the straights." This perspective illustrates this association of lesbians with uncontrolled, predatory hypersexuality. Possibly this association is the projection of some men who can use only their own perceptions of sexuality and women as sexual objects to imagine what it must be like to be sexually attracted to women and have access to the women's locker room. This enduring lesbian sexual predator image is a fabrication of early 20th century sexologists who believed that lesbians were, in fact, men trapped in women's bodies. Thus, lesbians are viewed as pseudo-men, exhibiting all of the worst aspects of heterosexual male sexuality.

Ironically, it is much more likely that women in or out of sport will be the targets of male sexual harassment or violence. Statistics on sexual harassment, sexual and other forms of violence against women, as well as sexual relationships between coaches and athletes show that heterosexual males are far more likely to be perpetrators than are lesbians. Unfortunately, until the last few years the abuse of power by heterosexual male coaches has not received nearly as much attention as has the assumption that, by their very presence, lesbians pose a sexual threat to their heterosexual teammates. (See chapter 10 for a more detailed discussion of these issues.)

If this stereotype were true, it would be difficult to see how lesbian athletes could maintain their performance level in their sports if they are always thinking about sex and how to lure their heterosexual opponents and teammates into bed. In fact, most lesbian athletes and coaches in the locker room are thinking about the same things their heterosexual counterparts are: What is my strategy against this opponent? How do I feel today? Is that nagging injury going to affect my play? How can I focus my concentration on the game?

WANDA, SMITTEN WITH THE SECOND BASEWOMAN, DISGRACES HER TEAM BY FORGETTING TO RUN.

Lesbians Are Immoral and Are Poor Role Models for Young Women

Probably the most public expression of this stereotype occurred in 1990 when former tennis great and born-again Christian Margaret Court publicly called Martina Navratilova a poor role model for young girls following Martina's record-breaking ninth Wimbledon championship (Associated Press 1990). Court's outburst was apparently provoked by Martina's spontaneous trip into the stands after her victory to hug her lover, Judy

Nelson. Though Court was criticized in the press for her remark, many parents of athletes and heterosexual coaches agree with her: Lesbians, regardless of their individual character and accomplishments, are inherently bad role models.

Lesbians in sport are held to a different standard of morality than heterosexual women or men in sport. Displaying any open acknowledgment of lesbian identity or relationship is all that is necessary to be labeled immoral. All other character attributes immediately become secondary: charitable work or contributions, service to the sport and community, or exemplary behavior on and off the playing field. Though heterosexual women athletes are also held to a higher moral standard than male athletes, they are still given more latitude as long as they can prove their heterosexuality, or perhaps *because* they can prove their heterosexuality. Tennis player Chris Evert, for example, was known for her salty sense of humor and several highly public relationships with different male celebrities during her career: Jimmy Connors, Burt Reynolds, and Jack Ford, to name a few. Nonetheless, she was widely admired as a wonderful, wholesome role model for young girls. Evert herself acknowledged this perception, "I don't think there is any doubt that one of the reasons I became the girl-next-door to the public was my sexuality. People could relate to the fact that I was dating men" (Feinstein 1992, 455).

In contrast, male athletes get drunk, take drugs, fight in bars, have sex with numerous women, cheat on, beat, and rape their wives and girlfriends, flip spectators the bird, grab their crotches, wear dresses, swear at officials, kick photographers, moon fans, get into fist fights with opponents, spit at umpires and fans, harass female sportswriters, yet few male sportswriters or fans express any concern that they are serving as role models for young boys or damaging the image of men's sport.

The irony of the "poor role model" stereotype is that many lesbian coaches and athletes are serving as excellent role models for young girls, but they are able to do so only because they keep their lesbian identities carefully hidden. Acknowledging that lesbians already are serving as good role models for young girls runs counter to the negative lesbian boogeywoman image.

Lesbian Cliques Dominate Sports and Discriminate Against Heterosexuals

In 1994 Denise Annetts, a member of the Australian women's cricket team, claimed that she was dropped from the team because she was heterosexual and married (Burroughs, Ashburn, and Seebohm 1995). Annetts' charges received coverage from newspapers and other media all over Australia that typically never cover women's sports. Burroughs,

Ashburn, and Seebohm claim that the widespread media attention paid to Annetts's charge was motivated not only by homophobia and male sports reporters' prurient fascination with lesbianism, but also by a "homosexual backlash." These authors proposed that this backlash was in response to lesbians' and gay men's increasing visibility and demands for employment rights and a harassment-free environment. The incident also provided heterosexuals frustrated with the negative lesbian image associated with women's sports an opportunity to vent their anger at lesbians for "creating" public relations problems.

Similarly, in the United States some men and women softball coaches claim that men are discriminated against by a "lesbian mafia" in the National Softball Coaches Association. A 1996 posting on a softball coaches' bulletin board went so far as to name a number of prominent and successful women softball coaches and insinuate that they were lesbians who had received their coaching positions because they were part of the lesbian in-crowd controlling college women's softball.

Part of CBS golf analyst Ben Wright's criticism of lesbians on the LPGA tour was that homosexuality "is paraded, there is a defiance to them in the last ten years." His comments followed the Nabisco Dinah Shore tournament, which may have in part provoked Wright's comments. This LPGA tournament is well known as a major lesbian social event to which thousands of openly lesbian women flock for a week of parties and other events planned to coincide with the golf tournament. One can only speculate what it must be like for homophobic TV commentators (and the image-conscious LPGA leadership) to have this tournament associated with so many open and proud lesbian spectators in the gallery. Since the deeply closeted LPGA lesbian players can hardly be accused of flaunting or parading their sexuality, it makes sense that Wright might have been responding more to the spectators than the golfers. Proud and unapologetic lesbians are far more threatening than lesbians who are trying to conceal their identities.

As these examples illustrate, when anyone in women's sport has a grievance or when they want to explain why women's sport is not more popular, lesbians are always a vulnerable and convenient scapegoat. Playing "the lesbian card" in this way almost always places those who must respond to these charges on the defensive and taps into the generalized discomfort that surrounds any discussion of lesbians in sport. It matters little whether or not the women accused are lesbians. Such lesbian baiting is used to discredit strong women in or out of sport. Hillary Rodham Clinton, Janet Reno, and Donna Shalala are all women in powerful positions who have been called lesbians in an attempt to discredit them.

Since most lesbians in sport are securely locked in the closet, it is amazing that they are perceived to wield such power. This assumption speaks to the expectation that lesbians, if they are to be tolerated at all in sport, are expected to be invisible and grateful for any acceptance they are accorded. Any action that reflects an expectation that lesbians should be able to be as open about their identity as heterosexuals are is called "flaunting," "parading," or "taking over," and lesbians who insist on their right to be visible and treated fairly are discounted as "activists."

Lesbians Have an Unfair Advantage in Sport

The association of lesbianism with masculinity and masculinity with outstanding sport performance feeds into the assumption that lesbians are not "real" women. This image is based on the belief that lesbians have extraordinary strength and competence that enable them to dominate women's sport or to beat men. Dennis Connor, recognized as one of the premier competitors in America's Cup sailing competition, called the all-women crew of the Mighty Mary "that lesbo boat." Connor's name-calling came after the Mighty Mary crew defeated him in one of the 1995 America's Cup trials. Connor's comments were intended to discredit the women's performance and to make the crew of the Mighty Mary defensive about their accomplishment. Calling them lesbians questioned their status as "real" women, thereby softening the sting of being beaten by an all-women crew.

When Martina was dominating women's tennis in the mid- to late 80s, Hana Mandilokova suggested publicly that Martina should be playing on the men's tour. The implication was that she was not a real woman and therefore had an unfair advantage when playing other women. Sports commentators also remarked about her muscular appearance in ways that made it clear that they considered her to have an unfair advantage over the other women on the tour (Navratilova and Vecsey 1985). The same criticisms were leveled at Babe Didrikson and her multisport accomplishments in the midcentury. More recently, in addition to his antilesbian comments about LPGA players, Ben Wright also opined that women were inferior golfers because their "boobs" get in the way, impeding their golf swing. The implication again is that "real" or "normal" women (with breasts) are inferior athletes.

All of these images stigmatize lesbians and drive a wedge between lesbians and other women in sport. In the short run, it might appear to benefit heterosexual women to distance themselves from lesbians and to condemn lesbian participation in sport. This position, however, ignores the societal function of heterosexism and homophobia and their connection to sexism. No woman who challenges traditional gender roles and male supremacy or threatens men's exclusive sexual access to women is safe from accusations that she is a lesbian. In the end, the lesbian boogeywoman stereotype and the fear and discomfort it provokes serve male dominance in sport and the rest of society, not the expansion of opportunities for women.

How do women and men in sport react to the lesbian boogeywoman image? How does the persistence of this image affect young athletes and their parents? How is the fear of the lesbian boogeywoman used as a recruiting tool by some coaches? In the next chapter I discuss these questions.

5

Full Court Press:

Defending Women's
Sport Against the
Lesbian Boogeywoman

Women's sport advocates historically have taken a defensive position in response to the lesbian boogeywoman. Rather than questioning the value of societal expectations of compulsory femininity and heterosexuality or acknowledging and valuing the diversity of women in sport, many supporters of women's sport continue to rely on the same defensive responses that have already proven to be ineffective in deflecting questions about the heterosexuality and femininity of women in sport. This defensive response, labeled the "apologetic" by Felshin (1974), has remained largely unchanged for almost 100 years. I have identified several variations of this apologetic response to the lesbian boogeywoman image: (1) silence, (2) denial, (3) promotion of a feminine, heterosexual image, (4) promotion of a heterosexy image, (5) search for heterosexual-only space, (6) attacks on lesbians, (7) preference for male coaches, and (8) acknowledgment but disassociation from lesbians. These responses are used by women's sports enthusiasts and advocates of all kinds—parents, coaches, athletes, administrators, men and women, both gay and straight—to defend women's sport against the lesbian boogeywoman.

SILENCE

Many advocates of women's sport use silence as a way to avoid addressing the issue of lesbian participation in sport. The lack of response from women's sport advocates to eruptions of public attention to lesbians in sport illustrates this reaction. In 1981 when Billie Jean King acknowledged her lesbian relationship, the flurry of media attention included no statements of public support from the USTA or WTA or any of the other women professional tennis players. In 1991 when the mainstream media revealed Penn State University basketball coach Rene Portland's "no lesbian" policy, the Women's Basketball Coaches Association (WBCA), individual coaches, and most other women's sport advocacy organizations were silent. A spokesperson for the WBCA reacted to the charge that Portland was discriminating against lesbian athletes by saying, "She is a good coach. As far as we are concerned, she remains in good standing. We have no knowledge of her position on lesbians" (Bull 1991, 66). Only the Women's Sports Foundation issued a clear public statement condemning discrimination against lesbians in sport in response to the Penn State story (Lederman 1991).

Even without the threat of public scandal, professional meetings for coaches and athletic administrators rarely address homophobia or heterosexism, and when they do, it is often treated as a controversial decision. For example, when I spoke to a women athletic directors' conference in 1989, I was told by the leaders of the organization that some women chose not to come to the conference that year because homophobia in women's sport was on the program. Likewise, the WBCA's decision to include a panel on homophobia in women's sports at the 1996 coaches' conference was treated as a highly controversial decision even though over 500 coaches attended this session. When leaders of coaching associations, college athletic conferences, or spokespeople for professional tours respond with silence to calls to address heterosexism and homophobia, they treat lesbians like nasty secrets who must be kept tightly locked away from public view.

1994 Gay Games in New York City. Women's ice hockey competition.

Many lesbians in sport choose to maintain this silence. Silence has provided at least the illusion of protection and is a survival strategy in the face of persistent hostility. If a woman coach or athlete identifies herself as lesbian, she risks ostracism, condemnation, loss of commercial endorsements, loss of employment, or loss of the opportunity to compete. With the potential for these dire consequences, many themselves prefer silence.

DENIAL

When asked direct questions by reporters or parents, some women's sport advocates and coaches deny the presence of lesbians in athletics, at least at their school, on their professional tour, or in their sport. The response of one LPGA tour director to Ben Wright's statement that lesbians on the professional tour limited the appeal of women's golf exemplified this denial. He asserted that he personally knew many of the "girls" on the tour and had never seen any evidence of "lesbian activity, overt or otherwise" (Associated Press 1995b). Readers were left to wonder whether he expected to see lesbian golfers having wild sex on the 13th tee. In the early 1980s Martina Navratilova and Nancy Lieberman, her trainer and lover, repeatedly denied their lesbian relationship in press conferences (though both acknowledged their relationship later). At the time, Martina was concerned about the effects of her lesbian identity on her application for U.S. citizenship. In another example, Billie Jean King called her seven-year lesbian relationship with Marilyn Barnett a "mistake" and denied that she was a lesbian. Likewise, many college coaches deny that they have lesbians on their teams when asked by the parents of prospective athletes.

PROMOTION OF A FEMININE, HETEROSEXUAL IMAGE

Even with the broader acceptance of women as athletes, concerns about femininity persist in 1997 as evidenced by a Reebok television ad in which Olympic and WNBA basketball player Rebecca Lobo reassures viewers that women can be athletes and still be feminine. Femininity, however, is a code word for heterosexuality. The concern is not that women athletes are too plain, out of style, or don't have good grooming habits. The real fear is that women athletes will look like dykes, or even worse, are dykes.

At some schools, parents and administrators scrutinize a woman coach's heterosexual credentials as carefully as they review her athletic accomplishments. At least three criteria are used in this "heterosexual security check." Individual women and women's sport organizations also use these criteria to defend themselves from suspicion and to disassociate themselves from the lesbian boogeywoman. Heterosexual credentials are determined by (1) visibility of relationships, (2) appearance and demeanor, and (3) attitudes and actions about lesbians in sport.

Visibility of Relationships

Women, both closeted lesbians and nonlesbians, attempt to "prove" their heterosexuality and distance themselves from the lesbian boogeywoman in a number of ways: dating or marrying men, being seen with men in social settings, having sex with men, or talking about their relationships with men. The presence of children, even for an unmarried woman, also provides evidence of heterosexuality. The high visibility of married women athletes and coaches flaunting their husbands and their children contrasts with the complete invisibility of lesbian partnerships in sport. The importance of presenting a heterosexual image is reflected in the number of media features about women athletes and coaches who are married or who are married with children that focus on their husbands and children. Nancy Lopez, Sheryl Swoopes, Nancy Lieberman-Cline, Chris Evert, and Pat Summit are some of the best examples of how the media plays up the "normal" heterosexuality of those women who can readily produce their heterosexual credentials in the form of boyfriends, husbands, and children.

When Chris Evert retired from professional tennis, *Sports Illustrated* did a cover story on her. Accompanying the story were pictures of Evert, not on the tennis court, but with each of the men she had been involved with over the course of her career (Evert 1989). Similarly, in 1994 a nationally televised college women's basketball game between the University of Tennessee and the University of Texas included a halftime show featuring profiles of married women coaches as wives and mothers. Newspaper coverage of the 1995 NCAA women's basketball finals included several pictures of Pat Summit's husband and son sitting in the stands. During the inaugural weekend of the WNBA, television coverage included an interview with Nancy Lieberman-Cline about the reactions of her son and husband to her decision to play accompanied by shots of them in the stands watching her play. During the postgame celebration of Tennessee's 1996 national championship, Summit's husband bubbled to a national TV audience about what a wonderful cook Summit was and how she loved nothing better than to whip up a fancy meal for him and their son.

A CBS Mother's Day special preceded the telecast of the 1995 LPGA Championship. This special program featured women athletes who are mothers and described how they manage their dual roles. The LPGA also calls attention to the heterosexual, young, and conventionally attractive married players on the tour and their traveling day-care program for presumably heterosexual players with children.

There are two reasons why a focus on the heterosexuality of women athletes is remarkable. First, we rarely see similar stories about male athletes and coaches unless they themselves or their children are facing tragic medical conditions or there is some other exceptional human interest twist to their family life. Features about heterosexual male coaches and athletes rarely focus with such predictability on how these men fulfill their family roles. Imagine Rick Pitino's wife at center court as

1930 U.S. National Women's Golf Championship.

the team celebrates a national championship describing how Rick loves nothing better than to tinker with his table saw or prepare a meal for the whole family to enjoy.

The second reason why the media attention given to the family lives of heterosexual women athletes is remarkable is the complete silence about the family lives of lesbian athletes and coaches. Lesbian athletes and coaches are treated and expected to act like single women whose family members include only mothers, fathers, sisters, and brothers. News stories about lesbian athletes or coaches are conspicuous in their silence about significant personal relationships as both the athletes and the media collude to maintain their invisibility. With the exception of Martina, whose lover Judy Nelson was often identified as her "companion," most lesbian athletes' lovers are trivialized as "roommates," "hairdressers," "business managers," and "secretaries" (if they are identified at all). These "marriage or mystery" contrasting portrayals of heterosexual and lesbian athletes and coaches reflect the pressure on all women in sport to both provide evidence of heterosexuality and deny any evidence of lesbianism.

Ironically, the complete absence of any mention of a woman athlete's or coach's personal life leads most people to assume she is a lesbian anyway. We assume that if she is heterosexual, she would be placing evidence of this on public display. Martina's trip into the stands to embrace her lesbian partner after winning the 1990 Wimbledon singles championship was remarkable because she forced the public to acknowledge her family by publicly embracing her lover.

Appearance and Demeanor

Conforming to traditional norms of femininity in dress and mannerism is another way women coaches and athletes provide evidence of heterosexuality. This "heterosexual drag show" includes wearing skirts, makeup, and—especially for college basketball coaches—high heels while coaching. While watching women basketball coaches teeter on high heels and squat in front of the bench while wrapping their skirts around their legs to avoid exposing their underwear, it is easy to see how important appearance is, even at the expense of practicality and comfort. Despite the fact that some of these "dykes in drag" may feel uncomfortable and out of place in the frilly costumes they wear, they comply with traditional standards of femininity to maintain a heterosexual front. As the camera focused on a woman basketball coach pacing the sidelines in high heels, Martina Navratilova said in the video *Out for a Change: Addressing Homophobia in Women's Sports* (Mosbacher 1992), "We should make men coach in those things." But earlier in her career, even Martina succumbed to the pressure to present a feminine front in her 1985 autobiography:

> People judge you by appearances, and since I was all woman underneath, I finally figured I might as well start dressing the part. . . . I was getting to like the new me—makeup, blond hair and frilly clothes . . . (Navratilova and Vecsey 1985, 214-215).

Many sport advocates want to focus attention on women athletes who meet white, heterosexual standards of beauty and behavior. To this end, women in sport have always been encouraged to engage in the protective camouflage of feminine drag to make their athleticism more acceptable. The LPGA employs an "image consultant" who travels with the golfers on the tour to provide consultation on makeup, hairstyle, and clothes selection (*Golf Illustrated* 1987). Charles Mechem, the former commissioner of the LPGA, defended the image consultant as a way to provide support for women professionals who are in the public eye and are concerned about "good grooming" (Mechem 1995). Why is it then that only women athletes need to be concerned with good grooming? Why don't the PGA, the NBA, or the NFL have image consultants?

At least one team, the California Dreams in the short-lived Women's

1902 Ivory Soap advertisement depicting a very "feminine" team of basketball players.

Professional Basketball league in the 1970s, sent players to the John Robert Powers Charm School, where players were instructed how to present a "feminine" appearance. College coaches often require athletes to wear dresses when traveling as a team and remind them to act like "ladies" when away from the playing field.

The Women's Sports Foundation sponsors a glitzy annual fund-raising dinner attended by well-known professional and amateur women athletes and the male corporate sponsors who support many of the WSF activities. Before the dinner, athletes have an opportunity to have "experts" style their hair and apply makeup. The men attending the dinner do not have an equivalent opportunity to "improve" their appearance. The message is that women athletes must be made up to be attractive to the male corporate sponsors who will, presumably, be more motivated to donate money to the WSF if they share the evening with "beautiful" women athletic celebrities.

Members of the 1996 Olympic softball team, in an appearance on the Oprah Winfrey show prior to the Atlanta Games, were introduced to the audience after they had undergone a "makeover" in which their hair was styled, makeup was applied, and they were costumed in dresses and heels. Their live "feminine" appearances were contrasted with action photos of the players in uniform on the softball field. Rather than focus on the athletic talent of these eventual gold medalists, they were presented as women who, despite their unusual sport prowess, could be made up to look feminine too. As if to reinforce their transformation, the audience greeted each made-over athlete with delighted applause.

I was asked to speak on one of the panel discussions at the New Agenda for Women in Sport in 1983 entitled "How Can We Disarm and Deflect Threats to Our Sense of Femininity?". The title of the panel says a lot about the conference organizers' perceptions of the defensiveness women athletes feel about their sport participation and how this issue is to be taken seriously. One of the other panelists, professional race-car driver Janet Guthrie, took the question quite seriously and encouraged audience members to wear dresses and be seen with men as "protective camouflage." When I reframed the panel topic as the wrong question and suggested that it was a code for concern about women in sport being perceived as lesbians, she insisted that the conference was "no place for a gay rights rally." Such uncritical and apolitical acceptance of traditional standards of feminine appearance and conspicuous heterosexuality as a measure of normalcy for athletes and coaches divides and keeps women defensive and tentative about their sports interests and talents.

Many young athletes also feel compelled to assert their feminine heterosexuality or camouflage their lesbianism by letting their hair grow long. Young, white athletes in particular place a lot of importance on hair length as a statement about sexual identity (straight women have long hair, lesbians have short hair). Based on the number of white college basketball, volleyball, field hockey, and soccer players who wear their hair long, spectators might assume that ponytails are a required part of their uniforms. A young lesbian basketball player described to me how, when she confirmed to nervous teammates that, yes, she was a lesbian, they told her that they would "accept" her presence on the team as long as she adhered to two rules. One, she could not "hit on" anyone on the team, and two, she could not cut her hair. Michele Timms, the point guard for the WNBA Phoenix Mercury was, with her blond crew cut, a refreshing contrast to this obsession with long hair among white athletes.

If women coaches and athletes could freely choose among a range of appearance styles without jeopardizing their heterosexual image, then the issue of coaching attire and hairstyles would be unimportant. Women could fashion their appearance according to their comfort, practicality, and individual sense of style. Homophobia and heterosexism in women's athletics, however, transform the choice of clothing, hairstyle, and other personal appearance decisions into important statements about sexual identity and gender. Crosset (1995) describes in rich detail how LPGA players "do gender" in an attempt to present themselves as unambiguously feminine and heterosexual despite their golf prowess. The assumption is that the general public is much more likely to accept a woman athlete if she "does gender well." Women athletes waste a lot of energy making sure they present a feminine heterosexual image as a way to defend themselves and women's sport in general from associations with the lesbian boogeywoman.

Attitudes and Actions About Lesbians

Actions or attitudes that reflect tolerance or acceptance of lesbians can raise questions about the sexual identity of the speaker or the program she represents. The assumption that if you speak out against discrimination against lesbians, you must be one has silenced many women of different sexual identities. Jody Conradt, the women's basketball coach at the University of Texas, has been outspoken about her refusal to discriminate against lesbian athletes, though she did soften this statement by talking about accepting "diversity" rather than actually saying the word "lesbian." As a result the UT team was labeled a "lesbian team" by some high school athletes and coaches. An article in the *Austin American-Statesman* (Bohis and Wangrin 1993) speculated whether or not this label was responsible for UT's failure to make the top 10 in the last few years after being a perennial fixture there for years before. No lesbians have identified themselves in the UT program, and there have been no reports of problems among the lesbian or straight players on the team. Yet, because the coach took a stand against discrimination, her team was labeled and possibly avoided by young athletes afraid of playing with lesbian teammates. Not only women's sports teams or individual coaches or athletes become stigmatized for taking a stand against discrimination. The Women's Sports Foundation has taken a leadership role among women's sports organizations with their stance against homophobia in women's sports. As a result, the WSF has been attacked on the Internet as the "Lesbian Sports Foundation" by a few people who believe lesbians are a threat to women's sport.

Conversely, silence about heterosexism and homophobia in sport or espousing antilesbian attitudes can have the opposite effect. That is, being silent or publicly antigay are ways both straight and lesbian coaches distance themselves from the lesbian label. No doubt having a "no lesbian" policy has helped some schools recruit young players whose parents believe their daughters are safer in these programs than with a coach who does not discriminate against lesbians.

PROMOTION OF A HETEROSEXY IMAGE

In 1989 the LPGA developed promotional material featuring photographs of women golfers posing pin-up style in swimsuits (Diaz 1989). The LPGA also published a calendar with photographs of selected golfers, such as Jan Stephenson, who presented a traditionally heterosexy image with plenty of skin and cleavage on display. Muffin Spencer-Devlin posed mimicking the famous picture of Marilyn Monroe standing over a floor vent trying without success to keep her dress from blowing up and revealing her thighs. Likewise, the Women's Tennis Association has published promotional photographs of tennis players, including Martina Navratilova, posing in glamorous evening clothes, heavily made up, and with hairstyles that made some of the athletes almost unrecognizable. The uniform of a short-lived women's professional basketball league in the 1980s was a skintight unitard.

One of the most extreme examples of the attempt to present a heterosexy image was a 1987 media guide for the Northwestern State University of Louisiana women's basketball team. The team picture showed the players in uniform with Playboy bunny ears and tails posing coquettishly and smiling at the camera. The brochure gushed, "These girls can play, boy," and invited (male) fans and reporters to watch these sexy women play in the "pleasure palace."

Some people ask what is wrong with women athletes being sexy or point out that male athletes are sometimes presented as sex objects too. The problem is that these attempts to heterosexualize women athletes by portraying them as sex objects for the enjoyment of men is demeaning to all women athletes regardless of their sexuality. The assumption underlying the heterosexualizing of women athletes is that they will not be acceptable unless they can present themselves as heterosexy. Men in athletics do not need to make this compromise. Their sport performances alone are taken as evidence of their masculine heterosexuality. Women athletes also should be respected for their sport accomplishments without apology.

THE SEARCH FOR A HETEROSEXUAL–ONLY ATHLETIC SPACE

Many parents, coaches, and athletes believe that lesbians are a threat not only to the image of women's sport, but to "normal" young women

Photo by Joan Bobkoff © 1994

1994 Gay Games in New York City. Water polo.

athletes. These fears are described by Michael Mewshaw (1993) and John Feinstein (1992) in their books about the professional tennis tours. Sending a daughter away to college is a tremendous rite of passage for both parents and child. In most cases the daughter will be living away from home without direct parental supervision for the first time. Parents have many understandable concerns at this time. Most parents with athletic daughters probably have had to contend with the lesbian stigma attached to women's sport, especially women's team sports, at some level. Perhaps they suspected that a high school coach or a high school teammate was a lesbian. Maybe the high school team had been dyke-baited at games or in school. High school coaches sometimes warn players about lesbians in college programs. In some instances parents are already worried about their daughter's sexual identity. Having a daughter leave home and enter an environment where "dangerous" lesbians might be present aggravates these fears and prejudices. Some young women athletes decide not to play on a college athletic team because of their fear or their parents' fear of lesbians in college athletic programs. One lesbian coach described such an interaction with the father of a high school recruit who was visiting her campus:

> I had the father of a recruit who made it clear that he was afraid for his daughter. When they came to visit, he came into my office and said, "This is

a good place for my daughter to be. No butch-type women hanging around. I wanted to see some good-looking women, and you have some on this team, none of those lesbian types." I wanted to laugh! I thought to myself, "Maybe you haven't brought your daughter to a team with lesbian players, but you have brought her to a lesbian coach!" I sort of glossed over it, and after I got over laughing to myself, I was a bit scared. I keep wondering what his daughter thinks of me.

—Division 1 tennis coach

A young woman who later came out as a lesbian told me about her father's warning to her as she left for college on a basketball scholarship: "He told me always be careful about your teammates, women who try and get close to you for reasons other than just friendship. So you always have to watch your back and be careful. I was like, 'OK, dad.' I wasn't even thinking like that."

It is not unusual for parents of prospective athletes to ask coaches of women's college teams, especially team-sport coaches, about lesbians in their programs. Many coaches assume that saying "yes, we have lesbians on our team" would severely damage their ability to recruit and would mark their team with a lesbian reputation that could jeopardize the entire program.

Parents ask you point-blank about your lifestyle. I've always handled it like it is not an issue whether I am single, straight, gay, or bisexual. That's how I answer the question, that it is not an issue for me, our administration, or with our athletes or students on campus, which may be true or false, but that is the party line for parents. It sets you back a bit because you don't want to lie, but at the same time you are selling a product here and you want them to believe in you. You don't want to outright lie to them, but at the same time there is no reason it should make a difference in the way we operate our program. I'm not going to make this kid gay. She's going to be herself and grow up to be whatever she's going to be. I get asked THE question about once every year in the home visit. They never ask the question in front of their daughter. I think it is more the parents' issue. You've got to be ready. Whether it works or not, who knows? Sometimes they ask how many athletes on the team are gay. I tell them I don't know, because I don't. I don't want to know. It is not a question I would ask them [her athletes] about their lifestyles. So I tell parents it is not an issue with me and it is not an issue with the team.

—Division 1 field hockey coach

Fathers are often the parent to ask the "lesbian question" of college coaches. Coaches report that fathers' attempts to find out about lesbians in a college program can range from direct to indirect. Some fathers ask coaches directly if they have lesbians on the team. Coaches have told me that some fathers have even asked women coaches directly if they were lesbians. Sometimes, if the coach is a woman who has not convinced the father of her heterosexuality, he will ask the athletic director, an assistant coach, or even a team member about the coach's sexual identity.

High school recruits, though less bold about asking direct questions about lesbians, are no less curious or concerned about it. They find out through friends who attend the school already what the team's reputation is like, or they make their own assumptions about team members and coaches based on their own lesbian stereotypes.

I heard a number of stories about first-year athletes who, after spending one season on a college team, transfer to another school because they discover that there are lesbians on the team. One of the most high-profile examples is Sheryl Swoopes, an outstanding collegiate basketball player, member of the 1996 gold medal Olympic Team and WNBA player. Sheryl transferred out of the University of Texas because, according to her mother, she did not want to play on a team with lesbians (Bohis and Wangrin 1993).

The search for a heterosexual-only athletic space limits all women in sport. Women athletes are encouraged to curtail or feel defensive about their sport participation, their femininity, and their heterosexuality. For young athletes who already know they are lesbians or who are questioning their sexual identity, the negative messages about lesbians from parents, coaches, and peers create tremendous fear and self-hatred. Women coaches also fend off suspicions and questions about their sexual identity. Lesbian coaches are at particular risk of being attacked by athletes, parents, other coaches, or administrators.

ATTACKS ON LESBIANS

Over the past 15 years or so, concerns about the lesbian boogeywoman have taken a nasty turn. Where innuendo and rumor once were the rule, now direct attacks on lesbians in athletics are more common. This change coincides with the rise in popularity and acceptance of women's sport. The legal clout provided by Title IX and changing gender-role norms enable more girls and women to explore and enjoy their athleticism. As more heterosexual women and men participate in women's sport, lesbians are increasingly a minority. When heterosexual women and men in sport view lesbians with suspicion or fear and blame lesbians for tainting the image of women's sports, these attitudes increase the inhospitable climate for lesbians in sport.

Discrimination Against Lesbian Athletes and Coaches

Some athletic directors fire women coaches if they suspect that they are lesbians. In many cases, athletic directors count on the coach's fear of being publicly named a lesbian to prevent her from challenging harassment or dismissal. Many women who are fired because they are lesbians do not challenge this discrimination because they assume that being open about their identity will make finding another job in athletics more difficult. Karen Weaver, the former field hockey coach at Ohio State University, is an exception. She filed a discrimination suit against OSU claiming that she was fired because of discrimination on the basis of gender and sexual orientation (Cronin 1996). The charge of discrimination based on sexual orientation was deferred, until her charge of gender discrimination is settled.

Penn State coach Rene Portland is not the only coach to prohibit lesbians from her team. Other college coaches also tell athletes and their parents that they will not allow lesbians on their teams. One of the athletes I interviewed remembered a coach who told her team she would not allow "sluts, whores, or lesbians." Some coaches follow through by dropping women they discover are lesbians from the roster, limiting their playing time, or ostracizing them.

Coaches who are willing to accommodate parents and athletes looking for a lesbian-free athletic experience by implementing "no lesbian" policies have different motivations: personal gain, personal beliefs, public image, personal protection, pragmatic concerns, and athletes' right to "choice."

Personal Gain

Coaches who are motivated by personal gain may not have any salient objection to lesbian athletes, but they believe that having a "no lesbian" policy gives them a recruiting edge. They believe that this policy makes their program more appealing to prospective high school athletes and their parents. By catering to these fears, coaches motivated by personal gain damage women's sport in the long run by perpetuating negative stereotypes about lesbians and fears about lesbians in sport.

Personal Beliefs

Some coaches are motivated by genuine personal convictions that lesbians are sinful, immoral, or psychologically deviant. These convictions are often based on religious beliefs. Such coaches base the development of team policy on their religious beliefs. Some of these coaches, such as assistant basketball coach Cheryl Littlejohn of the University of Alabama, believe that it is their duty as Christians to make their beliefs known to prospective athletes and their parents. (See chapter 7 for more discussion about this topic.)

I spoke with a producer for a 1997 ESPN special, "Women in Sport at the Crossroads," which included a segment on homophobia in women's sport. The producer described phone conversations with two prominent Division 1 basketball coaches who freely told her they did not allow lesbians on their teams. One coach did not want his players "exposed to it." The other coach believed that lesbian athletes "flaunted it." However, neither was willing to describe their perspective on camera, even in silhouette.

Public Image

Some coaches do not have any particular problem with lesbians. They might even have good lesbian friends or colleagues, but they are concerned about the public image of their team or women's sport in general. Image concerns motivate their "no lesbian" policy. They believe that adoption of a discriminatory policy protects them and their program from the taint of a lesbian image.

Personal Protection

Some women coaches adopt a "no lesbian" policy to protect themselves from association with the lesbian label. Sadly, both lesbian and heterosexual women coaches are motivated by this concern. Even if coaches do not adopt a formal "no lesbian" policy, some prefer to recruit athletes who present a "feminine" image as a way to distance themselves from suspicion and innuendo.

Pragmatic Concerns

Some coaches have nothing against lesbian athletes and are not concerned about losing recruits who are afraid of lesbians. However, they want to avoid what they see as the hassles that come with coaching lesbian athletes. They don't want to deal with coming-out issues or relationship issues among teammates that might interfere with athletic performance. They don't want to address potential antagonisms among lesbian and straight athletes on their teams. They believe that prohibiting lesbians from playing on the team eliminates these and other problems they associate with lesbian athletes.

Athletes' Right to "Choice"

Some coaches justify their discrimination against lesbian athletes by asserting that athletes have a right to choose an athletic environment where they can be "comfortable," as if college programs that discriminate against lesbians are just another acceptable criterion, like major fields of study offered, upon which high school athletes make their college choices. "We have some schools that accept lesbians and some that don't; you decide where you are most comfortable."

In the past, similar arguments have been used to defend discrimination against women, people of color, Jews, and other disadvantaged social groups. Imagine the same "freedom to choose" perspective in relation to these social groups: "We have programs that accept blacks and Jews and programs that prohibit their participation. You decide where you are most comfortable."

"No lesbian" policies do not always have the desired effect of persuading young athletes to come to a school that claims to be a heterosexual-only athletic team environment. In a conversation I had with a young woman recruited by Penn State, she described how, during a home visit with the athlete and her mother, Portland told them about her "no lesbian" policy. This particular recruit and her mother were surprised and put off by Portland's statement. The athlete decided not to attend Penn State, in part because of Portland's discriminatory policy. Unfortunately, many prospective athletes and their parents are relieved and reassured to hear that a college women's team will not knowingly include lesbians.

Though it is general knowledge in athletics that some coaches adopt these discriminatory policies, to date too few athletic governing bodies or coaches' associations have publicly stated their opposition to discrimination against lesbians in athletics. In 1993 the Minority Opportunity and Interest Committee of the NCAA recommended the adoption of an antidiscrimination principle that included gender, race, and religion. Patty Viverito, then the NCAA council liaison to the committee on women's athletics, moved to add sexual orientation to the list. Viverito described her surprise when what she thought was consideration of a routine motion quickly escalated into a controversial and heated discussion among the athletic directors, university faculty, and university presidents on the NCAA council. According to Viverito, "It was appalling. To my dismay, the motion failed, but they realized it would look bad to specifically exclude sexual orientation so they deleted all categories entirely." Instead, the NCAA adopted a bland and meaningless principle of nondiscrimination that reads, "The association shall promote an atmosphere of respect for and sensitivity to the dignity of every person."

The National Softball Coaches Association, the American Volleyball Coaches Association, the Women's Basketball Coaches Association, and the U.S. Field Hockey Association include sexual orientation in their statements of equal employment opportunity or nondiscrimination statements. The WBCA statement also "reminds and encourages athletic directors across America to follow the policy of the WBCA in the hiring of coaches of women's basketball at all levels" and to "operate free of discriminatory practices in all matters relating to recruiting, hiring, training, compensation, benefits, advancements, terminations, educational, social and recreational programs." Unfortunately, as illustrated by the WBCA statement, coaches associations and sports governing bodies may not have any enforcement authority beyond the direct employees of their organizations.

Negative Recruiting

Negative recruiting occurs when coaches try to persuade a potential recruit to choose their school by making disparaging comments about another school that the recruit might be considering. Though negative recruiting is prohibited by the NCAA, it is often used to attack lesbians in sport. Several lesbian coaches I talked with knew that negative recruiting was used against them by other coaches in their conference. This information is passed along through informal networks of athletes and coaches.

> Negative recruiting is huge. It happens when a coach is sitting there with her husband and two kids and knows another coach [at a rival school] is gay. She says to a recruit and her parents, "You know, that other school you are thinking of, the lifestyle on that campus, I'm not sure you want to get involved in that." That's all she has to say. You don't have to say what it is. You make insinuations and immediately the parents and the kid start thinking, "Oh shit." It taints how they feel about what goes on in your program. And they start looking for it at every turn. That really sets a negative tone when a recruit comes to campus. I know which coaches do this so when a kid arrives on campus and she is considering that school too, I have to be prepared to show them something that will negate their fears. I make sure I take them to mainstream places and that they meet the AD [athletic director, a man]. We select the athlete she will stay with in a different light. Usually it is random, whoever is free, but if I know this kid is being recruited by a coach who does this [negative recruiting], I know which pool of athletes I want that kid staying with and associating with.
>
> —*Division 1 field hockey coach*

In the wake of news articles about lesbians and the University of Texas women's basketball program, the basketball coach at Texas rival Baylor University sent a prospective player several postcards. Each card described a reason why the recruit should choose Baylor. One card said, "Coach is actively outspoken against lesbianism and won't accept it" (Bohis and Wangrin 1993). By playing on the fears of young women and their parents, coaches hope to gain an advantage in recruiting new talent.

Negative recruiting does not always have the desired effect, and this provides hope that parents and prospective college athletes are becoming less tolerant of this unethical practice.

I had an athlete who had already committed to my program. A coach from another school saw her father at a 16-and-under tournament and said, "You don't want to go there; the coach recruits all these lesbians, and if your daughter is not a lesbian, they'll try to make her one." The dad told him, "Even if my daughter wasn't already committed, she would never play for you." I actually had a mother call and tell me she wishes that more lesbian coaches would come out so her daughter would have more role models. That was really powerful.

—Division 1 softball coach

One coach found out negative recruiting was being used against her program because a first-year athlete in her program told her that a rival coach had warned her about lesbians in that program. She chose to attend the school despite his warnings. Ironically, her lesbian coach had written a letter of recommendation for the coach who was now using negative recruiting against her. Most lesbian coaches endure these attacks in silence, believing that challenging these unethical recruiting methods would only call further attention to themselves in ways they are not prepared to address.

Harassment of Lesbian Coaches and Athletes

Women athletes, regardless of sexual orientation, can encounter antilesbian harassment. Athletes who are, or are assumed to be, lesbians can encounter even more name-calling, taunting, physical harassment, and destruction of property. This harassment can come from heterosexual teammates, closeted lesbian teammates who are afraid of being labeled, male athletes, fans, and sometimes coaches. Some lesbian coaches receive anonymous harassing phone calls or find personalized antilesbian graffiti on locker room walls and office doors.

Particular teams at some schools are tagged with a lesbian label by male and female athletes from other teams. Sometimes lesbians are targeted by their own teammates, who fear that they will be harassed by association. Sometimes players on one team will harass players on the opposing team during competition. A softball player told me about competing against a school whose players called her team "lezzies" and "dykes" from the bench within earshot of their coach, who did nothing to stop them. At many schools, team-sport athletes in sports such as softball, basketball, soccer, and field hockey are more likely to be harassed. Athletes endure anonymous phone calls at home, have property destroyed or stolen, are targeted by antilesbian graffiti, and endure name-calling in public places on campus. This harassment frequently goes unreported because women, regardless of their sexual identity, are reluctant to call attention to the lesbian issue in general, and they are not eager to associate themselves in particular with it. In other cases the targets of antilesbian harassment do not expect or believe that they are entitled to protection from this kind of treatment.

PREFERENCE FOR MALE COACHES

The increase in the number of men who coach women's teams since the implementation of Title IX is at least in part due to athletic directors' attempts to avoid hiring lesbian coaches. Some athletic directors prefer male coaches for women's teams to "rehabilitate" a team whose image has been "tarnished" with a lesbian reputation.

Some young women athletes and their parents prefer male coaches in a lethal mix of sexism and homophobia that leads them to believe that male coaches are safer and more competent than women coaches. The belief that female athletes are safer with heterosexual male coaches than they are with lesbian coaches is open to question. (See chapter 10 for a more in-depth discussion of this issue.)

ACKNOWLEDGMENT BUT DISASSOCIATION FROM LESBIANS

Over the last few years the news media have paid more attention to homophobia and homosexuality in sport (Cart 1992; Denney 1992; Dozier 1995; Kaufman 1993; Riley, Anderson, and Garber 1992; Scarton 1992; Spander 1991; Wilstein 1996). In addition to numerous articles in mainstream newspapers around the United States and Canada, ESPN and ABC sports have done short segments on these topics. As women athletes, coaches, and other supporters of women's sport are called on to discuss homophobia and lesbians in sport, I have noticed that some responses are depressingly consistent with those already discussed in this chapter. I have also noticed some subtle changes in how many women athletes and coaches talk about lesbians in sport. More women now acknowledge that there are lesbians in sport but still disassociate themselves from lesbians, and lesbians themselves are largely and conspicuously absent from the discussion.

I Don't Mind Lesbians, Just Don't Call Me One

The media attention paid to America's Cup sailor Dennis Connor's antilesbian slur illustrates the response, "I don't mind lesbians, just don't call me one." The all-women Mighty Mary crew countered Connor's comment by refocusing attention on the heterosexuality of the crew and tried to sound supportive of lesbians too. They appeared in a full-page color photo in several national magazines accompanied by text that read in part

Their [the Mighty Mary crew's] presence in the race has inspired homophobic jerks to label them, in the words of Mr. America's Cup, Dennis Connor, "a bunch of lesbians."—For which he got a drink dumped over his head by one of the America3 sailors. Unfortunately, he is wrong. About a third of these talented athletes are married to men and the others espouse boyfriends before the media inquisition. Although they say there aren't any lesbians among them, the sailors claim it wouldn't make a difference if there were.

If it really didn't matter, why the full-page photo of the predominantly blond and long-haired crew in a national magazine, and why the insistence on telling readers that they were all heterosexual? One of the Mighty Mary crew, Anna S. Huntington, in a 1997 interview on National Public Radio confirmed that the crew and their sponsors "didn't want to risk the perception that there were lesbians on the boat" and were anxious to be seen as wives, girlfriends, and mothers despite their public nonchalance (Huntington 1997).

The interesting twist in the Mighty Mary response is that the crew apparently believed that it would not be acceptable to make such antilesbian feelings public. The insistence in the magazine text that it wouldn't matter if there were lesbians on the crew, even though there weren't any, was an attempt to both defend the crew's heterosexual image and avoid the appearance of being homophobic.

Several LPGA golfers used the same "acknowledge but disassociate" strategy in response to Ben Wright's comments. Rather than deny the presence of lesbians on the tour, most players acknowledged that, yes, there were a few lesbians on the tour and tried to minimize the issue rather than challenge the assumptions imbedded in his antiwoman and antilesbian comments. LPGA board president Mary Jo Jacobi defended tour players as "wives, mothers, single working women and some who happen to be gay." Patty Sheehan and Amy Alcott insisted that "it" (meaning being a lesbian) is a private matter. Some golfers insisted that lesbianism is no more an issue in women's golf than in any other area or that there are no more lesbians in golf than in law or medicine, for example. Several LPGA players insisted that lesbianism on the tour was a "nonissue" or was "irrelevant." (Associated Press 1995a; Potter 1996). One tournament director claimed that "lesbianism was not a problem" on the tour. Whether he meant that there was no problem because there are no lesbians or that there are lesbians, but this was not a problem, is unclear.

In an article in the Minneapolis *Star Tribune* the LPGA's media consultant said she was pleased with how well the players dealt with what she called the "lifestyle issue" during the Ben Wright affair. She coaches the golfers to deflect questions about lesbians by insisting that lesbians on the tour are a "non-issue" and then, with "grace and diplomacy," steering the interview back to a focus on golf (Blount 1995).

Reactions from LPGA golfers and officials to Muffin Spencer-Devlin's coming out in the March 18, 1996, issue of *Sports Illustrated* also acknowledged lesbians on the tour, but tried to disassociate the LPGA from Spencer-Devlin's coming out. New commissioner Jim Ritts said, "This is a personality story. This is not a story about the LPGA. When you get right down to it, I'm not sure who cares about this issue anymore." Former LPGA President Elaine Crosby said, "In my opinion, if she wants to do that, that's her life. That's what America is all about, so if she wants to do that, that's fine" (Potter 1996; Heath 1996; Szekely 1996). Spencer-Devlin herself seemed anxious to make it clear that her coming out was a personal decision for herself rather than a broader social issue of importance to the LPGA or women's sport in general (Garrity and Nutt 1996).

The primary objective in these responses is to return the topic to the closet, insisting that it shouldn't matter if a few women athletes are lesbians but making it clear that the speakers are disassociating themselves from lesbians.

Lesbian Label as Social Control Versus Insult

Recently, more women athletes and coaches express an understanding of how the lesbian label is used as means to control, discredit, and intimidate women in sport. Understanding the use of *lesbian* as a social control tool that supports sexism is progress. The problem is that this is an incomplete response because it does not question the negative stigma attached to the word *lesbian*. Unfortunately, some women athletes object to the use of the lesbian label to discredit heterosexual women athletes only because they consider it insulting to be called a lesbian. As a result, lesbians are still demonized, and heterosexual women are still disassociating themselves from lesbians. Golf pros Karen Peek and Helen Finn said they were "insulted" and "offended" by Ben Wright's comments about lesbians. Without attacking the stigma attached to the lesbian label, the twin images of lesbians in sport as dangerous sexual predators or abnormal deviants are left intact.

None of the public comments from players, the commissioner, or tournament directors could be characterized as supportive of lesbian golfers, even comments by closeted lesbian golfers themselves! Commissioner Mechem called Wright's allegations "absurd, ugly and demonstrably untrue" (Associated Press 1995a). Nancy Lopez lamented, "I wonder why it is that men can room together and women can't. I don't even feel comfortable having a woman roommate on tour anymore. Why doesn't he talk about all the men on the tour who fool around on their wives?" (*San Francisco Chronicle* 1995, A13). In addition to equating lesbians with sex and infidelity, this response reflects the reluctance on the part of everyone affiliated with the LPGA to encourage any association between lesbians and the LPGA. Some players, such as Laura Davies and Dottie Mochrie, criticized the woman reporter who wrote about Wright's comments for sensationalism (*Daily Hampshire Gazette* 1995; Hodges 1995; Kupelian 1995; *New York Times* 1995; Phillips 1995; White 1995; Yelaja 1995). Some newspaper columnists took the LPGA in general and lesbian players in particular to task for their failure to affirm lesbians on the tour or to come out (Knapp 1995; Price 1995; Rotello 1995).

Even a 1997 research report by the President's Council on Physical Fitness and Sports dealing with physical activity and sports for girls included only two sentences about lesbians in a section on the sociological dimensions of sport and left unchallenged the assumption that lesbians are bad people. Both sentences focused instead on reassuring readers that women interested in sport are not lesbians:

> *An erroneous but particularly persistent and long-standing belief is that sports are masculinizing and that physically active girls are more likely to become lesbians or that all successful female athletes are lesbians. Though this homophobic belief is unfounded, it leads some girls to avoid physical activity. (Duncan 1997, 40)*

It is important to understand how the lesbian label is used as a scare tactic, but the complete absence of any challenge to the lesbian stereotype in these discussions reinforces fears about the assumed danger and menace lesbians in sport pose to other women and to women's sport in general. In the April 1997 ESPN segment on homophobia as part of the special, "Women in Sport at the Crossroads," the host for the show kept referring to the "threat of the lesbian label," the "pervasive fear" of opening up the issue, "the lesbian problem," and the "power of the lesbian label" to deter young women from playing sports. Challenging the social control function of the lesbian label without understanding the connections between sexism and heterosexism leaves intact the division between lesbian and nonlesbian athletes. As long as being called a lesbian is taken as an insult, the label maintains its power to intimidate, and lesbians continue to be demonized as a threat to "normal" (heterosexual) women in sport.

Lesbian as Invisible Space Alien

In the absence of any publicly out, prominent lesbian athletes and coaches, save Muffin and Martina, the reluctance of women in sport to challenge the lesbian stereotype makes lesbians a central but mysterious focus of the discussion about heterosexism and homophobia. Some athletes and coaches are now talking *about* lesbians, but few lesbians are speaking for themselves. Lesbian athletes and coaches remain in the shadows, mysterious alien creatures whose voices are muffled by the closed closet door (Knapp 1997).

The WBCA sponsored a homophobia panel discussion for the second year in a row at their 1997 convention. However, none of the panelists identified themselves as lesbians. When a lesbian in the audience asked why there were no out lesbians on the panel, she was cut off by the moderator as if this question was breaking some kind of rule, and in fact it was, in a sport where publicly identified lesbians are assumed to pose a threat to the entire sport. In contrast, it would be unthinkable to organize a panel to discuss racism in women's sport without including women of color to speak for themselves.

Likewise, in the ESPN special mentioned earlier, none of the women who spoke were identified as lesbian. In fact, one of the women interviewed for the special, Nancy Boutilier, a high school basketball and softball coach, spoke openly of her lesbian identity in her ESPN interview. She described how her school community, teams, and parents accept both her and her partner. She was outraged to see that all references to her lesbianism were edited out of the final segment shown on the air.

On the same ESPN special, Lisa Leslie, a member of the 1996 gold medal Olympic basketball team and WNBA player, said, "I'm not saying *it* doesn't exist. *It* is *out there,* but not everyone playing sports is a lesbian." It? Out there? Can anyone else hear "The X-Files" theme music? This response reflects the acknowledgment that lesbians are in sport but disassociates the speaker from lesbians. Lesbians are presented as something "out there"—mysterious aliens who we know are there but are invisible. Many women and men in sport cannot even say the word "lesbian." Instead they refer to lesbians with indeterminate referents such as "it," "they," "that"—as in "that" is no longer a problem, or "it" isn't an issue. Lesbians in sport are reduced to discussions about labels, threats, problems, and images. Remember those old sci-fi movies with titles such as "It Came From Beneath the Sea," "Them," and "Creature from the Black Lagoon." That's how lesbians are treated in many of these discussions: menacing aliens lurking in the shadows of sport threatening innocent women and children.

As with most forms of social injustice, heterosexism and homophobia are not sustained merely by virulent "homophobes" who intentionally discriminate against lesbians. These injustices are also perpetuated by the larger number of well-intentioned people who do not understand how their fears about lesbians in sport form the basis for an acceptance of an athletic climate that forces a significant number of participants to live in fear of their colleagues' or teammates' prejudice and the institutional climate that supports that prejudice.

These defensive reactions to the lesbian boogeywoman create a climate that is threatening for all women, but particularly for lesbians in sport. Not all athletic contexts are the same, however. Some teams or athletic departments are more hostile to the presence of lesbians than others. The next chapter describes in more detail different climates for lesbians in sport.

6

Life in the Shadow of the Lesbian Boogeywoman:

The Climate for Lesbians in Sport

T he lesbian boogeywoman casts a large shadow over the experiences of all women in sport, but she has the most effect on the lives of women who identify themselves as lesbians. Reactions to the lesbian boogeywoman create an atmosphere in which lesbian coaches, athletes, and athletic administrators devote enormous energy not only to athletics, but also to protecting themselves from potentially career-threatening discrimination and prejudice. The focus of this chapter is to describe, from the perspectives of lesbians in sport, the climates that are created by the reactions described in chapter 5.

I have developed a continuum to describe different climates for lesbians in athletics (see table 6.1). This continuum can be used to describe an individual team, an athletic department, a school, or a professional sport tour. These climates are rarely determined by formal institutional policy. Instead, they develop out of and are guided by informal norms that coaches and athletes learn through their experiences in athletics. These climates are (1) hostile, (2) conditionally tolerant, and (3) open and inclusive. The conditionally tolerant climate includes two subcategories: family secret and "don't ask, don't tell." Several articles in the mainstream press over the last several years describe different aspects of the hostile and conditionally tolerant climates in particular (Cart 1992;

TABLE 6.1
Climates for Lesbians in Athletics

Hostile	Lesbians are the problem even if they are concealing their identity. • Discrimination • Harassment
Conditionally tolerant	Lesbian visibility is the problem. • Glass closet • Acceptance contingent on invisibility and silence
Open and inclusive	Homophobia and heterosexism are the problems. Open lesbians are welcome. • Nondiscrimination • Women of all sexual identities affirmed

Kaufman 1993; Riley, Anderson, and Garber 1992; Scarton 1992; Spander 1991).

HOSTILE CLIMATES: LESBIANS ARE THE PROBLEM

In a hostile athletic climate, lesbian participation is prohibited. The underlying assumption in a hostile climate is that lesbian participation in sport is a problem. If lesbians do participate in this climate, they must conceal their identity from everyone. They must be especially careful about revealing their identities to anyone in a position of authority who controls important requisites of participation (coaching jobs, team membership, playing time, scholarships, corporate sponsorship). Other writers have described the hostile climate in athletics for lesbian athletes and coaches (Blinde and Taub 1992; Brownworth 1994; Cahn 1996; Griffin 1992a, 1994, 1996; Krane 1996a, 1996b; Lenskyj 1991; Palzkill 1990; Rankin in press).

I had just finished showing the video *Out for a Change: Addressing Homophobia in Women's Sports* (Mosbacher 1992) to a group of teachers and coaches attending a professional conference in the spring of 1995. Several members of the audience stayed to ask a question or talk more about the topic. As I spoke with each of these people, I noticed a young woman who seemed to be waiting until everyone left. She stood patiently at the edge of the cluster of people around me. Finally, she was the only one left. I smiled at her, waiting for her question. She tried several times to speak, but stopped each time as tears filled her eyes and her throat constricted with emotion. I suggested that we go sit down. When she had regained her voice, she said, "That video was about my life right now. I could relate to everything they said. It has all happened to me, and I don't know if there's anything I can do." As a young girl, Susan had a goal: to play college basketball. All through school she worked hard on both her academics and her basketball. She achieved her goal when she earned an athletic scholarship to play basketball at her state university. The first couple of years were great, everything she had hoped college would be. She was doing well in school, enjoying basketball, and taking a leadership role in her physical education major program. During this time Susan also fell in love with another woman. She felt good about who she was and decided to tell her basketball coach, whom she respected and liked, about herself. To her shock and dismay, when she came out to her coach, Susan was thrown off the team. As Susan left her office the coach told Susan she would pray for her. Susan was then ostracized by the rest of the team. She was cut off from what she loved most, and her dream was smashed for trusting her coach, feeling good about who she is, and wanting to be honest. In subsequent phone conversations with Susan, I put her in touch with a lesbian lawyer from her state to see if she had any legal recourse. This lawyer told Susan that it was unlikely that they would be able to challenge the dismissal because the state where Susan lives does not provide legal protection from discrimination on the basis of sexual orientation.

Susan disclosed her lesbian identity in a hostile environment. It is dangerous even to be suspected of being a lesbian in this climate. Women suspected of being lesbian are questioned about their identity or even sanctioned and ostracized without confirmation.

> I was being interviewed for a coaching position at a private college. The AD [athletic director] assumed that I was straight, I guess. He told me about the previous candidate and how she had short hair and had arrived for the interview on a motorcycle. From this, he assumed that she was a lesbian. He thought I was straight because I have long hair and drive a Toyota Corolla instead of a Honda 360. I sat there terrified as he told me about the previous candidate and his relief at finding a woman coach "who would be a good role model for woman athletes."
> —Division 3 lacrosse and field hockey coach

A lesbian participating in a hostile climate must be prepared to deny her lesbian identity and act in ways that lead others to believe that she is heterosexual. This tyranny of heterosexuality can cause women athletes and coaches to spend as much time worrying about how they are perceived as they do honing their athletic skills. One coach talked about attending the men's basketball games, a big social event on her campus:

> All coaches are given tickets to the home games, and they are all in one block of seats. I had a discussion with another lesbian coach about how many times you can bring your partner to the game without raising suspicions. I mean how many times can you casually say, "Oh, my friend just happened to be free and so at the last minute I asked her to come to the game with me" without people raising their eyebrows.
> —Division 1 tennis coach

Many athletes are careful about how friendships with other women might be construed and how their appearance might affect perceptions about them. At one college where the basketball coach's antilesbian policies were explicitly spelled out to her players, athletes were afraid to share apartments or dorm rooms because their living arrangements might lead the coach to suspect that roommates were lesbians. Athletes on this team described how some players served as "moles" for the coach, reporting any evidence that teammates might be lesbians.

One coach told me about intentionally avoiding association with other women coaches to minimize the chance that someone might suspect that she is a lesbian. Another coach described how her male athletic director called her in and encouraged her not to spend so much time with the other women coaches. It is difficult to imagine a male coach being warned about spending time with other men. In a hostile climate all women's casual and professional relationships with each other might raise suspicions about lesbianism. In this way homophobia and heterosexism discourage women from bonding as colleagues, friends, lovers, or political allies against sexism in athletics.

At one university, coaches talked about "shooting the silver bullet." This code referred to instances where male administrators tried to find out if women candidates for coaching or administration positions were

1994 Gay Games in New York City. Physique competition.

lesbians with the intention of using that information against them. Administrators typically called male friends at other institutions to find out a woman's sexual orientation.

I was being considered for a position as an associate commissioner of the athletic conference we were in. The communications director called our male athletic director and asked, "Who does she hang around with?" The AD came to me and said, "Well, Marge, he was asking about your social life, who you hang around with, and I told him that every time I see you, you make a great impression." So he was telling me they were checking me out. This was fairly typical any time a woman was being considered for a leadership position. The men's athletic director network would get activated, and they would try to find out if the woman is a lesbian. They ask questions, and the better they know each other the more frank they are about asking. Social or personal life never comes up when they are hiring a man.

—Division 3 athletic director

I was on a search committee to hire a coach for the women's basketball team. There was one woman whose credentials were so much better than any of the other candidates. One of the men on the committee, an administrator, kept trying to push one of the male candidates instead. It was ridiculous, so I knew something else had to be going on for him. He finally volunteered to call the AD at the school where she was an assistant coach to ask about her. He never came right out and said anything, but I know he wanted to find out if she was gay or straight. He didn't seem at all interested in calling the male candidate's AD.

—Division 1 athlete counselor

Sometimes the hostility is more direct, as this lesbian coach describes:

My AD was really putting the pressure on me trying to find out if I was gay. I felt like I was walking on eggs. He suspected that one of the other women coaches and I were together, and he was right, we were. I even found out that he followed me a few times to see if I spent the night at her house or if her car was parked at my house overnight. We had this whole elaborate thing about never parking in each other's driveway and being really careful about not being seen together in town.

—Division 2 basketball coach

Often hostility toward lesbians comes from male athletes, as the following story told by a lesbian athlete illustrates:

I dated a football player my sophomore year. Then we broke up, and that summer I came out. It was big gossip among the football team. Football players were calling my roommates and asking if it was true that I was gay. These guys were friends of mine, I thought. We had socialized together, and they were teammates of the guy I had dated. To my face, if we ran into each other, they were, "Hi, how are you doing?" Meanwhile, they were making my former boyfriend's life miserable. They called him "the converter." It really offended them that I am gay. They stole my backpack from outside the weight room. I had everything in it: my journal, my books, my wallet. That was a $400 expense for me to replace everything. Two weeks later my ex-boyfriend brought me my wallet but wouldn't say where he got it. I knew he didn't take it. He found out some of his teammates had taken it and had confronted them and asked them not to harass me. I felt totally violated. A hundred men I don't even know read my journal, passed it around the locker room, and then threw it all in the back of some guy's truck. I wanted to go to the police, but my roommates convinced me that the football team would beat the shit out of my ex, which was probably true, if I did. Plus, I had mentioned my closeted girlfriend in the journal. Not only that, but things had just started getting better with my own team accepting me as gay. So I didn't go to the police. I thought about going to the football coaches about it, but I found out that they were the ones who started calling my ex "the converter." Until then I thought I was going to just come out and be proud. I was so amazed that these 100 men discussed and made fun of me, harassed me, hated me just because I chose not to sleep with one of them. That was my first experience with terror. I'm proud of who I am, but I don't want my car windows smashed in because I have a rainbow flag on my bumper.

—*Division 1 basketball player*

Some lesbian coaches or athletes are harassed with anonymous graffiti, notes in their mailboxes, or phone calls.

I came home one night late after a road trip, and as my headlights hit the garage door I saw the word "Dyke" spray painted in huge letters. I want to tell you that scared me really bad. I had no idea who did it, but I kept a really low profile in the (athletic) department after that.

—*Division 1 softball coach*

Sometimes male coaches are enormously curious about the sexuality of women coaches.

I was standing around the coffee nook with a bunch of the men coaches when they started talking about some of the other women coaches, you know, wondering who was gay. They think I'm straight, and I haven't discouraged that impression, so I guess they thought they could talk about this in front of me. Finally one of them asked me if this other woman coach was queer. I was so uncomfortable. I said something like, "How would I know?" and just got out of there as soon as I could without making it obvious I was uncomfortable.

—Division 1 track coach

Unfortunately, closeted lesbians can also make the climate hostile for other lesbians. One bisexual athletic director described how the only woman coach on her staff dealt with the lesbian issue on her team:

She is the most homophobic of all. I am certain she is a lesbian herself. She was being very negative toward anyone who was a lesbian on her team. She had a policy against it. Not openly, not visible, but some of the athletes were upset because she had said, "I don't want that kind of behavior on my team." I think she called it a perversion. It surprised me when I heard about it.

—Division 3 athletic director

Coaches and teammates, regardless of sexual orientation, are sometimes hostile to lesbian athletes' participation.

After joining (the campus lesbian and gay student group) I enjoyed the sense of community I had with other students. I was an anomaly, an out lesbian softball player who wanted to take on the world. I became one of the poster children who were invited to classes or dorms to talk about lifestyles and answer questions. While I was becoming more and more open about who I was, I found myself sitting on the bench more and more. I was there (on the team) as an athlete not a lesbian, but no one on the team could separate the two in their minds and accept me for who I was, so I had a pretty horrible season. On away trips no one wanted to stay in the same room with me at hotels. Other players preferred sleeping on the floor in other rooms rather than staying in a room with a lesbian. Players shunned me and generally made my life miserable. My coach, who was also rumored to be a lesbian, was no help. When I was in the health center with a back injury, no one on the team checked on me.

—Division 3 softball player

My girlfriend and I were the only lesbians on the team. One summer before the season started during two-a-day workouts, my girlfriend and I went back to the dorm just to take a nap. My whole team burst into the room and threw the blankets and sheets off of us, trying to catch us in some type of sexual position. It was really embarrassing and rude. My girlfriend and I never flaunted our relationship. . . . I had a lot of paranoia about losing my scholarship because of my sexuality. I know I suppressed a lot of my personal life in the community where I went to school. I did not go anywhere in the community that was lesbian identified until my senior year. I believe my athletic director was a big dyke, but of course, she was not out and I don't believe she would have supported me being out.

—Division 1 volleyball player

The rest of the team started figuring out that Jane [one of her teammates] and I were lovers, and everything changed. No one talked to us. They wouldn't change clothes near us in the locker room. One time there was a team party. Neither Jane nor I had a car, so some of the girls were supposed to pick us up outside the residence hall. We waited and waited, and they never showed up. The next day at practice, I asked what happened, and one of them said, "Oh, we came by, but you weren't there." Well, there is no way they could have missed us if they had really come by.

—Division 1 soccer player

Parents can also help to create a hostile climate for lesbians. A high school basketball team picture caused a group of players' parents to suspect that the assistant coach was a lesbian. In the picture the assistant coach's hands were clasped together in front of her with her index fingers and thumbs together forming a triangle. Some of the parents had heard that a triangle was a secret gay symbol. They went to the school principal and accused the assistant coach of intentionally making a gay symbol in the picture. When the assistant coach was asked about this, she was stunned and had no idea what anyone was talking about. Nonetheless, to avoid controversy, the picture was retaken with everyone's hands in less-threatening positions. This incident might have been laughable except for the fear it must have created for any of the players or coaches on this team who might have been lesbian or unsure of their sexual identity to hear parents express such paranoid and hostile attitudes about lesbians.

In a hostile climate lesbians must keep their identities carefully hidden. As these stories demonstrate, lesbians in hostile athletic climates are subjected to different kinds of discrimination and harassment ranging from blatant to subtle. The consistent message, however, is that their presence is not welcomed.

CONDITIONALLY TOLERANT CLIMATES: LESBIAN VISIBILITY IS THE PROBLEM

The problem in a conditionally tolerant athletic climate is lesbian visibility rather than the presence of lesbians. If lesbians are willing to abide by an implicit set of "rules," their presence is tolerated and even welcomed. These rules require lesbians to be silent about their identity even though others in athletics or the general public know about them. Mariah Burton Nelson (1991) in her book *Are We Winning Yet?* used "A Silence So Loud It Screams" as the title for a chapter describing the experiences of an anonymous lesbian golfer on the LPGA tour. This title is an apt description of the climate for lesbians in a conditionally tolerant climate. In this climate lesbians live in a glass closet; they keep their identities "secret," but everyone knows they are there. Women coaches and athletes construct elaborate charades that enable everyone to act as if there are no lesbians present or to maintain that lesbians in sport are a "non-issue." This collaborative denial maintains a delicate balance that allows heterosexuals not to confront their prejudices and enables lesbians to participate in sport as long as they are willing to keep their identities "secret." Maintaining this bargain affects everything from how women's sports are marketed to interpersonal dynamics on school teams. This "open secret," as Sedgewick (1990) calls it, leaves lesbians dependent on the willingness of others to ignore their presence, making

Courtesy of Mariah Burton Nelson

Former professional basketball player Mariah Burton Nelson is now an openly lesbian best-selling author who writes about women in sport.

lesbians vulnerable to discrimination and harassment from anyone who chooses to violate the implicit contract of invisibility in exchange for participation.

In her first meeting with her assistant athletic director after being hired, a lesbian coach was told that she was expected to avoid going to gay bars, being seen at any kind of gay-related event, or developing friendships with other women who were "not careful about who knows about them." This closeted lesbian administrator was warning the new lesbian coach to remain invisible. The implication was that her job would be in jeopardy if she broke these rules. Another lesbian, who had been coaching tennis at a private club as an out lesbian, told me how surprised she was to learn that she was expected to be closeted in her new position as a university coach. She believed that the other lesbian coaches were avoiding her because they thought that she was too open about her identity and that she threatened their safety because she didn't immediately understand the unspoken rules of silence she was expected to abide by in college athletics. In both cases these women learned the rules quickly and felt pressure to conform to expectations of invisibility.

In the "don't ask, don't tell" athletic climate, as in the military, lesbians are expected to keep their identity to themselves. Even though teammates, competitors, or coaches might know a lesbian athlete's secret, they expect her never to make her lesbian identity obvious in appearance, discussion, or association. A lesbian athlete talked with me about the pressure she felt from her teammates to pretend that she was heterosexual even though they all knew she was a lesbian.

The majority of the team was straight and knew that I am gay. I had told everyone. One day the team was in the locker room listening to music, getting ready for practice. They were talking about men's butts and were going around and everyone was saying if they thought men's butts looked better in football or baseball pants. I just didn't pay any attention. I was getting dressed, tying my shoes. One of the younger players insisted on asking me, "What about you, whose butts do you like better?" I didn't answer, and she asked again. I finally said, "I'm kind of partial to softball players myself." There were all these groans and "awwwws." Then I got mad, and I said, "You guys are trying to force me to say football or baseball when you know I'm not attracted to men." They would get mad at me because I would be up front about that. They were kind of OK with me being gay, but they were like, "Do you have to talk about it?" They could talk about guys they were seeing, but it wasn't OK for me to talk about my girlfriend.
    —Division 1 basketball player

In a conditionally tolerant climate, even though others know there are lesbians in the department or on the team, it is understood by everyone that lesbians are not supposed to call attention to their sexual identity. Athletic department social events where heterosexual colleagues bring their significant others are uncomfortable for many lesbian coaches. They often attend these functions alone and feel awkward and out of place in social settings where their heterosexual colleagues bring partners.

In the family-secret climate, lesbians may tell teammates, competitors, or coaches, even athletic directors, but this information is carefully guarded to prevent outsiders from finding out. This unspoken pact of silence is maintained as a secret within the immediate athletic "family." Everyone affiliated with that climate goes into the closet with the lesbian participants. Everyone assumes that it is in the best interest of all concerned to protect the secret from outsiders.

> I assume everyone in the athletic department knows about me. When you are in the same place for any length of time and you never appear at any social functions with a male escort, I would gather that people assume you are gay. I have tried to be very careful about what I do and where I go in public. Just to make sure I'm not too blatant because I think that is the kind of thing that people worry about, if you are too open or too outrageous and don't care. That's when it comes back on you professionally.
>
> —*Division 1 field hockey coach*

> I was at a volleyball game. It was mandatory because we had a basketball recruit visiting. I was sitting with the basketball team and this recruit, but they were all acting really obnoxious and loud. So I said good-bye to the recruit and went to sit with my roommates, who are all softball players. I ended up leaving the match with them. Later we had basketball practice, and the assistant coach was all over me about why did I walk out of that public event with softball players. Ironically, at the time most of the softball team was straight, but she didn't want me associating with them in public because everyone thinks softball players are gay.
>
> —*Division 1 basketball player*

For athletes who were out as lesbians in high school, the expectations of a conditionally tolerant college climate are particularly painful.

> Everybody in athletics here is real hush-hush about it [lesbians]. It was hard to deal with because in [hometown], everyone was out. There were a lot of lesbians, and it was much easier to be yourself. When I came here [to the university], everybody was like, "Don't say that" or "You can't do this." It was more "keep it to yourself."
>
> —*Division 1 basketball player*

Lesbian athletes are often pressured by teammates, both lesbian and heterosexual, to keep their identity hidden. Being out as a lesbian and being an athlete are perceived to be completely incompatible. A lesbian softball player who had chosen to be active in campus lesbian and gay student groups received a lecture from one of her older more closeted teammates:

> One senior, who was the most respected player on the team, laid it out, "Watch what you say. You don't know what you are playing with. You only make it worse for everyone else. Either play on the team or be out. It's your choice." My heart sank because I knew I had lost and was never going to be a part of the team. I spent many nights alone in hotel rooms on road trips. Leaving the team was the hardest thing I have ever done. It was like I gave up the good fight.
> —*Division 3 softball player*

In the conditionally tolerant climate any breach of secrecy voids the informal contract of protection and solidarity, making lesbians vulnerable to potential discrimination or harassment. This discrimination can come from teammates or coaches who are willing to be tolerant only as long as a lesbian's identity is kept within the athletic family. During a workshop with the athletic department at a Division 1 school, the women's track coach described to me how she did not "mind" lesbians on her team. When a lesbian athlete on her team spoke at a campus gay pride rally, however, both she and the rest of team were angry at the lesbian athlete for this breach of the family-secret code. A Division 1 lesbian basketball player told me that her assistant coach warned her to avoid attending lesbian and gay social or political events, joining lesbian and gay organizations, or wearing buttons, clothes, or jewelry that would identify her as lesbian.

Neither the hostile nor the conditionally tolerant climate is safe for lesbians. In either situation lesbians who do not follow the rules risk losing their jobs, a spot on the team, the support of others in the athletic environment, or—for professional athletes—commercial endorsements.

OPEN AND INCLUSIVE CLIMATES: DISCRIMINATION AND HOMOPHOBIA, NOT LESBIANISM, ARE THE PROBLEMS

In an open and inclusive climate athletic directors and coaches make it clear that homophobia and discrimination against lesbians are the problems, not lesbians. Institutional policy sometimes backs up this stance, but more often an open and inclusive climate depends on individual coaches or administrators who are personally opposed to discrimination against lesbians. These coaches are brave and often lonely pioneers navigating uncharted waters with little guidance or support in terms of institutional policy or leadership. Nonetheless, lesbians in this climate can be more open about their sexual orientation without as much concern about the kinds of discrimination or harassment experienced by lesbians in the hostile or conditionally tolerant climates. All participants are treated fairly and with respect so that discrimination against and harassment of lesbians is not tolerated.

> My first lover and I were teammates. We were freaked out so I suggested we go talk to our coach. We thought she was probably gay, but we didn't know. So we went to her and told her we were having these feelings. She said, "Whatever you do, be respectful of each other." She was someone I really felt confident to go to. It was good to have her as a resource person. She was someone we could talk to.
>
> —*Division 3 soccer player*

> I did not hide or cover up who I was to the team. I talked freely about my partner, and for team dinners, parties, or the end-of-the-season banquet, if partners were invited, I always brought Meg. Our head coach was a black man. He was supportive from the first time that he figured out that I was gay. Being black, I think he was more sensitive to being inclusive. He just wanted you to be a good student and a good athlete. He would ask how Meg was. He gave her passes to get into meets free, and he always spoke to her. He could have been a real jerk and said, "No, you are not a part of the team." I was out in talking about our relationship with anyone who wanted to talk about it. I fielded questions from anyone who was questioning themselves.
>
> —*Division 1 track athlete*

Helen Carroll, an out lesbian athletic director at Mills College, is convinced that directly addressing homophobia with athletes helps teams to perform better. She believes that when teammates learn to respect and accept each other, these relationships are reflected in how the team works together in competition. Every year at Mills, each team chooses a topic and organizes a dialogue about that topic for all of the other teams and coaches. These dialogues occur throughout the school year, led by teams in their off-season. Homophobia is one of the most requested topics, along with racism, media images of women in sport, and eating disorders among women athletes. Her goal is to make the athletic climate more open and accepting.

> We want to make the environment more inviting to everyone. We can take our time. Each coach can do this in their own way. There are lots of opportunities to continue the dialogues: van trips, weekends. Our focus is learning together about these issues.
>
> —*Helen Carroll, athletic director at Mills College*

Helen Carroll, athletic director at Mills College and an out lesbian, promotes an "open climate" in which homophobia is outspokenly addressed.

Not all open and inclusive climates are as affirming as these examples suggest. Caught between the belief that lesbian athletes should not be discriminated against and the fear of negative consequences to the program, some coaches and athletes are more tentative in their acceptance. Lesbians who are open about their identity are not punished, but their openness makes coaches, other athletes, or administrators a little nervous.

My coaches don't know quite what to do with me. I make them a little nervous. I have rainbow flags on my car. The first time I wore a gay T-shirt to practice, I thought my head coach was going to lose it, but then after a while they [her coaches] couldn't wait to see what I would wear the next day. She said she admires me for being so out, but she thinks I push it on people sometimes.

—Division 1 lacrosse player

My coach is a little uncomfortable with me being out. It seems like whenever I'm having a conversation with my teammates [about being gay], he gets fidgety and blushes, but he never says anything negative.

—Division 1 rower

Silence about lesbians does not necessarily reflect acceptance. As with most issues of social justice, a public statement of intention to be open and accepting is required and must be backed up by specific actions that communicate the policy to all participants. Unfortunately, the number of open and inclusive athletic climates is small. Most athletic climates are hostile or conditionally tolerant. The more media attention a women's team or sport receives, the less likely the climate is to be open and inclusive as coaches and athletes try to "protect" their image and maintain public approval.

Until Muffin Spencer-Devlin came out in the spring of 1996, the LPGA was conditionally tolerant. As long as no lesbian golfers came out publicly and everyone participated in efforts to camouflage their identities through the use of makeup, feminine hairstyles, and clothes, lesbians were tolerated on the golf tour. Though other golfers knew who the lesbians on the professional golf tour were, this information was hidden from the press and public. After Spencer-Devlin came out, LPGA officials had no choice but to edge toward a tentative acceptance and acknowledgment that there are lesbians on the tour. Perhaps as other golfers come out, the LPGA will move toward being more open and inclusive. Time will tell.

Most college teams are either hostile or conditionally tolerant. Highly visible Division 1 programs whose teams compete at the national level are less likely to be open and inclusive. I have found that smaller, less-visible Division 2 or 3 programs are more likely to be working toward being open and inclusive.

In both the hostile and conditionally tolerant climates the underlying assumption is that lesbians in athletics are a problem. In the hostile climate the inclusion of anyone suspected of being lesbian is a problem. In the conditionally tolerant climate, inclusion of closeted lesbians is not a problem, but the inclusion of open lesbians is. In the open and inclusive climate the problems are defined as homophobia and discrimination against lesbians. Because most women's athletic contexts are either hostile or conditionally tolerant, suspicions about lesbians and lesbian fears of being publicly identified create an atmosphere in which a lot is happening below the surface of public silence.

Contradictions in a particular athletic climate make its classification difficult. For example, within a hostile athletic department, there might be individual teams whose coaches create a climate that is conditionally tolerant of lesbians on that particular team. Another example is an athletic department that claims to follow a school nondiscrimination policy, but one or more teams in that department are openly hostile to lesbians. These inconsistencies point out the importance of developing and enforcing institutional policy to prohibit discrimination against lesbians rather than leaving the decision of whether to discriminate or not up to the personal whim of individual coaches or athletes.

In addition to the lesbian boogeywoman image, religious beliefs also affect how lesbians are treated in sport. What happens when coaches or teammates see lesbians not only as sexual predators, but also as sinners? The next chapter extends the discussion of athletic climates for lesbians by focusing on the potential for the evangelical Christian influence in sport to add to the hostility many lesbian athletes and coaches experience.

7

We Prey,
They Pray?

Lesbians and
Evangelical Christians
in Sport

Many athletes and coaches express their religious beliefs as a part of their sport experience. Sport fans are used to watching football players drop to one knee and bow their heads in the end zone after scoring a touchdown or basketball players crossing themselves before a foul shot. Pre-and postgame prayers are a traditional part of many team rituals, and athletes thanking God for an important victory are practically a sport interview cliché (Davis 1996; Rutkoski 1996).

The integration of religion into sport is not only a matter of individual expression. Two evangelical Christian organizations, the Fellowship of Christian Athletes (FCA) and Athletes in Action (AIA), have a huge presence in professional and amateur athletics. The FCA is an interdenominational evangelical Christian athletic ministry encouraging athletes and coaches from junior high school through professional sports to develop a personal relationship with Jesus Christ. As such, its goal, as described on the FCA Internet home page, is to "present to athletes and coaches, and all whom they influence, the challenge and adventure of receiving Jesus Christ as Savior and Lord, serving Him in their relationships and in the fellowship of the church" (Fellowship of Christian Athletes 1996a).

The FCA statement of faith asserts that the Bible is "the inspired, the only infallible, authoritative Word of God" and "that for the salvation of lost and sinful men (women) regeneration by the Holy Spirit is absolutely essential." The FCA claims to have over 5,000 "huddles," or campus-based groups, with an estimated 250,000 to 400,000 student participants across the country. The FCA's goal is presence on "every school campus in America" (Fellowship of Christian Athletes 1996a).

The FCA sponsors prayer breakfasts and distributes Christian literature at many college coaches' association meetings, national championships, and football bowl games. In addition, the FCA sponsors men's and women's sports camps that attract junior high through college coaches and athletes "brought together by their love for sports and their life in Christ." High-profile coaches and athletes such as Joe Gibbs (former Washington Redskins coach), Tom Osborne (University of Nebraska football coach), Bill McCartney (former University of Colorado football coach), Michelle Akers (Olympic soccer player), Jennifer Azzi (Olympic and professional basketball player), Betsy King (LPGA golfer), and Sheryl Swoopes (Olympic and professional basketball player) are featured in testimonials on the FCA home page and in the FCA publication, *Sharing the Victory.*

Athletes in Action is affiliated with the international evangelical Christian organization Campus Crusade for Christ and its leader, Bill Bright. Bright is one of a number of high-profile leaders—including Pat

Robertson, founder of the Christian Coalition, and James Dobson of Focus on the Family—who have shaped the increasing influence and visibility of the Christian right over the last 20 years (Cantor 1994; Diamond 1989, 1996). Like the FCA, AIA believes that to be saved, it is necessary to develop a personal relationship with Jesus Christ, live a Christ-centered life, and accept the Bible as the literal word of a Christian God (Athletes in Action 1996). AIA also bases its recruitment efforts in athletics, with campus-based groups at colleges and universities throughout the United States. On their home page AIA describes itself as "having capitalized on society's love for sport, using the platform of athletics to win many to Christ." AIA seeks to "reach the United States and resource the world for Jesus Christ through the influence of sports." AIA also runs summer camps for Christian athletes and coaches and sponsors touring teams of Christian athletes who play exhibition games against men's and women's college basketball, baseball, track and field, volleyball, tennis, swimming, wrestling, soccer, and softball teams throughout the United States. The AIA women's basketball team also played against the 1996 women's national basketball team.

Both the FCA and AIA are among more than 100 sport ministries in a coalition known as Sports Outreach American (SOA). SOA distributes a Super Bowl kit for home-viewing parties. The kit includes a video to be played at halftime, activities, and selected biblical scriptures. In 1997 more than 6,000 kits were sent out, and SOA claimed that over 300,000 people participated in kit activities during the Super Bowl (Shapiro 1997).

So, in a nation where freedom of religion is protected, what is the problem with the expression of Christian faith among athletes and coaches and the proliferation of sports organizations that support that faith? And what does the growth of evangelical Christianity in sport have to do with lesbians in sport? Certainly, individual athletes have a right to express their faith as they choose, and groups of athletes who share a religious faith can choose to gather and celebrate that faith. Sport ministries affiliated with a particular religious perspective, such as the FCA and AIA, also have a legitimate role to play for athletes and coaches who share that faith. Problems arise, however, when one religious perspective is affiliated with school teams and with sports governing bodies. Problems also arise when athletes or coaches feel pressured to participate in religious activities or are discriminated against on the basis of a particular religious perspective. The increasing influence of evangelical Christian coaches, athletes, and organizations intensifies an environment that is already hostile to lesbians and can discourage expressions of spirituality that conflict with evangelical Christian beliefs.

In this chapter I want to address four areas of concern that I have about the influence of evangelical Christianity in sport: (1) the belief

that homosexuality is a sin that must be "overcome," (2) sports governing bodies and schools providing the FCA and AIA access to coaches
and athletes, (3) FCA and AIA affiliation with Christian right organizations professing antigay, antifeminist agendas, and (4) the pressure exerted on athletes to participate in evangelical Christian practices or adopt
evangelical Christian beliefs.

I want to acknowledge a few important points that make discussions
about lesbians in sport and religion complex. First, the title of this chapter, "We Prey, They Pray?", implies that Christians and lesbians are
incompatible social groups, when no real separation neatly divides Christians and lesbians or gay men. To the contrary, lesbian, gay, and bisexual
people come from many different spiritual perspectives and have formed
groups even within conservative denominations to celebrate both their
faith and their sexuality (for example, Dignity for Catholics, Affirmation
for Mormons, Integrity for Episcopalians, Baptists Concerned, and Am
Tikva for Jews). Their spiritual beliefs and practices are important to
many lesbian, gay, and bisexual people. Evangelical Christian leaders'
portrayal of gay people as spiritually impoverished sinners in need of
salvation causes a great deal of pain and anger, especially among lesbians, gay men, bisexual people, and their families for whom religious faith
is central to their lives.

Several lesbians I interviewed for this book identify as Christians. Some
of them participate in either FCA or AIA activities. Most of these women
viewed their participation in FCA or AIA events as a way to express their
love of sport and their Christian faith with others who shared their perspectives. They were either unaware of an antigay perspective in these
organizations or choose to participate in spite of it, taking from their
experience what they find useful and ignoring the rest. A few women
who are now self-accepting lesbians remembered their past participation in FCA or AIA as an attempt to "overcome" their sexual attractions
to women. Others no longer participate in FCA events because they can
not reconcile their participation in an organization that does not accept
who they are.

Second, I want to acknowledge that not all Christians, or even all evangelical Christians, are intolerant of lesbians. There are many varied Christian denominations with differing perspectives on sin in general and
homosexuality in particular. For example, I spoke with one heterosexual
coach who is an active FCA member. She does not agree with the FCA's
organizational perspective on homosexuality, and she challenges FCA
practices that she believes are antigay. My intentions here are not to
polarize lesbians and Christians or to demonize Christians. Rather, I want
to identify ways in which the uncritical and privileged acceptance of
any religious perspective in sport, in this case evangelical Christian perspectives, can encourage or exacerbate an already hostile atmosphere

1994 Gay Games in New York City.
Martial arts competition.

Photo by Joan Bobkoff © 1994

for lesbian athletes and coaches and ignore or discriminate against other spiritual perspectives.

HOMOSEXUALITY IS A SIN THAT MUST BE "OVERCOME"

The FCA Internet home page includes a list of questions to guide discussions during campus "huddle" meetings and the FCA perspective on how to respond to these questions. On homosexuality, the FCA answers the question, "How should I as a Christian regard homosexuality?" as follows:

The Bible gives two very clear statements about homosexuality. 1. It is a sin. The old testament saw it as a sin demanding capital punishment. New Testament words say: "indecent ... abandoning the natural function ... burning in desire ... strange ... depraved ... not proper ..." 2. Homosexuals can be converted from homosexuality. Paul spoke of homosexuality among the perverse Corinthians and said, "... and such were some of you. But you were washed, you were sanctified, you were justified ..." Notice the word "WERE" (past tense). Men were not saved in their perversion, but from it. Our day has done much to give "hearty approval"to what God abhors (Romans 1:32). But the Word of God abides forever. In our church are numbers of former homosexuals who have been converted. Though they may struggle with this area as the "sin that so easily entangles" (Hebrews 12:1). Yet they have been given wonderful victory by the Lord Jesus Christ. "His blood can make the foulest clean." (Fellowship of Christian Athletes 1996c)

The FCA's position on homosexuality supports several organizational practices that target lesbian athletes and coaches. While preparing to speak about homophobia in sport at the 1991 National Softball Coaches Association conference, I browsed through the exhibit area. Among various softball equipment and clothing exhibitors, both the FCA and AIA had tables with their organizations' publications available to coaches free of charge. One of the free publications available at the FCA table was a small booklet titled *Emotional Dependency: A Threat to Close Friendships* (Rentzel 1987). This pamphlet is published by Exodus International, an "ex-gay" Christian ministry devoted to "liberation from the sin of homosexuality" through conversion to Christianity and prayer. The pamphlet described the perspective that all lesbian relationships are based on dysfunctional emotional dependency and lead to "bondage," "manipulation," and "destruction." The characteristics and causes of dependent relationships are described, as is the path back to heterosexuality, "God's creative intent for humanity."

Another publication available from Exodus International (1996), *Overcoming Lesbianism—Women and Femininity,* describes the importance of femininity as an "outer reflection of inner wholeness" and promotes "make-over" seminars on color analysis, applying makeup, nail care, clothing selection, and hairstyling as important skills for overcoming lesbianism. For men, involvement in sport and other masculine pursuits is prescribed as a way to overcome homosexuality. This simplistic view and conflation of masculinity, femininity, and sexuality rely on the adoption of stereotypical gender-role behaviors to "cure" homosexuality. The *Emotional Dependency* pamphlets were also placed on the plates of all attendees at an FCA-sponsored prayer breakfast during the Women's Basketball Coaches Association conference at the Final Four in 1992. The speaker at this prayer breakfast was an "ex-lesbian" who described her struggle to overcome her "sin" and her salvation in Jesus Christ and heterosexuality. Among the attendees were many closeted Christian lesbian coaches who endured this event in uncomfortable silence. They were afraid that if they got up and left, it would be tantamount to announcing to all present that they were lesbians, a step they were not ready to take. But as one coach said, after I told her the pamphlet was published by a Christian "ex-gay" ministry called Exodus, "Talk about an exodus, there were a lot of people who left FCA as a result of that. People were steamed." However, according to WBCA executive director Betty Jaynes, there were no complaints made to the executive board about this speaker or the pamphlets.

The FCA also distributed the *Emotional Dependency* pamphlet at the prayer breakfast held at the National Softball Coaches Association annual conference in 1991. This time, however, there was a different response. A lesbian softball coach explained,

> The pamphlets were on everyone's plates at the breakfast. All these closeted lesbians sitting there. We were really angry and brought it back to the executive board. The NSCA leadership didn't know the FCA was doing that [distributing the pamphlets]. This is supposed to be a breakfast about athletes. To my knowledge it has never happened again.

I spoke with a Christian lesbian coach who was a counselor at one of the FCA summer camps. She described what she remembered of an orientation lecture given to all staff at the beginning of the camp session:

> The lecture went something like, "The issue of homosexuality may come up during this sport camp. You, as coaches and counselors, are not to attempt to field these questions. If a camper brings up the topic direct them to [a specified staff member]. The FCA position is that homosexuality is an abomination. The Bible is very clear. If you yourself are struggling with this issue, you are also encouraged to talk with [specified staff member]. Do not discuss it with campers or other counselors. Such behavior will not be tolerated." The implication was made that any coaches or counselors who were found to be openly gay would be dismissed.

This coach asked how the camp directors reconciled the notion that not all Christians agree on this perspective about homosexuality. She was told that the FCA leadership had adopted this position and there was no room for discussion. Since she was filling in for someone else, she felt uncomfortable challenging the FCA position more strenuously but recalled being "infuriated" by it. When she was asked to work for FCA camp again, she refused, citing FCA intolerance for homosexuality and her philosophical differences with the organization's policy.

A heterosexual woman soccer coach who worked at the same FCA camp challenged their position on homosexuality as well and received a similar response: There was simply no room for discussion. She added,

> I don't remember FCA having this policy when I first became involved. It has evolved over the years. There is this belief that lesbianism is running rampant in women's sports. The FCA has always been an old boys' network, and it is getting more conservative and more polarized. There are assumptions that if you are in FCA, you believe everything down the line. I don't see it that way, and a number of my straight friends don't see it that way. We are extremely frustrated by it. I would like to be a person who stays and fights, but if my efforts are in vain, I'll move on. I'll leave FCA unless I see some changes.

She also found out in the process of challenging FCA that the "gay lecture" was not given at the boys' camp, only the girls' camp. She reported that this lecture is now given at both the girls' and boys' camps. (Can we call this gender equity?) She added,

> This year the statement was a little different. They talked about "sexual purity" in relationships without a lot of detail. They needed to put a blanket term on it. There were men at the boys' camp involved in relationships out of wedlock and a few women coaches who were offended by the FCA position on homosexuality so they just came up with different terminology. I don't think their stance changed. They were just being more politically correct.

A lesbian coach sent me an article in *Competitive Woman* titled "A Controversial Lifestyle: Clearing the Fog of Homosexuality" (despite the efforts of reference librarians, questions on women's sports computer lists, and phone calls to the FCA headquarters, I have not been able to track down any information about *Competitive Woman*). In the article, Jane (not her real name), an "ex-lesbian" who competed and coached at the college level, is interviewed by *Competitive Woman* about "the events that led to her 'controversial lifestyle' and her insights and understanding about why homosexuality is prominent in women's sports." Jane describes several clichés about lesbianism: that she was unpopular with boys because she was a jock; that she had tried to be the boy her unloving father wanted; that, rejected by men, she sought love and acceptance with female teammates; and that she was seduced by a female teacher. She then reports that when she was a college coach, the mother of one of her athletes wrote her a letter asking how she could call herself a Christian and live "that way?" Jane describes her devastation, "I was deceived into thinking other people saw me as, 'yes, she may be homosexual, but she is a really good person.'" Soon after this, her mother's death devastated Jane. She reported that the turning point came when she was asked to be a basketball counselor at a Christian sports camp, presumably either FCA or AIA sponsored. With the help of one of the Christian speakers at the camp, Jane came to see her lesbianism as a form of "emotional dependency" and gave her life to Christ. She was able to "change her circle of friends" and now has "some new Christian friends who have been wonderful to me." Jane's advice for other women "experiencing unnatural desires" is to say, "Satan, just get out of here! You are not ruling my life anymore. Jesus Christ is Lord of my life." The article ends with a summary of the characteristics of a "dependency relationship" taken from the Exodus *Emotional Dependency* pamphlet. Examples of the characteristics listed are "refers frequently to the other in conversation," "displays physical affection beyond that which is appropriate for a friendship," "prefers to spend time alone with this friend and becomes frustrated when this does not happen," and "experiences romantic or sexual feelings leading to fantasy about this person." Hmmm, sounds like it might be love to me, regardless of sex or sexuality.

The clear organizational message from the FCA and AIA and from other fundamentalist Christians in sport is that homosexuality cannot be tolerated and that lesbians need to be counseled and prayed for so that they can overcome their unnatural desires and emotional dependency. The only way to overcome this "affliction" is to accept Jesus as one's Lord.

Some women, like "Jane," having internalized all of the negative societal messages about homosexuality, are troubled by their attractions to women, and feel forced to choose between their religious faith and their sexuality. They are receptive to the antilesbian messages delivered by the FCA and AIA. For these women, in the absence of support from coaches, teammates, or family, denying their sexual and emotional attractions is the only way they can resolve their discomfort with their feelings for women. For many others who refuse to renounce either their sexuality or their religious faith, this message becomes the basis for secrecy and deception to avoid condemnation or discrimination at the hands of other members of their religious communities.

Throughout history, selected excerpts from the Bible have been used to rationalize social injustice. Selective readings of the Bible have been used to justify enslavement of African people, subordination of women, persecution of Jews, stigmatization of people with disabilities, and the superiority of white European Protestants and their cultural values and destiny (Hill and Cheadle 1996). Approximately eight Biblical verses are typically used to justify discrimination against lesbian, gay, and bisexual people (Hill and Cheadle 1996). Progressive religious writers take the perspective that these verses are taken out of historical context and used selectively, while other prohibitions in the same sections are ignored (Scanzoni and Mollenkott 1994). Scanzoni and Mollenkott are evangelical Christians who base their views on the Bible and come to very different conclusions from other Christians who condemn homosexuality.

Christian fundamentalists' belief in the inerrant authority of the Bible as they read it is only one perspective among many. Other religious perspectives that accept and affirm homosexuality focus on the quality of love, caring, and responsibility in a partnered relationship rather than on the sex of the people involved (Arguelles and Rivero 1996; Gomes 1996; Scanzoni and Mollenkott 1994; Spong 1992; Wilson 1995). Progressive religious denominations such as Unitarian Universalists, United Church of Christ, and the Society of Friends have embraced lesbian, gay, and bisexual people. Other mainstream denominations are engaged in heated discussions about what role lesbian, gay, and bisexual people should play within their faith. The freedom of religion guaranteed by the Bill of Rights includes the freedom to read and interpret sacred religious texts in different ways. The challenge in a pluralistic society that values this freedom is to find a way to live with our differences rather than try to impose one set of religious principles on others who do not share them. This is the challenge for evangelical Christians in sport.

FCA AND AIA ACCESS TO COACHES AND ATHLETES

At the 1996 Women's Basketball Coaches Association conference, the WBCA organized a panel discussion entitled "Are You Putting Your Head in the Sand? An Educational Dialogue About Homophobia." Approximately 500 people attended the session. Four people were on the panel: Molly O'Neil, cofounder and leader of Husky Hoops, a lesbian fan club for the University of Washington women's basketball team; Cheryl Littlejohn, a Christian fundamentalist assistant women's basketball coach at the University of Alabama, Tuscaloosa; Jim Bolla, the women's basketball coach at University of Nevada, Las Vegas; and me. During the panel presentation, Molly and I argued that lesbians are discriminated against in sport and that this must be addressed as an issue of social justice. Cheryl shared her perspective that homosexuality contradicts the teachings of the Bible. As a coach, she believes that she has a responsibility to tell prospective athletes and their parents what her position is, especially when directly asked if lesbians are on the team. "Then," she said, "the kids can discriminate. It's their life. It's their choice. I believe that a Christian athlete's parents have a right to know that their daughter will be on a team with Christian values. So, I tell them I am a Christian and that I do not condone homosexuality." Jim Bolla stated that he had no problem with lesbian athletes as long as they respect the rights of other athletes.

The composition of the panel and its title reflected the WBCA leadership's efforts to provide balance to what they perceive to be a controversial topic. The WBCA was careful to include on this panel a fundamentalist Christian, a man, and two lesbians so that a range of perspectives would be presented. This so-called balanced approach is often taken by organizations grappling with how to address antigay discrimination in an attempt to avoid appearing to be "progay" or "promoting homosexuality." Yet the WBCA and other sport organizations promote Christianity by regularly including FCA prayer breakfasts in their annual conference programs. The WBCA did not insist that, for balance, the FCA breakfast where an "ex-lesbian" spoke also include a lesbian speaker who embraces her identity. By providing a forum for the FCA to distribute antigay literature and air their views on homosexuality, the WBCA and other sports governing bodies who sponsor FCA events provide tacit, if not explicit, approval of discrimination against lesbians.

When I proposed a homophobia and heterosexism seminar for the 1997 WBCA coaches' conference, the executive board considered my proposal for several months. They finally decided that the topic was so controversial that they wanted me to give the workshop for the executive board first before they would decide if it was appropriate for the general membership. In contrast, the continued participation of the FCA on the basketball coaches' conference program is unquestioned, despite their sponsorship of an "ex-lesbian" speaker, their distribution of antilesbian material, and their explicit position that homosexuality is a sin that cannot be condoned.

Athletes in Action also has unquestioned access not only to athletes and coaches at public colleges and universities, but to their fans as well. During the early part of the 1996-97 basketball season, the University of Massachusetts women's basketball team played an exhibition game against the AIA touring women's team, of which former Olympian and WNBA player Nancy Lieberman-Cline was a member. During the first half several young people fanned out in the stands handing out an AIA pamphlet describing the AIA touring team's purpose, philosophy, how easy it was to accept Jesus Christ as one's savior, and a suggested prayer if we wished to do so. The pamphlet also listed several AIA corporate sponsors including Nike and Champion.

The AIA pamphlet highlighted a testimonial from Lieberman-Cline about her conversion to Christianity and how her life was meaningless despite a successful Olympic, collegiate, and professional basketball career until she abandoned her Jewish heritage and chose to live a "Christ-centered" life. Lieberman-Cline is now married with a child, though in the early 1980s she was involved in a lesbian relationship with Martina Navratilova. Lieberman-Cline disclosed her relationship with Martina in her autobiography, *Lady Magic* (1992). She wrote of this relationship, "There was an instant attraction, and instant level of comfort. . . . Maybe for that particular time in my life, that's what God wanted me to experience. I honestly don't know." Now, presenting her as a Christian heterosexual woman with a child, AIA can claim Lieberman-Cline as a "twofer." She is both an ex-Jew and an ex-lesbian. A lesbian coach who is active in FCA observed, "AIA is going to get a lot of leg work out of her. She has been 'fixed.' It is possible to be 'fixed.' That is the kind of approach they will take."

I was a little uncomfortable with the distribution of religious material at a basketball game, but I had no idea how much more uncomfortable I would be at halftime. That's when the Christian tent revival really got under way. After the UMass team went to the locker room, the AIA team lined up on one foul line and Lieberman-Cline took center court with a microphone. She elaborated on her testimonial in the pamphlet, emphasizing how her life had changed for the better since she accepted Christ and learned to live according to the Bible.

After Lieberman-Cline spoke, one of her teammates took the microphone and encouraged all spectators to consider taking Jesus Christ as their savior right there in the Mullins Center. She invited us to fill out the tear-off section of the pamphlet and give it to the young people who would be circulating through the stands later. On this tear-off section we were asked for our names, addresses, and phone numbers and invited to check one of three boxes:

- I have just placed my faith and trust in Christ for the first time.
- I would like to know more about the person of Jesus Christ.
- I would like to know how I can grow in my relationship with Christ.

I was astounded at what seemed to me to be a clear violation of church and state. We were being openly proselytized by an evangelical Christian touring basketball team at a public university–sponsored athletic event. I learned later that this halftime event is a standard part of the AIA touring-team agenda at all their games, as is a visit to the host team in the locker room following the game to talk with the college players about their faith. The AIA touring schedule for the 1996-97 season included games with Ohio State, West Virginia, Penn State, Vermont, Rutgers, Old Dominion, North Carolina, Georgia Tech, Auburn, and Alabama—all public institutions who have a responsibility, like UMass, to avoid promoting any one religious perspective over others.

The university athletic department claimed not to know that AIA's halftime program and distribution of Christian material were a standard part of their appearance. The associate athletic director said she was as surprised as I was. She assured me that AIA would not be asked back, and the university chancellor wrote a letter of apology to everyone who complained that the AIA halftime program was a violation of the principle of separation of church and state at a public educational institution.

The easy access to coaches, athletes, and fans enjoyed by FCA and AIA through events sponsored by schools and sports governing bodies raises a number of issues. Do schools and sports governing bodies who sponsor FCA or AIA events support the FCA and AIA positions on homosexuality? Do college athletic departments and sports governing bodies see their affiliation with Christian-oriented groups as good public relations for alumni, parents, and recruits? What kind of work and competitive environment is created for lesbian athletes and coaches when their schools and sports governing bodies affiliate with evangelical Christian sport ministries that condemn homosexuality? The answers to these questions are particularly important, given that many schools and sports

Photo by Joan Bobkoff © 1994

1994 Gay Games in New York City.
Women's backstroke competition.

governing bodies are not on the record as being opposed to discrimination against lesbians in sport nor do many of them support educational programs for athletes and coaches focused on homophobia and heterosexism in athletics.

Are public institutions and sports governing bodies who sponsor FCA or AIA events promoting a particular religious faith? Both the FCA and AIA are evangelical Christian organizations whose mission includes the recruitment of athletes and coaches to Jesus Christ. What about athletes who are Jews, Muslims, Catholics, agnostics, or Christians who are not evangelical? The affiliation of public educational institutions and sports governing bodies with evangelical Christianity is an association that needs to be evaluated far more carefully if the rights and safety of all members of educational and professional communities are to be respected.

Given the explicit antigay position taken by both the FCA and AIA, how do sports governing organizations and public institutions reconcile their sponsorship of FCA and AIA events at their conferences and schools? By the same token, how do these public organizations and institutions reconcile their association with a particular religious perspective, in this case, evangelical Christianity? Why are these sport ministries, despite their discriminatory policies, provided unquestioned access to athletes and coaches by such national organizations as the NCAA, the Women's Basketball Coaches Association, USA Basketball, and College Football Bowl sponsors?

CHRISTIAN RIGHT ORGANIZATIONS WITH ANTIGAY, ANTIFEMINIST AGENDAS

Both the FCA and AIA have informal and formal affiliations with a network of Christian right organizations and leaders who actively oppose civil and family rights for lesbian and gay people and promote a traditional view of gender roles and heterosexual married relationships in which the husband is dominant and the wife is submissive (Berlet 1995; Herman 1997; Pharr 1996; Vaid 1995).

Bill Bright, the founder of Campus Crusade for Christ (CCC), which is the parent organization of AIA, was one of the original organizers of the movement to organize evangelical Christians in the early 1970s to exert their influence in politics (Diamond 1989). In addition to athletics and politics, Bright's organization has a strong presence in the military. His stated goal is to reach every person in the United States with the gospel. He described his goals in the following statement:

As the head of a large international movement I am involved with thousands of others in a "conspiracy to overthrow the world." Each year we train

UPI/Corbis-Bettmann

Original 1927 newspaper caption read: "Prize class of gymnasts at Bryn Mawr College, Bryn Mawr, PA., who were awarded first prize in a recent contest, demonstrating their athletic and aesthetic abilities in this pretty pyramid."

tens of thousands of high school and college students from more than half of the major countries of the world in the art of revolution, and daily these "revolutionaries" are at work around the globe, spreading our philosophy and strengthening and broadening our influence. (Plowman 1972, 38)

The Campus Crusade for Christ is known on college campuses across the United States for an aggressive style of "two-on-one" recruitment called "spiritual multiplication," in which two CCC members write their names on two sides of a triangle and the name of an unsaved friend, whom they pray for and witness to, on the third. Crusaders are trained to take any opportunity to witness to unbelievers by explaining the "four spiritual laws." (1) God loves them and has a wonderful plan for their life. (2) We are all sick and separated from God. (3) Jesus Christ is God's only hope. (4) Each person must individually accept Jesus Christ as personal savior in order to know God. These "spiritual laws" were described practically word for word on the AIA pamphlet distributed during the AIA basketball game with the University of Massachusetts women's team.

With Pat Robertson, founder of the Christian Coalition, and Jerry Falwell of the Moral Majority, Bright was one of the organizers of "Washington for Jesus" in 1980. This day-long prayer rally was attended by 200,000 fundamentalist and charismatic Christians. This event marked the rising influence of the Christian right and the coming together of factions of Christians who had not previously joined together for common political goals. Bright was also on the executive board of the American Coalition for Traditional Values, an organization with an explicitly antigay agenda. The executive board also included such antigay luminaries of the Christian right as Jerry Falwell, James Dobson, Donald Wildmon, Jimmy Swaggart, Rex Humbard, and James Robison (Cantor 1994).

The FCA is affiliated with the Christian right primarily through individuals who participate in both FCA and other Christian right organizations. Bill McCartney, a prominent FCA member and the former football coach for the University of Colorado, was in the national news in 1992, but not for football. He allowed his name and university affiliation to be used in a fund-raising letter for Colorado for Family Values, the statewide group organized to prohibit and repeal state and local laws protecting lesbians and gay men from discrimination. At a news conference McCartney called homosexuality "a sin" and an "abomination before Almighty God" while wearing his coach's sweater and standing at a podium with the university's logo on it (de Mers 1992; Monaghan 1992). As a result, McCartney was subsequently charged with, but cleared of, violating a university policy prohibiting employees from using their job titles or university affiliation in activities not related to the university's business.

McCartney was profiled in the FCA magazine, *Sharing the Victory*. This article, titled "A Heart Yielded to God's Game Plan" is available on the FCA home page (Fellowship of Christian Athletes 1996b). In this article the author praised McCartney for how he "took hold of the position God had given him in the sports world to use it for His glory. One reason McCartney understood his position of influence was by being influenced himself through FCA."

In 1990 McCartney and Colorado state FCA director Dave Wardell organized the first of an increasingly popular series of sport stadium rallies for Christian men. McCartney is now recognized as the founder and leader of Promise Keepers, a "Christ-centered ministry dedicated to uniting men through vital relationships to become godly influences in their world and to take their rightful place among society's leaders" (Bellant 1995; Novosad 1996). The Promise Keepers' two-day conferences are held in sports arenas and attract thousands of men who sing hymns, pray, listen to sermons, cheer, and pledge themselves to uphold the Seven

Promises of a Promise Keeper, published by James Dobson's prominently antigay Focus on Family organization. National leaders in the Christian right are regular speakers at these events and contributors to the Promise Keepers' publication, *New Man*. Bill Bright of the Campus Crusade for Christ and Athletes in Action is a member of the Promise Keepers' board of directors, speaks at Promise Keeper events, and writes articles for *New Man*.

The Promise Keepers' conferences blend the energy of a football game and the power of a church service to appeal to Christian men to reclaim their manhood by taking back their "rightful role" as heads of their families. Women are encouraged to submit to their husbands for the "survival of the culture." Though they claim not to be political, the Promise Keepers' affiliation with other more politically active Christian right organizations and McCartney's leadership in supporting Colorado's antigay referendum send clear messages to participants. Moreover, in his addresses to Promise Keeper conferences, McCartney directs attendees to "take back the nation for Christ."

As with other fundamentalist Christian groups, the Promise Keepers espouse an "inerrant" perspective on the Bible that judges homosexuality as a sin and evidence of a culture in decline. Speakers at Promise Keeper conferences condemn homosexuals as immoral. "Godly" men are explicitly heterosexual or homosexuals who "overcome" their "perversion."

Many, maybe even most, individual athletes and coaches who participate in FCA or AIA activities may not be aware of or agree with the antigay, antifeminist, right-wing political agendas associated with these sport ministries. Nonetheless, the FCA and AIA formal and informal affiliations with Christian right political organizations and leaders inform their philosophy and programming. This association, combined with the evangelical Christian belief in the importance of "witnessing" to bring unbelievers to Christ, creates the potential for increasingly hostile climates in athletics for lesbian and gay athletes, as well as anyone who does not share evangelical Christian beliefs.

THE PRESSURE TO PARTICIPATE IN EVANGELICAL CHRISTIAN PRACTICES: WHO'S RECRUITING WHOM?

One of the prevalent stereotypes about lesbians in sport is that we pressure other women to become involved in lesbian relationships. Some of the people who accuse lesbians in sport of recruiting women to a "gay lifestyle" are actively involved in recruitment efforts of their own.

Evangelical Christians believe that they are called to "recruit" nonbelievers to a "Christian lifestyle." Though not all evangelical Christians are equally aggressive about saving souls for Christ, this call to evangelize can take the form of pressure and even harassment of team members or coaches perceived to be nonbelievers (Manasso 1994). This pressure can be particularly difficult when evangelizing Christians are in positions of power: athletic directors, head coaches, team captains, or star players, for example. This pressure and judgment is intensified for young women who are unsure of their sexual orientation or who are identifying themselves as lesbian or bisexual for the first time.

In much of the FCA literature, coaches and athletes talk about integrating their Christian beliefs into their athletic careers or living their Christian values through their roles as coaches or athletes. Certainly, anyone with strong spiritual beliefs strives to live daily by these spiritual values. When does sharing the Gospel cross the line and become harassment? When does living one's understanding of Christian beliefs in athletics become imposing these values on others? When does practicing one's faith in athletics infringe on the rights of others not to participate in those practices or even be exposed to them? These are difficult questions that need deeper exploration in athletics than they have received. When the participation of sport ministries such as FCA and AIA in the NCAA, coaches' associations, or individual school-sponsored events is not respectful of different religious perspectives or tolerant of other differences, there is great potential for offending non-evangelical Christians and making athletics unsafe for those who evangelical Christians believe are sinners.

On an individual level, coaches use the power of their position to influence the beliefs and behaviors of their athletes. Much of this influence has a positive effect on athletes, but pressuring or requiring athletes to participate in religious activities is an inappropriate use of coaching authority. High-profile evangelical Christian coaches like Bill McCartney and Tom Osborne of the University of Nebraska are praised in FCA publications for creating a "Christ-centered" team environment (Fellowship of Christian Athletes 1996b, 1996d). McCartney conducted team prayers at meals and before games until a student complaint forced him to stop in 1985. He talks about the importance of coach participation in FCA-sponsored student huddles: "If you take a coach who is lukewarm for the Lord, those players know, and the students in that school know. They know this coach isn't the 'real deal,' so it doesn't have the same impact" (Fellowship of Christian Athletes 1996b). In 1992 McCartney was named in a wrongful dismissal lawsuit filed by a former assistant coach who alleged that McCartney told others that "God had told him to discharge" the assistant (Gallagher 1992).

Tom Osborne describes on the FCA Internet home page how he leads his coaching staff in a "short devotion for a few minutes before we start our day. We try to get together with a few other people and have a Bible study once a week with the FCA Adult Chapter" (Fellowship of Christian Athletes 1996d). Osborne also describes his team's expected participation in FCA events at bowl games: "For the last 12-15 years, I can't remember when there hasn't been some type of FCA function each year. And in recent years, FCA events have been scheduled like any other event, with all players attending." This from the coach who defended Heisman Trophy candidate Lawrence Phillips, who was convicted of assault and trespassing after he physically assaulted his former girlfriend (a Nebraska basketball player) and dragged her down a flight of stairs.

Several of the women I interviewed for this book described encounters with evangelical or fundamentalist Christian coaches or athletes that ranged from uncomfortable to threatening. In some cases all athletes were expected to participate in team prayers or Bible studies. Usually this pressure was informal rather than an explicit team requirement and was exerted by either older teammates or coaches.

> The team captains were Christians, and they led a prayer in the locker room before every game. Some of the team didn't feel completely comfortable with that, but I was only a freshman, and it was easier just to go along. Christianity was woven throughout everything by some of the starters on the team. The coaches were completely out of the picture. We would pray before they came into the locker room. I don't know if they even knew about it.
>
> —*Division 3 basketball player*

Condemnation by and isolation from teammates or coaches is especially painful for women who have only recently identified themselves as lesbian.

> She [a Christian teammate] gave me quotes from the Bible and told me I was a sinner. She told me I was hurting the team. It was pretty horrifying. I had a lot of shame at that point about who I was and to have to deal with this on top of that. I had no way of defending myself. I thought, "She must be right. I do have something to be ashamed of." I told her I didn't want the Bible quotes, and she stopped. It wasn't like she accosted me every day, but I was worried about things she said to other players, and I never felt safe. I had this team that was supposed to be a source of support and camaraderie, but I had to look somewhere else to find support.
>
> —*Former Division 1 basketball player*

> I think it is perfectly normal for Christian athletes to gather together, but I think the strong connection between athletics and Christianity can add to the pressure of coming out or not. Not being accepted by peers is one thing, but when your peers believe you are damned to hell, there is a lot more

pressure. I was approached on more than one occasion to go to FCA meetings and join. The presence was definitely there.

—Division 1 golfer

Sometimes coaches feel uncomfortable with athletes who want the team to pray together before games.

I had a majority of players on my team who wanted to pray as a team before games. I told them they needed to realize that everyone might not feel comfortable with that. They did it anyway in the locker room. What if I had a Jewish player?

—Division 3 basketball coach

Sometimes the pressure to "overcome" homosexuality becomes harassment and discrimination, as described by a lesbian coach who also taught women's studies courses:

I was told I was not an appropriate role model. A colleague told me I needed the healing hand of God. Another told me he couldn't support the textbook I was using for my class because it condoned homosexuality. I had a Stonewall flag and women's posters in my office, and these colleagues told students not to go into my office, especially after I started teaching women's studies. I never knew how to confront it directly. Whenever I did, they would say, "Let's pray together." They started putting things in my mailbox, like daily prayer books, stuff saying affirmative action was bad for women, antifeminist literature. I was told I needed prayer counseling. They could get rid of me as a coach, but not as a teacher because I had tenure, so they made my life miserable. Other lesbians were afraid to speak to me. Guilt by association. Some faculty wrote letters to the president of the college about me and told him they had prayer meetings to help him handle this burden, meaning me. Every day I went into a war zone.

—Former Division 3 basketball coach

I spoke with a heterosexual woman soccer coach who belongs to the FCA. She described a situation in which members of the FCA were partly responsible for the dismissal of a coach rumored to be a lesbian:

The coach was taking a sabbatical, so she brought in a replacement who was with FCA. This was a religious school where you signed a "purity statement" as a coach. The replacement coach heard rumors that the sabbatical coach was a lesbian. She believed them and went over the sabbatical coach's head to report it. The sabbatical coach had to deal with this whole underground thing going on all season while she was gone, and she finally resigned. Before it was over there was this whole group of FCA coaches and athletes involved. Several of us went nuts about this and complained to the state

FCA headquarters and told them this was an FCA issue because it was FCA people spreading the rumors. They said it wasn't an FCA issue. This coach resigned coming off a stellar year. Basically her coaching career is over. The replacement coach still doesn't think she did anything wrong. I challenged the FCA to look at their stand and statements (on homosexuality) and how their silence about this situation had added fuel to the fire when it was FCA members who were spreading rumors and calling for the coach to resign. They didn't have the courage to let the coach know what was going on so she could decide to respond or not.

Another Christian lesbian softball coach joined the AIA chapter on her campus and described an experience with a Christian athlete:

> A number of the athletes who were in FCA or AIA would come and talk with me. I started meeting with one athlete every couple of weeks for breakfast and prayer. She came to me one day, and she was really down. She said, "I heard this in the dorm … are you gay?" I said yes. She said she didn't get how you could be gay and a Christian. We talked about that for several weeks. She didn't believe you could be Christian and gay. I lost touch with her for awhile, then I saw her, and she was so happy. I asked who he was, assuming she must be in love with a guy. She said, "He is a she." Her minister called her mother saying I was a bad influence on her because I was a lesbian and I was converting her.
> —*Former Division 1 softball coach*

This coach also described her interactions with other gay athletes who struggle with reconciling their Christian identity and their gay identity:

> Say you are a softball player and you are a Christian, then you start to think you might be gay. That's a lot to deal with and play ball and get good grades. Many of these kids totally disavow their sexual orientation and focus on being good Christians. They don't date. They are totally nonsexual beings. I've dealt with a number of athletes like that. They buy into the "I am gay, but I don't act on it" thing. They go around and give testimonials about how they used to be gay.
> —*Former Division 1 softball coach*

Organized athletics, as is true of the larger culture, must take on the challenge of sorting out the relationship between the freedom to express religious faith and the need to protect lesbian and gay athletes and coaches from discrimination. Over the last several years the call for lesbian and gay rights and the rise in political influence of the antigay Christian right highlight the conflict between apparently contradictory positions.

My belief is that there is room for all perspectives in sport as long as all participants can respect the rights of others, even those with whom they disagree. This requires that evangelical Christian participants honor the rights of other participants to express their religious faith or lack of it as they choose without formal or informal pressure or sanction. Evangelical Christians must also respect the rights of lesbian and gay athletes and coaches to participate free from discrimination and harassment. By the same token, participants who do not share evangelical Christian beliefs must honor Christians' right to practice their faith.

Coaches and athletes affiliated with public institutions are bound by the broader rights of all participants, regardless of religion or sexual orientation, to compete in a safe and equitable environment. In public educational institutions, athletes, coaches, and administrators must differentiate their personal beliefs from their professional responsibilities to ensure that all athletes and coaches are safe and treated equitably when those beliefs and responsibilities conflict. Fundamentalist Christians in public institutions have a right to practice their faith, but they also have an obligation not to impose their personal beliefs on others.

Before the WBCA homophobia panel, Christian fundamentalist coach Cheryl Littlejohn and I introduced ourselves to each other and spent about 30 minutes engaged in a spirited but respectful discussion about our widely differing perspectives on homosexuality and the appropriate role for coaches when addressing homosexuality in sport. Though neither of us was able to change the other's perspective, I left the discussion a little more educated about Cheryl's perspective, and she knew more about mine. More important, I think we liked each other. I heard her passion and the depth of her faith. I hope I became more than an immoral and willful sinner to her. I hope she saw my humanity and integrity. I sensed that dialogue might be possible and that, given time, we might even be able to come to some agreement about how our differences could be accommodated without either of us feeling compromised.

This hope was sustained at a workshop I led for the NCAA women's educational committee. I met another African-American fundamentalist coach who described her belief, based on religious convictions, that homosexuality is wrong. As I braced myself for a difficult discussion, she said she has several openly lesbian athletes on her softball team. She described these lesbian athletes as "good people whom she respects." She went on to say that she does not agree with the choices these athletes have made about their lives but believes everyone has a right to make their own life choices. She talked about believing that she does not have the right to judge those choices. She does not allow women on her team to treat each other with disrespect, and that includes how the lesbian players are treated. She also expects her lesbian players to treat others respectfully. I felt myself relax as she spoke. Her description is my vision of how we can work together and honor our differences.

These encounters give me hope that similar discussions in individual athletic departments or teams could help us find a way to make room for all. Several research studies support this optimism. These studies indicate that there is a positive relationship between increased interpersonal contact with openly lesbian and gay people and more accepting and affirming attitudes towards lesbian and gay people (Grack and Richman 1996; Herek and Capitanio 1996). Rankin (1995) found this to be the case even for those who believe that homosexuality is immoral based on their religious beliefs.

I hope that the questions raised in this chapter can initiate a discussion in athletics that is long overdue. Though many coaches, administrators, and athletes would like to believe that athletics is somehow separate from the political and social struggles facing other institutions in the United States, it is not so. Until we face up to how these conflicts are played out in athletics and the effects of our silence on the lives of athletes and coaches, we run the risk of alienating many women from the joy that sport participation can bring when we are free to bring all of who we are to the experience with the expectation that we will be treated with respect and dignity. Pervasive stereotypes of lesbians and the belief that lesbians are sinners create climates in athletics that affect how lesbians are treated. Given the prevalence of hostile and conditionally tolerant climates, how do lesbians in college athletics manage their identities? What strategies do they use to protect themselves from discrimination? What is it like for lesbians who choose to reveal their identities to others in athletics? These questions are the focus of the next chapter.

8

The Culture of the Closet:

Identity-Management Strategies of Lesbian College Coaches and Athletes

Sport is a passion for many lesbian athletes. For these women, being denied the opportunity to coach or play is unthinkable. Many lesbian coaches and athletes accept as fact that being publicly out and being in athletics are entirely incompatible. This certainly was my experience as a high school and college coach. Though I did come out to a few lesbian athletes and coaches while a college coach, I would never have considered revealing my identity to anyone else in the athletic department. Being a coach was too important to me, and I did not want to forfeit the opportunity to do work I love.

Given the overt hostility or conditional tolerance characteristic of many athletic departments, this belief is not merely a reflection of individual lesbian athletes' and coaches' internalized homophobia. There are real risks in revealing one's lesbian identity in athletics, and significant social pressures support the hostility and conditional tolerance most lesbians in sport face (see chapter 2).

HOW LESBIAN COLLEGE COACHES MANAGE THEIR IDENTITIES

I had been coaching in a private tennis club for a number of years when I got this job. I knew it was a very liberal area and that some of the coaches were lesbians. I thought it would be great and that there would be some closeness among us. I found that there was no difference between being out now as a lesbian coach in 1996 than there was in 1975, the last time I coached in college. The lesbian coaches clearly give the message that no one is to speak of this. You are not to be out, and you are not to make waves, and you are not to identify each other as lesbians. There are times when an issue comes up and it seems that the lesbian coaches should stick together or talk about it, but all the coaches go quietly into their offices and close the door.

I think that women coaches believe that in order to get ahead, you have to shut up. The lesbian coaches here believe that they have gotten this far because they were quiet about who they are, and they are not willing to take a chance to see if they were wrong. The career path is everything, and the career path means that you shut up. I think lesbian coaches here believe that they have their jobs not because of how well they do, but how careful they are, how they act. Coaches don't socialize or even go out to lunch together. We are isolated from each other. I go in, I do my job. I hang out with my male assistant coach. I go home. I don't talk about my life with anybody.

—*Division 1 tennis coach*

This quote captures much of the pressure many lesbian coaches feel to protect their identities in athletics. Though there are many different kinds of strategies lesbian coaches use, the primary conflict is about the questions, How much of myself do I need to hide and with whom? Whom can I trust? What will be the consequences of people knowing I am a lesbian?

A few years ago, as part of a research project, I developed a continuum of identity-management strategies used by lesbian and gay school teachers (Griffin 1992b). This continuum is useful in describing the ways that lesbian college coaches and professional athletes manage their identities. By identity management I refer to the decision-making processes lesbians go through every day in determining how much of their lesbian identities to reveal or conceal. These processes include self-monitoring as well as monitoring the reactions of others to gauge the safety or risk in each new relationship or situation a lesbian encounters. The continuum describes six different strategies that range from being totally closeted in athletics to being publicly out and includes four strategies used on a case by case basis: (1) passing as heterosexual, (2) covering lesbian identity, (3) implicitly coming out, and (4) explicitly coming out (see table 8.1).

Few lesbian coaches or professional athletes fit into either of the two extreme ends of the continuum, totally closeted or publicly out. However,

TABLE 8.1
Lesbian Coaches' Identity-Management Strategies

Completely closeted	Concealing lesbian identity from all in athletic context
Passing as heterosexual	Intentionally leading selected others in athletic context to see self as heterosexual
Covering lesbian identity	Concealing lesbian identity from selected others in athletic context
Implicitly out	Allowing selected others in athletic context to see self as lesbian without naming self
Explicitly out	Intentionally revealing lesbian identity to selected others in athletic context
Publicly out	Revealing lesbian identity to everyone in athletic context

one woman I interviewed, who is the athletic director at a small conservative college, captures the isolation of being totally closeted at her school:

> After two years I have never been open with anyone, except a lesbian who happened to be leaving the institution. I only know of one other person on campus who is gay. I am out there with absolutely no network. I hide just as much as I ever have, maybe more. I never talk about my home life. I never talk about my partner.
>
> —*Division 3 athletic administrator*

At the other end of the continuum, few college coaches or administrators have chosen to publicly identify themselves as lesbians. Women who have—such as Helen Carroll, the athletic director at Mills College in Oakland, California, and Sue Rankin, the former softball coach at Penn State—are among a small minority of publicly out lesbian coaches or administrators in college athletics. In contrast, many lesbian coaches or administrators are out to at least a few trusted peers in athletics. Les-

Courtesy of Sue Rankin

Sue Rankin, former Penn State softball coach, said she gained a sense of empowerment after coming out of the closet.

bian coaches and administrators use the strategies in between the two extremes of being totally closeted or publicly out on a case by case basis, depending on the specific circumstances. Consequently, many lesbian coaches and administrators are constantly assessing and monitoring how to present themselves depending on who they are with and where they are. Most lesbian coaches and administrators are always vigilant, assessing subtle changes in colleagues' or athletes' behavior: Do they suspect? Can I tell them? I know they know, but can I actually tell them? The energy required to maintain this constant vigilance is enormous. The deception and secrecy required to hide or camouflage one's identity is debilitating. Managing this constant vigilance becomes part of the everyday experience of coaching for most lesbians, and the energy used to maintain this vigilance is diverted from attention to athletes and coaching and can affect a coach's relationships with everyone in athletics. Sometimes lesbian coaches are perceived as aloof or lacking spontaneity because they are diverting so much energy into monitoring the reactions of others and protecting themselves from potential exposure.

Passing as Heterosexual

Coaches or administrators who are passing as heterosexual intentionally and actively encourage the perception that they are heterosexual. As one coach described herself earlier in her coaching career:

> I was very conscious of how I looked, whether I did or did not touch the athletes. I was conscious of the things I chose to wear. I had very long hair. I think pretty much throughout my career I've been very aware of the fact that people don't think I look like a lesbian and therefore see me as safe and sometimes say things that reveal that they think that. In my early coaching years I was very self-conscious about living with another woman. We both dated men throughout that time to throw people off. People want to see you as heterosexual, so you just let them.
>
> —*Division 3 athletic director*

Lesbians who are passing as heterosexual lie about the significant relationships in their lives, changing pronouns when they discuss personal relationships or describe weekend plans. Some lesbians ask male friends to whom they are out to serve as escorts for social events where attendance as a couple is expected and encourage the perception that they are romantically involved with these male escorts. In some cases lesbians who are passing as heterosexual marry men, or if they are divorced, continue to use *Mrs.* or invoke their divorced status as needed to maintain a heterosexual front. Lesbian coaches with children sometimes use their status as mothers and the assumptions of heterosexuality that go with having children to promote the perception that they are straight.

Susan Cayleff's (1995) biography of Babe Didrikson describes how later in her career, Babe intentionally cultivated a heterosexual image to "rehabilitate" earlier perceptions that she was masculine and therefore a lesbian. During the last six years of her life, however, Babe's primary relationship was with golfer Betty Dodd, not her husband George Zaharias. Dodd, not Zaharias, slept on Babe's hospital room floor and cared for her in her fight against the cancer that eventually took her life.

Covering Lesbian Identity

Covering is a middle ground between passing as heterosexual and actually coming out. In this middle ground the intention is to cover one's lesbian identity without actively promoting a heterosexual image. Lesbian coaches and administrators who are covering do not change pronouns or conjure up mythical boyfriends. Their intention is not to actively mislead, but to prevent others from seeing any evidence of their lesbian identity. Instead, they avoid referring to significant personal relationships at all or downplay a woman lover's importance by calling her a "roommate" or describing her as a casual friend.

> I don't talk about my personal life. If they [athletes] ask if I am married, I say no, even though I am in a committed relationship [with a woman]. I don't live near the school. I really separate the two. With colleagues I don't do a lot to protect myself. I talk very vaguely about my personal life, "My roommate did this or that." I won't lie. I don't flaunt it or rub their noses in it. I don't have bumper stickers.
>
> —*High school coach*

Covering lesbians attend social events solo or in groups rather than pretend to be heterosexual.

> One of the things I find particularly difficult is, because I am not out and open, I don't have a partner to take to social functions at work. There is a lot of discomfort with me always showing up as a single woman. It makes women uncomfortable; it makes men uncomfortable. It makes me uncomfortable. When you go into those fund-raising functions as a single lesbian with your honey at home twiddling her thumbs because you are busy that night, it's just not much fun. Not that it would be easier for me to go into this conservative environment and say, "Hi Joe and Jill, I'd like you to meet my partner, Sally." I just can't even envision that except in humor. I've been pipe-dreaming for a few years now; when I hit 50, get ready honey, because that's it. Fifty is the day. I'm not going to hide anymore. When they ask me these questions about family and home, it's going to be, "This is Sally, and

we've shared a home for 15 years, and what else would you like to know?"
By then I'll be ready to get out of athletics anyway.
  —Division 3 athletic director

Covering lesbians present themselves as women who do not have significant family relationships other than parents or siblings. In moments of celebration—winning a championship, for example—covering lesbians do not feel free to publicly share their joy with lovers or acknowledge the role that lovers play in providing support. For many covering lesbians it is inconceivable to imagine being out and remaining in athletics. A choice must be made between the two.

I was told during my interview for a coaching position that the previous coach was gay and that she was no longer there because of that. There was also another candidate who was not hired because they suspected that she was gay. There are a limited number of positions that I am qualified for and want, so I made a decision to live in the closet at that school. It was difficult. I constantly felt like I was living a double life. It was always hanging over my head. Even in a losing season, I felt threatened because I was gay. They could always use that because the fear was already there.
  —Division 3 athletic director and former basketball coach

This fear is not irrational. Especially for lesbians who work in hostile and conditionally tolerant conditions, covering and camouflaging their identity is a safety mechanism that does provide at least an illusion of protection against discrimination and harassment. Covering one's lesbian identity, however, does not eliminate the possibility of being discriminated against. In fact, most lesbian coaches who lose their jobs are trying to pass or cover. Few are trying to call attention to their lesbian identities.

British comedian Tracy Ullman did a skit for her HBO special in the spring of 1996 in which she played the lover of an LPGA golfer, played by Julie Kavner. The golfer's fear of being identified as a lesbian and her lover's growing impatience with pretending to be her nutritionist leads to an argument between the two women. They fantasize about Kavner's first win on the tour and how wonderful it would be for Ullman to be able to run out onto the green and kiss her victorious partner as heterosexual golfers can. When Kavner finally wins her first big tournament, she spies her lover standing in the crowd and with a big wave of her arm invites her onto the green and plants a big kiss right on her lips in front of the national TV audience. Several other lesbian golfers and their partners join them on the green and kiss each other, much to the surprise of the male TV commentators. In this skit Ullman captures the real fear that so many lesbian athletes and coaches feel about even the simplest public expressions of love and affection with their life partners, and then provides a vision of what it could be like if lesbian golfers stopped hiding who they are. Mariah Burton Nelson also describes this fear in her account of the experiences of an anonymous lesbian LPGA golfer (Nelson 1991).

Covering and passing lesbians often do not want to be seen in the company of other lesbians who are out or associated with attempts to address homophobia and heterosexism in sport. At the last several WBCA conferences, Husky Hoops, a lesbian booster club for the University of Washington team, has had a booth and display in the exhibit area where they make available educational materials about homophobia and heterosexism in women's sport. Molly O'Neil and her partner, Margaret King, of Husky Hoops describe how most closeted lesbian basketball coaches give the booth a wide berth rather than risk being seen talking

Courtesy of Margaret King and Molly O'Neil

Margaret King (left) and Molly O'Neil are the founders of Husky Hoops, a lesbian fan club that supports the University of Washington women's basketball team.

with Molly and Margaret or appearing to be interested in the material at the booth.

Both passing and covering require secrecy and hiding. Lesbians who use these strategies carry the burden of deception and inauthenticity in their professional relationships as their personal relationships and lives go unacknowledged. Lesbians who think that they are covering success-fully often are actually assumed to be lesbians by colleagues, athletes, or competitors. In the glass closet a lesbian coach might assume that no one knows, but in fact most people do know, or at least assume, that she is a lesbian. One college athlete assured me that all of the athletes at her school know who the lesbian coaches are, even though these coaches are covering their lesbian identities.

> When you come to this school you get a tour: This is the locker room, this is the weight room, the coach is gay. . . . It's just a fact. It is just known. Every-one knows who the gay coaches are and their partners too.
>
> —*Division 1 basketball player*

Differences between coaches and athletes in their comfort about be-ing out can create tension in the coach-athlete relationship.

> Our assistant coach came from another school where she had been fired or resigned because there was a rumor that she was having a relationship with a woman. A woman would come and visit her [the assistant coach], and we always wondered if it was her girlfriend. We'd ask who she [the visitor] was, and our coach would say she was a friend. Then her "friend" got an intern-ship here, and she came to all of our meets. Since our coach left the other school under those circumstances, she was so right-wing. She was a total bitch. She didn't want to be close to anyone because of what happened at the other school. We did not click at all from the first because I was out and she was not. I think she was afraid of anything being misconstrued about relationships with athletes. She was hard and not close to anyone. When I talked about my girlfriend, I think that pissed her off. So for two years she probably lived in hell because I was so out and she was so in [the closet].
>
> —*Former college track athlete*

Many women in sport cover their lesbian identity, not because they are ashamed about who they are, but because they either fear discrimi-nation or believe that the prejudice against lesbians is so deep that be-ing out would damage their ability to do their jobs effectively. Their choice to cover their identity is pragmatic.

> As an administrator, I am in a position of having to raise some money, and I think from the perspective of interacting with the public it would feed into all the stereotypic negativism that is already out there. I think it would make

it very difficult for the overall athletic program to do the things that need to be done to build the program in a positive way. That is the greatest fear I have today, and I think my being out would get in the way. It's hard enough being a woman. To be out on top of that would just compound it.

—*Division 3 athletic director*

Being Implicitly Out

Being implicitly out falls between passing as heterosexual or covering and actually coming out. When a coach decides to be implicitly out, she stops passing and covering but does not actually name herself as a lesbian. A lesbian who is implicitly out lives her life in a way that allows others to see what they want to see without spelling it out explicitly. She does not name herself as a lesbian but assumes that colleagues know that she is or that they will figure it out if they want to. An administrator described her thoughts:

I think probably everybody on my staff either knows [she is a lesbian] or thinks they know. I've never been open with any of them. And most of them just don't care. Some may. Who knows what they say behind my back? I may be very naive.

—*Division 3 athletic administrator*

She uses the appropriate pronoun to refer to her woman partner. She brings her lover to athletic department social functions, and though she would not introduce her partner as such, she would not pretend that she is "just a friend" either. She might even invite colleagues to her home, something a covering lesbian would probably not do. A lesbian middle school basketball coach describes her experience:

My partner comes to all of my games and sits with the parents. They see us arrive and leave together. I think they are not stupid, and some don't want to see [that we are gay]. We have matching rings, and I don't take my ring off.

—*Middle school basketball coach*

Athletes are enormously curious about their coach's sexual identity if they believe she is a lesbian. The coach's sexual orientation is sometimes a major topic of conversation among athletes.

The coach and the assistant coach were lovers, and everyone knew about it, and they had us over to their house for dinner sometimes. Everyone talked about that, you know, "Do they share the same bed?" One player used to clean house for them, and we'd always be asking, "Were there two beds unmade or just one bed?"

—*Division 1 basketball player*

Being implicitly out enables a lesbian coach some flexibility in choosing future strategies. Because she has not actually identified herself as a lesbian, she could, if she thought she needed to, return to passing or covering. Because she is no longer lying about her identity, however, being implicitly out affords more self-integrity.

Being implicitly out also allows a lesbian coach's heterosexual colleagues to continue to pretend that they do not know that she is a lesbian. In many situations lesbians are tolerated as long as heterosexuals do not have to directly deal with the explicit knowledge that a colleague or an athlete is a lesbian. This unspoken pact of implicit knowledge allows heterosexuals to avoid addressing their discomfort and enables a lesbian coach or athlete to be out without being explicit. Some lesbian coaches talked about how, though they had never explicitly come out, they assumed that the parents of their athletes knew about them. This knowledge did not seem to influence the affection and respect parents had for these coaches. As long as the knowledge was implicit and the coach had a stellar professional reputation, her lesbian identity did not seem to matter to parents. As one implicitly out lesbian coach told me,

> I assume that the majority of the parents of my players know. They see me in a variety of situations; there are no boyfriends, no men. I'm sure they have formed their opinions. I've never had it be an issue with a parent of any athlete who has played for me.
>
> —*Division 1 field hockey coach*

Being Explicitly Out

Coaches who use this strategy directly tell selected others that they are lesbian. For many lesbians this strategy is an important step because there is no retreating to passing, covering, or being implicitly out once the line that separates direct disclosure from the other strategies is crossed. Lesbians who decide to come out explicitly do so with careful consideration of the potential consequences and are deliberate in choosing whom in the athletic context they tell. Typically, coaches choose to tell trusted colleagues or coaches from other schools. They most often choose to tell other coaches who they know are lesbian also, though they might choose to tell trusted heterosexual colleagues as well. Most lesbian coaches do not tell their athletes that they are lesbian, and many maintain a social distance from athletes' lives unless personal issues affect athletic performance.

> My athletes don't talk to me about their personal or social lives. The gay kids might stop by my office more. They need more attention, but it is not attention I seek from them. They do not come by to talk about gay issues. They just come by to say hi. I don't want to know about it [athletes who are

lesbian] unless it is affecting performance. The farther I keep from that, the more fair I can be with everyone. That's my rule of thumb. I've sent kids to mental health who had their relationships going down the tubes and were really struggling, but they don't say whether it is x, y, or z [heterosexual, lesbian, or bisexual], and I don't want to know.

—*Division 1 field hockey coach*

Few college or high school coaches are publicly out. Most lesbian college coaches and professional athletes are passing as heterosexual or covering their lesbian identities with the public and media, though they are more likely to be either implicitly or explicitly out to nonlesbian colleagues, teammates, or competitors.

Coaches who decide either to be explicitly out to selected colleagues and athletes or to come out publicly do not typically get public support from more closeted colleagues. They do not know what kind of support they would get inside athletics if their outspokenness resulted in discrimination or harassment against them.

They [other closeted lesbian coaches] think I am crazy. While they are supportive, they are quietly supportive. If push came to shove and I asked them to speak out on my behalf, which I wouldn't do because it makes for an awkward situation for them, I don't think they would. I get private support, not public. At first it was difficult to know that, but I'm used to it. I got past that. I understand. My support network is out of coaching. It's not in coaching even though all of my friends in coaching are lesbians. They say they are glad I am speaking out, but it's not for them. I think some are upset that I am upsetting the apple cart. I'm not following the tradition of what it is supposed to be like to be a lesbian coach: You leave your private life out of it. I think it makes them look in the mirror, and they don't like that.

—*Division 1 softball coach*

My lesbian friends in coaching say, "Good for you. We could never do that [be out]." They think it is empowering. They encourage me to be public, to say things that they can't say. It feels like support even though I know I'll be alone at least out loud, but not in sentiment.

—*Division 3 athletic administrator*

Many lesbian coaches and professional athletes have made some serious compromises in how they live their lives in order to stay in sport. They have separated their personal and professional lives, opting for silence and duplicity in most of their professional relationships. They have endured antilesbian prejudice and turned their backs on bigotry, afraid to challenge these injustices for fear of revealing their lesbian identity.

The literature on the psychological toll on self-esteem, spontaneity, and openness that the closet exacts from its inhabitants documents the cost that lesbian coaches and athletes pay for their participation in sport (Ellis and Riggle 1996; Krane 1996a). Helen Carroll expresses this perspective well:

> I was closeted most of my coaching career. Now [being out] I feel more peaceful with myself. I don't feel like I'm trying to prove things all the time. I can accomplish more. I have a higher energy level to give to the work I do, instead of spending time making sure people don't know who I am.

Similarly, athletes who have chosen to come out publicly, such as Greg Louganis, Rudy Galindo, Martina Navratilova, and Muffin Spencer-Devlin, describe the sense of relief and integrity that comes with laying down the burden of maintaining cover. Maintaining these protective strategies requires an enormous expenditure of energy. That they have accomplished as much as they have from the closet is amazing. What might these great athletes have accomplished if they did not feel compelled to divert so much energy to protecting themselves from prejudice and discrimination because of whom they love?

HOW LESBIAN COLLEGE ATHLETES MANAGE THEIR IDENTITIES

Meg had a dream she nurtured since she was old enough to hold a basketball. After school in all kinds of weather Meg shot baskets and played against imaginary opponents, as well as playing on every available local team. In elementary school she played on coed recreation department teams and later on all-girls town teams. Meg idolized the girls on the local high school team. She knew their favorite colors and foods. She wore the number of her favorite player. She went to all their games and dreamed of the day she would play for the town high school.

In high school Meg fulfilled her dream. She played point guard for the high school team. She was on the honor roll and had an active social life with a gang of boys and girls in her class. College coaches began writing to her and sending information about their schools. Two schools were seriously interested, and the coaches visited her home and invited her to come to their campuses. Meg eventually signed to play with the state university and eagerly anticipated her college career.

Meg had lunch with her high school coach the week before leaving for college. After the meal he pushed away his plate and said, "Meg, I know your college career is going to be great, and I will follow what's happening very closely. But I need to warn you about something you might run into at

State. In college sports you will probably come in contact with . . . other girls . . . who are . . ." Coach seemed so uncomfortable; Meg waited for him to finish, wondering what he was trying to say. He continued, "I know Joan Stevens, and she is a great coach, and she is married with two kids, but sometimes there are players on college teams who like girls." Meg stiffened. Coach said, "I just want you to know this so you can make sure you choose your friends carefully. You don't want to get in with the wrong crowd." Meg felt embarrassed and uncomfortable. She mumbled something to Coach to the effect that she would be all right and not to worry. Meg had been keeping a secret for some time, not sure what to make of feelings she had for her teammate Peg. In fact she and Peg had grown apart over the last season, and Meg knew it was mostly her doing. Meg was uncomfortable with the feelings she had for Peg.

When Meg got to campus, she quickly learned that some of her teammates were lesbians. She was told who by an older teammate, who warned her about whom to watch out for. Meg thanked her new teammate and made a derogatory remark about "dykes." As the semester progressed, Meg dated several football players, bragged to her teammates about her heterosexual exploits, and bad-mouthed the lesbians on the team whenever the opportunity arose. Meg also had a major crush on one of her teammates, which she told no one about. Her feelings scared her, and the more intensely she felt toward this teammate, the more she expressed antilesbian feelings to her teammates.

Meg's grades started to suffer, and so did her basketball. Finally Meg decided to forgo her scholarship and quit the team. She told friends that the reason was that there were too many dykes on the team and that they were always hitting on the straight players.

This story captures some of the differences in the issues that college athletes face in managing their lesbian identities as compared to the issues of their lesbian coaches or older professional athletes. Because they are younger, away from home, and living independently for the first time, many young women are either identifying themselves as lesbians for the first time or are acting on their attractions for the first time. These identity issues can affect their experiences and how they manage their identities. In addition to coping with all the confusing joys and terrors of falling in love for the first time, young lesbian athletes often must cope with antilesbian hostility or pressure to be closeted from parents, coaches, and teammates.

Athletic contexts that are either hostile or conditionally tolerant present numerous external barriers to young lesbian or bisexual women (see chapters 5 and 6). In addition to external barriers, lesbians also must deal with their own internal feelings and perceptions about their lesbian identities. Living in a society where homosexuality is stigmatized and despised, many lesbians internalize feelings of self-hatred and shame learned from religion, schools, parents, media, and peers (Schwartz 1997).

Lesbian athletes whom I interviewed described a variety of identity-management strategies they use to overcome both internal and external manifestations of homophobia and heterosexism. Lesbian athletes' experiences were also described by therapists and coaches who work with lesbian athletes. I have categorized these management strategies as (1) antigay/denying, (2) special friends/ashamed and self-hating, (3) member of a secret "club," (4) prudent and proud, and (5) out and proud.

Antigay/Denying

Some young women athletes who are sexually attracted to other women are terrified by these feelings and can be quite hostile toward lesbian teammates or coaches as a way to disassociate themselves from their own feelings or to keep others from suspecting that they might be lesbians.

> I can't say I was someone who didn't make homophobic comments. If you didn't stand with the crowd, you were next on the hit list. I heard rumors about someone's scholarship being taken away. I wasn't going to spend time in a hostile environment. Women went to great lengths to talk about their boyfriends, and then I'd see these same women in a gay bar. I would be a hypocrite if I said I wasn't part of that too. When you are 18, the pressure of wanting to be accepted is intense.
> —*Former Division 1 golfer*

> I chose State University because my host [a current member of the team who escorts a high school recruit during a campus visit] told me that they didn't have any dykes on the team. I knew I needed to go somewhere where there weren't any [lesbians]. I was too threatened. I didn't want to be around them. I think she told me there were no dykes because she thought that would be something that would get me to come to State because I was really peppy and foofy—a Dallas debutante back then. . . . I came out the summer after freshman year.
> —*Former Division 1 college basketball player*

This set of coping strategies is characterized by denial of lesbian identity and vocal expression of antigay sentiments. The goal is to push the issue of lesbian identity as far away as possible. Several of the women I interviewed who are now comfortable with their lesbian identity remembered their early experiences of struggling to accept themselves. They recalled consciously dating men with the intention of creating a heterosexual front to camouflage a secret relationship with a woman. Lesbian athletes who struggle with self-acceptance sometimes embark on intentional campaigns of conspicuous heterosexual sex to "prove" to themselves and others that they are not lesbian.

These young women use antigay slurs and put-downs to ward off any suspicions about themselves and to distance themselves from other lesbians. In some cases women quit teams or transfer to another school to avoid playing on teams with lesbian athletes or coaches.

> Looking back, the ones of us who were gay, but couldn't admit it then, were the ones who talked down the openly gay players the most. I think we were afraid we would be lumped with the gay players. So you made sure everyone knew that you were dating, or you were seen with guys just enough. My roommate was my lover, but no one questioned that. You have roommates in college and it's OK.
>
> —*Former Division 1 basketball player*

These women have internalized an image of lesbians as sexual predators and generalized this image to all women they assume are lesbians. These women and their fears can be dangerous when they make accusations about lesbians "hitting on them" or "leering" at them in the locker room based on these projections.

> When I was first coming out, I went through a phase of homophobia. I was really offended by being around lesbians, being in the locker room with them. I remember the first time the team took showers together and there weren't individual stalls. I insisted on going back to my dorm room. It took about two months for me to shower in the locker room. I had it in my head that I was [a lesbian], but I didn't want to acknowledge it.
>
> —*Former softball and basketball player*

> We talked about the ones on the team who we knew were gay behind their backs, made fun of them. You know, "They're probably sleeping together" or "She looks like a man; she probably wears a jock strap." Just different mean things you can say about somebody. We always talked about the ones we thought were dykes. When we had our team get-togethers, they [the lesbian athletes] wouldn't come. I don't think they felt comfortable. I'm sure they knew we talked about them. And on road trips, we were like, "I'm not sharing a room with her." In the showers, either we waited until they were done, or we took private showers. Some girls were really scared.
>
> —*Division 1 basketball player*

Unfortunately, many coaches and parents share a perception that lesbians hit on and leer at heterosexual teammates; these coaches and parents are predisposed to uncritically accept these accusations as truth without checking into them. Often these accusations are the result of the extreme homophobia of young players who are unable to face their own sexual attractions to other women. Blaming other lesbians is a way to protect themselves from acknowledging or taking responsibility for their feelings.

> We had a freshman on the team who transferred during that first year. She was freaking out. She told the coaches that she was transferring because the team was going to make her gay. She said that lesbians on the team were making her go out to gay bars with them. I knew this wasn't happening. The whole team knew this kid was gay. She was asking gay players on the team if she could go out to the bar with them. I had seen her out with her girlfriend. The coaches were nuts because they were afraid this would get us a gay reputation.
> —*Former Division 1 basketball player*

Among self-hating lesbians (and antilesbian straight athletes) any dispute with coaches or teammates who they assume are gay can be blamed on lesbianism. For example, if players have a dispute with coaches over playing time or with another player about passing the ball to her, athletes sometimes resort to antigay name-calling.

> We were really mad at this one gay player because the coach, who was also gay, told us to pass the ball to her more. We were like, "No way, this is favoritism just because she's a dyke. I'm not passing the ball to that dyke." We really made it hard for her [the lesbian teammate].
> —*Former Division 2 basketball player*

> The team was OK with the coach being gay unless we got pissed off at her about something, and then it was, "Oh, she's nothing but a dyke!" Anything she did that we didn't like, we blamed on her being a dyke. Or it was, "It's because she hasn't had sex with a man, that's her problem."
> —*Division 1 basketball player*

Special Friends: Ashamed and Self-Hating

Lesbians who use the "special friends" strategies are in sexual relationships with women but do not identify as gay, much less lesbian. To many lesbian athletes (and some coaches) *lesbian* connotes a feminist or political perspective with which they are uncomfortable. These women associate *lesbian* with gay rights marches, activism, political groups, and an openness they do not choose for themselves. Instead, many young women think of their relationship with another woman as a "special friendship" or talk about being "best friends." They are secretive and do not talk about their relationship with anyone. A therapist who counsels lesbian athletes told me that when she worked with such young women, she often needed to use a different language.

They do not use the words *lesbian* or *gay* to describe their feelings for women. When talking about their relationship, they talk about being "that way" or describe their relationship as being "with" someone. They talk about being in bed with a woman and "it happened," as if they had no control over their actions.

—*University therapist*

One lesbian athlete, recalling her own feelings of shame and ambivalence, referred to women who have lesbian relationships that they do not acknowledge as "straight dykes."

My freshman year we [she and her roommate] were in a gay relationship, but we weren't gay. At least we didn't think of ourselves as gay. I just thought it was a special case, just her, and that if we split up, I'd be with men again. My partner, who was a star on the softball team, was obsessed with keeping it a secret. I'd go to her games and sometimes wanted to sit with the other girlfriends of the players, but I didn't. She would have been mortified. I was supposed to just be her friend, but everyone knew.

—*Former Division 1 basketball player*

I was [in a relationship] with a teammate freshman year. At first we weren't open because she was having a hard time coming out and we didn't know how the other players would react. We found out later that everyone knew. Being in denial, I didn't know how it looked to the other players.

—*Division 3 volleyball player*

Member of a Secret "Club"

Some lesbian athletes, despite their secretiveness, still manage to expand their social network to include other lesbians athletes who are out only to each other. Members of this exclusive "club" do not want anyone outside of this small circle to know about them. Socializing occurs at off-campus apartments and more rarely in local women's bars. Often the basis for membership in this secret club is shame or fear.

Members of the group discourage other group members from being open about their lesbian identity or choosing friends or lovers outside of athletics.

None of the other athletes belong to [the campus gay group]. They don't join. They would come to one meeting and then not come back any more. It's rare for them to come. We try to keep in touch with them, and maybe they'll show up again.

—*Division 2 lacrosse player*

The closed nature of this group, combined with the demands of athletic participation and academics, leaves little time or energy to pursue other interests. Also, since this secret "club" of athletes provides social and emotional support, they may feel less need than other lesbians on campus to join outside lesbian and gay groups. The athletic secret club provides friendship, love, sex, and a social life among other women athletes who share a need for secrecy.

In a hostile environment this community can also provide young lesbians with an important source of support and validation.

> I looked to other lesbians who were athletes. There were several of us who hooked up from spotting each other at different sporting events. I spent a lot of time at sport events. We talked about what we were going through. We were all going through the same things. We were all pretty scared. I believed I should be in the closet and that I shouldn't rock the boat. We all believed that and were pretty ashamed. I drank a lot during my sophomore year. I can remember going out to clubs three or four times a week.
>
> —*Former college basketball player*

Prudent and Proud

Prudent and proud lesbian athletes have developed a sense of self-acceptance. They like who they are and are less concerned with secrecy. They often come out to teammates and coaches. They refuse to tolerate antigay locker room talk or other antigay treatment. Instead, they expect fair treatment from coaches and teammates.

> I came out right away to the whole team my freshman year. They were pretty shocked, but I didn't want anyone to blurt out some comment about gay people.
>
> —*Division 1 basketball player*

Prudent and proud lesbian athletes accept their more-closeted teammates' preference for secrecy, even though they themselves are more comfortable with heterosexual teammates or coaches knowing about them.

> Three other players on the team have come out to me, but not to anyone else on the team. I don't think they would call themselves lesbians. When they go home they act like nothing's going on, but back at school, it's a different story. They're confused, I guess.
>
> —*Division 1 basketball player*

Prudent and proud athletes avoid being identified as lesbians outside the athletic context for the sake of their teams. They believe that they have a responsibility to avoid associating the team with lesbianism by being too out, which they perceive to be synonymous with being too political. This perspective is less the result of a sense of shame about being lesbians than the result of believing that the association of lesbianism with the team might be used against the team or coach.

> I'd like to get involved with campus gay groups, but I won't. I don't want to cause problems for the team. I can't represent the team and the gay rights movement. It's just easier to stay with the gay athletes. It's fun. We support each other and go to each other's games. It's kind of understood that you have to wait until after graduation to do that other stuff.
> —*Division 1 basketball player*

> I have a friend who is a lesbian on the basketball team. They are not encouraged to hang out with the rugby team. If they have a basketball party, they can't just be who they are. It has to do with the gay thing. They are afraid of a bad name.
> —*College rugby player*

> The coach would be nervous if people thought the whole team was gay because I was too out on campus. I don't want to do that to the team.
> —*Division 1 basketball player*

In some cases prudent lesbian athletes with antigay coaches believe that being too out could jeopardize their position on the team.

> I was told by my coach that I was not allowed to make political statements, which meant I was not allowed to be out. I went by the rules. Someone told me they can't force me to be closeted, like if I wore a school basketball jacket and a gay pride T-shirt. I don't know; they [the coaches] might be able to say that's a political issue maybe.
> —*Division 1 basketball player*

Out and Proud

Lesbian athletes who are out and proud have a sense of entitlement to be as out as they want to be. They do not accept attempts by coaches or teammates to discriminate against them or to insist that they hide their lesbian identity. They wear gay-identified symbols such as pink triangles or rainbow flags. They are openly affectionate with lovers on campus; join campus lesbian, gay, and bisexual organizations; participate in campus or community lesbian, gay, and bisexual events; speak out about lesbian, gay, and bisexual oppression. They challenge the necessity for secrecy and coaches or teammates who try to enforce it.

Occasionally, out and proud athletes work with supportive coaches or administrators to arrange for homophobia workshops in the athletic department. Out and proud lesbian athletes often identify more with the larger lesbian, gay, and bisexual community than with only the gay athlete community and have more friends from outside the lesbian athlete community. They often educate other team members who are curious about what it is like to be a lesbian.

> We had this freshman player who was totally out when she joined the team. She knew who she was and was so OK with it. She didn't care who knew. She didn't push it in their face, but she didn't hide it at all. Everyone knew who her girlfriend was, so the team had to address it and become comfortable with her. She wasn't ashamed of it and didn't try to hide it at all. I think they [the team] saw this person who was really comfortable with who she was, and they felt comfortable. She talked about being gay with the team. On road trips in the van, they'd all be asking her questions like, Have you ever been with a man? Why don't you like men? What do your parents say? What do two women do in bed? And the van would get really quiet. She was really up front with them, and it was fine. They were all very fascinated.
>
> *—Division 3 basketball coach*

> Most of the time we'll be traveling to games or eating in a restaurant and in the middle of a conversation someone will ask, "How do you know?" I'm like, "What?" They say, [whispered] "How do you know you like women?" I say, "You don't have to whisper, everyone at the table already knows." They ask questions like, "How do you meet other women? Did you ever like a teammate? If you did, what would you do about it?" One time they asked, "Who's the man?" I say, "There isn't a man; that's the point." Then they say, "Then who acts like the man?" I say, "There is no man; we are two women."
>
> *—Division 1 basketball player*

> I was out to the whole team. I didn't exactly tell everybody, but I told four or five people, so the whole team knew eventually. I was out to my coaches too. I had three good friends on the team, and they totally supported me. One of my straight teammates went with me to a gay party on New Year's Eve. She felt a little uncomfortable, but she had a good time anyway. We also went out together, my teammates and their boyfriends and me and my girlfriend. We had a good time, and being gay was never a problem. I didn't get that many negative reactions from my team. Just sometimes some of them would think I was picking up on them. They think all gay people just do one thing: pick up on straight people. Yeah, right! But that only happened with the people I wasn't close to. I would explain that I wasn't picking up on them, and things were OK.
>
> *—Former Division 1 basketball player*

I meet comparatively few out and proud lesbian athletes. These young women are on the cutting edge of change, charting new territory for athletes to follow and in many cases leading the way for their closeted lesbian coaches as well (Griffin 1997; see also chapter 9).

In 1994 a University of Maryland field hockey player brought a lawsuit against her coach, the athletic director, and the university, charging that she was forbidden by the coach from joining a campus lesbian, gay, and bisexual speaker's bureau. She also charged that she was told by the coach to wear clothes that were less "dykey." The suit was settled out of court by the university, so the facts of the case never became public. The warning to coaches who forbid lesbian players from being out and proud is clear: As lesbian and gay issues are discussed more openly and more lesbian and gay people come out, there will be increasing numbers of young lesbians who come into college athletics with a sense of entitlement to fair treatment and the right to be out and to associate openly with lesbian, gay, and bisexual campus or community organizations.

Unfortunately, many of these young women are out and proud without any tangible institutional support from within athletics. Without institutional policies to protect their right to live openly, they are still dependent on the goodwill and tolerance of coaches who control their access to team membership and playing time.

These courageous young women challenge the old norms, passed from generation to generation of lesbian athletes and coaches, that rely on secrecy and silence in exchange for tolerance. Their determination to live out and proud will eventually help to change the culture of the closet and make sport more welcoming and safe for all women.

> Things are changing slowly. I think more people are educating themselves about being lesbian and gay. It's getting harder and harder to kick lesbians off teams. A lot of people are coming out. Some teams might have four or five lesbians, and the coach can't kick them all off. And the coach wants them to play because they are good athletes and good people, but the coach just doesn't like that one thing about them. But that is a part of what makes them who they are.
>
> —*Division 1 basketball player*

THE CLOSET AS A COMFORTABLE COMPROMISE

It would be a mistake to assume that all closeted lesbian coaches and athletes are either afraid or strive to live more open lives. Some very successful coaches and athletes who either cover their lesbian identities or are implicitly out are comfortable with the compromises they have made. Many would not even agree that they have made compromises. They do not feel a need to be more open about who they are.

Some like it the way it is. They don't want to rock the boat. They coach their teams; they go to coaching conventions; they have their social events associated with that. They separate their social and professional lives.
—*Former Division 1 softball coach*

These coaches and athletes have found a middle ground in which they can be successful in the sport they love and lead satisfying personal lives that they carefully keep hidden and separated from their public lives. One coach referred to herself as a "tweener." To her, this meant being neither totally closeted and isolated nor, to use her words, "out in the streets waving banners." She lives between these two ends of the continuum intentionally and quietly. She relies on her impeccable professional record and her ability to avoid controversy of any kind to protect her. For coaches with this perspective, the issue is not whether administrators, athletes, or even athletes' parents know they are lesbians. They probably do. Instead, the issue is abiding by an unspoken contract not to be too open and not to make demands that force others to deal with homosexuality directly: the essence of the glass closet compromise.

Over and over I heard college coaches or athletes talk about not wanting to "make waves," "upset the apple cart," "rub people's noses in it," or "rock the boat." All these images call forth a sense of a delicate equilibrium that many lesbians are reluctant to disturb. These coaches and athletes have taken out long-term leases on their closets and have settled in with no plans to leave. It is a tough sell to convince them that the potential risks to career, recruiting, playing time, or corporate sponsorship posed by publicly coming out are worth it. From their perspective, drawing attention to lesbians in sport is like standing atop a mountain while extending a nine iron into a thunderstorm: a foolhardy and dangerous action leading to certain disaster.

For lesbians outside of sport this decision is often difficult to understand. Lesbian sport fans looking for more visible and outspoken role models in athletics are often frustrated with coaches and athletes who seem to be comfortably ensconced in their closets. When closeted athletes and coaches react with hostility to openly lesbian fans in the stands or noisy political demonstrations protesting homophobia in sport, it is confusing and infuriating to lesbians who think they are acting on behalf of their closeted sports sisters.

Is it fair to judge lesbian coaches and athletes who have made this compromise to live comfortably in their glass closets? What is their responsibility to young women athletes confronting homophobia and heterosexism in sport? How will sport change if older lesbian coaches and athletes model living in the closet as the only way to be a successful lesbian in sport? When will a successful Division 1 college coach or athlete in a highly visible sport come out? Chapter 9 describes in more detail how some lesbian athletes and coaches are choosing to work, coach, and compete as open lesbians despite the hostility and lack of institutional protection against the discrimination characteristic of many schools.

9

Unplayable Lies:

Lesbians in Sport Choosing Truth

Much of this book focuses on the discrimination and harassment faced by lesbians in sport and the deception and secrecy lesbians use to protect themselves. A fair question at this point might be, "Why would any lesbian choose to reveal her sexual identity when there is so much individual prejudice and institutional discrimination against lesbians in sport?" Despite these obstacles, the climate for lesbians and gays in athletics is changing. Though the closet is still deep for many lesbians, some athletes and coaches are choosing to make their presence in sport known and insist on their right to be open about who they are (Woog 1995, 1998).

Lesbians choosing to name the truth about themselves have decided that secrets and deception have become, to use a golf metaphor, unplayable lies. In golf when a shot lands near an obstruction such as a tree or a fence that presents an unplayable lie, the golfer can drop the ball away from the obstruction and take a penalty stroke. Often, even after the drop, the ball is still in the rough, and there may not be a clear shot to the green. Usually this detour off the fairway means that the golfer will not score a personal best on the hole and must try to compensate for this penalty stroke on a later shot. In similar ways, lesbians in sport are faced with obstacles that penalize their ability to perform their best as athletes and coaches. For lesbians who choose to intentionally and explicitly reveal their identities, hiding and deceiving have become unplayable lies for which the penalty is a loss of authentic relationships and self-integrity. The closet, even the glass closet, has become intolerably confining and uncomfortable.

This chapter highlights some experiences of lesbians in sport who choose to come out. These women provide hope and challenge the assumption that lesbians cannot be out in athletics without being ostracized, harassed, or discriminated against. As pioneers, they are exploring new territory for others who will follow them out of the closet in the future. They are the role models who, by their openness, invite others to confront their stereotypes and to stretch their conceptions of social justice in sport. These lesbian coaches and athletes and their heterosexual allies are training, competing, and socializing in ways that respect the different perspectives and lives of all participants. We need to hear more of these kinds of hopeful stories.

Many heterosexuals (and some lesbians and gay men) ask why coming out to others is important. Heterosexuals sometimes ask, "I don't announce that I am heterosexual. Why do you have to make an issue of being gay?" However, heterosexual women *do* announce their heterosexuality all the time by talking about husbands and boyfriends, dates, wedding plans, and family trips. They wear wedding rings and put pictures of loved ones on their desks. Their husbands and children are often part of the team family who attend team social events or visible fans sought out by the media.

Coming out is also important because lesbian silence and invisibility allow discrimination and stereotyping to continue. When lesbians in sport are closeted, other women and men are not called to confront their own fears and prejudices about lesbians. They are not challenged to examine the contradictions between what they have learned about the lesbian boogeywoman and the reality and diversity of lesbian experience.

Coming out is also important because young women and men of all sexual orientations need self-affirming lesbian role models. I have a friend whose daughter is an outstanding high school volleyball player. She went to a summer volleyball camp where two of the coaches she worked with were lesbians. She came home and told her mother that she really admired and enjoyed working with these two lesbian coaches. She was surprised because her image of a lesbian coach was that she would be gruff, loud, and unfriendly. These coaches had been friendly and soft-spoken. Because this young athlete knew her coaches were lesbians, she had to reconcile the image of lesbians she had learned with the real women with whom she was working. This kind of confrontation between myth and reality cannot occur if lesbians remain closeted.

Young lesbians especially need role models who can contradict the shame and isolation so many young women feel when they first identify themselves as lesbian. Young lesbians and other women struggling with their sexual identity need to see adult lesbians living happy and productive lives in which they can integrate their personal and professional selves in ways that encourage pride and self-acceptance.

Coming out is a self-affirming act for lesbians who choose to do so (Anderson and Randlet 1994; Kavanagh 1995). Regardless of how friends, colleagues, teammates, or families respond to a lesbian's coming-out announcement, many women gain an increased sense of well-being as a result of stepping out of the closet. No one should be denied the sense of freedom and integrity that comes from being open and authentic about who she is.

Every time I have made a conscious decision to be more out and live my life more honestly, miraculous things have happened. Every time I have taken a step, a real gift has been given back. I'd sure love to see that happen for other women. I think it can. You don't hear about the good things that happen. People assume that bad things will happen. No wonder more people don't come out.

—*Helen Carroll, athletic director at Mills College*

WHAT MOTIVATES LESBIAN ATHLETES AND COACHES TO COME OUT?

The lesbians I interviewed who had come out to teammates, coaches, colleagues, or the community had different motivations for taking this step. However, one theme ran through all of their accounts: the simple desire to be truthful about their lesbian identity. Several women I talked with shared this perspective.

> Being out is a lot easier than being in. I feel like I can be a whole person. When I am in the closet, I feel like I am not quite being myself. I am much more myself [out of the closet]. Being in the closet for me was like living half a life. It is freeing to be out. It's just not that tough. I can't imagine going back. I have never regretted my decision to be out.
> —*Beth Emery, Wesleyan University crew coach*

> It feels good, a relief. I am more confident. I've finally accepted who I am.
> —*First-year college basketball player*

> I have to be honest. I can't lie anymore.
> —*Division 3 lacrosse player*

> I am more empowered. I can look in the mirror in the morning and say, you are doing the right thing.
> —*Sue Rankin, former Penn State softball coach*

> No one has the right to ask you not to be who you are. Be true to the person that you are. You have to live out loud. The most important thing is what is inside. Am I a good person?
> —*Division 2 assistant softball coach*

A few women mentioned that part of their motivation for coming out was that staying in the closet required too much work: needing to be on guard, keeping track of lies, searching every word others say for some indication that they suspect something, trying to figure out who can be trusted and whom to be wary of. A related motivation for some women was having survived an incident in which they were harassed or discriminated against for being a lesbian even though they had not revealed their lesbian identity. This critical incident led these women to realize that being closeted offered no protection anyway. Other women recalled incidents in which they believed that being in the closet had diminished their effectiveness and had hurt athletes on their teams. Sue Rankin recalled such an incident before she came out:

I had a lesbian athlete early in my career who was ostracized by the team. No one would room with her. We had a team meeting where she told everyone what it was like for her to be a lesbian. I tried to be supportive without coming out, and I'm sorry about that. I have since called her and apologized.

In another case a lesbian high school girls' basketball coach was falsely accused of sexual harassment by one of the players on her team. Though she was subsequently cleared of this accusation, the event was "horrifying." She described her reactions:

My belief is that I was so closeted that I created a situation where there was room for rumor and confusion about who I was. Because I wasn't talking about being a lesbian, there was fear. I think I helped create a situation where there was room for that, plus her own fears about what was going on in her life. What if I had been out? Maybe I could have been an ally instead of a source of confusion and hurt. This event taught me in very clear terms why it is important to be out and honest.

Other women were motivated by a need to do what they could to help change the hostile climate in athletics and prevent lesbian athletes or coaches from enduring the traumatic experiences they had. Some women wanted to be an adult with whom young lesbians could talk. A former basketball coach who lost her coaching job and has endured several years of antilesbian harassment and isolation as a teacher at her college said,

I knew I would never let another student go through what I had been through. I don't want anyone to go through that just because of who they are; even one kid is too many.

The winds of change can be heard in the comments of some young lesbian athletes. Their sense of entitlement to be out and their expectation that others will just have to deal with their openness is refreshing and provides hope for change. These young athletes see coming out as merely the next step after claiming their lesbian identity.

I came out with a vengeance. I felt like if I was going to be a lesbian, then it was an important part of who I am. It feels bad for people not to know because I feel like I'm hiding a part of myself and they don't know who I am.
—*Division 1 rower*

I am out to anyone who wants to know. It's fine. I don't believe in making a big deal of coming out. Sometimes it's just easier for people to find out in conversation or something. I never told my coach. She just figured it out through conversation, me mentioning a girlfriend. I don't remember exactly; it was not a big thing.

—*Division 1 volleyball player*

I'm pretty much flaming. I don't really care. I say yes if someone asks if I'm a lesbian. I'm out to everyone on the team and the coaches. I've never heard anything negative.

—*Division 3 lacrosse player*

WHO ARE LESBIANS IN SPORT WHO CHOOSE TO BE OUT OF THE CLOSET?

The women I talked with ranged from 18-year-old, first-year college students to women coaches or administrators in their 50s. They competed in or coached a range of sports, some team and some individual. Some were women of color; others were white. They came from large and small schools in many different parts of the United States and Canada. For every generalization one could make about lesbian coaches and athletes who choose to come out, I spoke with a woman who was an exception to the rule. Nonetheless, there are some broad generalizations about personal and contextual factors that affect whether or not lesbians choose to come out.

Generalization 1: It is easier to come out in sports that do not depend on recruiting, give scholarships, or receive a lot of media attention.

Many of the out athletes and coaches I spoke with who have come out are involved in so-called minor sports such as crew, rugby, and track and field. In comparing their experiences with those of lesbian friends on other teams at their schools, several women thought it was easier to be out in sports that receive less money and attention and in which the pressure to recruit high school athletes is less intense.

Crew is different from softball or basketball. I don't know why, but it does seem to be true. In some ways, there are just so many of us out in crew. My sense is that there is an open enough attitude so that no one seems to have a problem with it. I don't worry about recruiting at all. The recruiting for rowing doesn't make or break the team. Eighty to eighty-five percent of the team are freshmen that we teach to row.

—*Division 1 crew coach*

We are not a varsity sport. It is easier because we don't worry about scholarships and funding. I know a lot of women on the basketball team who cannot be as out. They worry about the coaches. The basketball coaches would not be supportive, though they are gay too. Basketball players are told they are representing the school and they can't act too crazy in any way.

—*Division 1 rugby player*

Generalization 2: It is easier to come out in a Division 2 or 3 school than in a Division 1 school.

I spoke with out lesbian athletes or coaches who compete in volleyball, softball, basketball, lacrosse, field hockey, and soccer, but with few exceptions, these women were in Divisions 2 or 3. Many of the Division 1 team-sport coaches and athletes I spoke with were much more closeted than their Division 2 or 3 counterparts. Again, the presence of scholarships, big budgets, recruiting, and media attention increased the pressure for athletes and coaches to hide their sexual orientation.

When I first got to school, I was so happy to be with other lesbians. One of the seniors who was a lesbian told me to calm down. She said I was drawing attention to the team and that the team would get a reputation.

—*Former Division 1 basketball player*

It's very different being in the public eye. At Division 1 schools athletes are told they have a certain image. The more visible the sport, the more control there is over the athletes and anything that might come up in public. Division 1 athletes are more isolated. They are told how to dress, what campus groups they can join or not.

—*Division 3 athletic director*

Generalization 3: It is easier to come out at a school where there are lesbian, gay, and bisexual student or staff groups and the overall campus climate is not politically conservative or does not have a strong fundamentalist Christian presence.

Many of the athletes who came out noted that the support they received from campus lesbian, gay, and bisexual groups was very important to them. In most cases these women did not look to other athletes for support for being out. If they had been on campuses where lesbian, gay, and bisexual groups were not allowed or were discouraged, they would not have received the kind of support they needed to come out.

Generalization 4: Identity factors such as race and class affect the decision to come out.

Almost all of the white athletes and coaches I spoke with did not consider race to be a factor in their decision to come out on campus. This is not surprising, since whites are rarely conscious of the effects of white-skin privilege. Lesbians of color, however, did consider race when they thought about coming out. They sometimes experience homophobia in their racial community and family as well as racism among white lesbians that complicate the decision to come out.

For lesbians of color the triple-threat identities of woman, person of color, and lesbian present issues of identity and community that make becoming visible as a lesbian a complex decision. More is at stake in deciding how to manage their lesbian identities. The families of athletes and coaches of color frequently are their most important source of love and support in a racist society. White lesbians often do not understand what a privilege it is to assume that they will be welcomed into a primarily white lesbian subculture if their families withdraw their support. Athletes and coaches of color may also feel pressures to choose their social justice battles selectively rather than taking on racism and heterosexism at the same time. There is no closet for most lesbian athletes and coaches of color in which to hide from racism, and the dailiness of confronting racism sometimes takes priority over living as an out lesbian.

Athletes on scholarship who are from poor or working-class families also must consider other factors in deciding whether or not to be publicly out. Some athletes are afraid that coaches who are not supportive could jeopardize their scholarship and, with it, their only opportunity to attend college. Coaches can cut lesbian players or make life so miserable that a lesbian athlete quits the team, forfeiting her scholarship in the process. As one African-American lesbian basketball player, who now is in graduate school, said,

> I'm from the projects. Basketball wasn't my whole life. It was a way to get me where I wanted to go. Basketball was my saving grace. I see where my friends from home are now [still in the projects].
> —*Division 1 basketball player*

Calls for lesbians in sport to come out must take into account the complexities and differences between the experiences of white lesbians and lesbians of color. The color of our skin and our access to economic resources can have a huge impact on how we choose to present our lesbian identity to others. As a white, middle-class lesbian, I can rely on my whiteness and my access to economic resources to shield me from some of the consequences of coming out in a racist and classist society. Lesbians of color and poor or working-class white lesbians do not have this cushion. These and other identity differences, such as having a disability or being a member of a religious minority, can drain our inner resources and diminish our ability to cope with homophobia and heterosexism as an out lesbian.

PROFILES OF COURAGE: LESBIANS CHOOSING TRUTH

To provide a more personal and integrated understanding of the experiences of lesbians in athletics who choose to come out, I have included profiles of a few of the women I interviewed. These profiles are by no means intended to be representative of all college lesbian athletes' and coaches' experiences. It would be impossible to capture the rich diversity of experience in a few selected profiles. They are for the purpose of bringing to life, in a few women's own words, their experiences, thoughts, and feelings. I believe these profiles are important for at least two reasons. First, so few lesbian athletes and coaches are out of the closet that it has become accepted common wisdom among many lesbians in sport that you cannot come out and survive professionally. Second, given the pervasive stereotype of lesbians in sport as immoral sexual predators in combination with so few out lesbians to contradict this image, it is important to hear the real stories of lesbian athletes and coaches. These women are no more exceptional than any of the other lesbians in sport I know or met through the interview process. I picked their stories to provide some diversity in experience and to highlight some of the issues many of the lesbians I spoke with must deal with on a day-to-day basis. Each of these women is out to her team, her athletic department, or the entire campus and community. These women made different decisions about how they wanted to be identified in these profiles. One asked that her first name be used, one chose to use her initials, three decided to include their first and last names, and two chose to use pseudonyms. I honored each woman's decision about how she chose to be identified. Coming out to your basketball team is different from coming out in a book to an unknown audience of thousands, and I respect each woman's need to decide when and where to reveal her lesbian identity.

 Lisa is white. She is a basketball coach at a Division 2 college. Previously she had coached in other Division 2 and 3 schools. She has been coaching for six years. In college she played basketball, field hockey, and softball in a Division 3 school.

I am cochair of the queer issues committee on campus. I am pretty out. I came into the job deciding to be out because I had problems at another school. At my previous school, a small Division 3 school, I was hired as women's athletic director and head basketball and softball coach. The second day on campus the chair of the physical education department, a closeted lesbian, said, "If you are a lesbian, you want to be careful, cover your tracks, don't say anything wrong." I wasn't going to start dating students. I wasn't going to go be an activist on campus, but I was not going back in the closet. I said thanks, but I have to live my life. Things were going fairly well, then I started meeting the parents of my players. They didn't like me, that was clear. I didn't know why. Right after Christmas I got a letter that was sent to the president of the college, the provost, the athletic director, the chair of the PE department, and me. It was a three-page letter from 14 of 15 parents of my team. It started out comparing me with the previous coach. They liked her. They didn't think I was an acceptable replacement. They said I lacked "professional image" and that was reflecting on the college. They said I was a deterrent to recruiting, and students on campus didn't want to play for me. The physical education chair told me it was because I was a lesbian. They had talked with her. The provost indicated the same.

I have a rainbow sticker on my truck. I am relatively dykey-looking, which stood out on campus. I am not real feminine, not a fluff chick. People knew who I hung out with on campus, mostly the lesbian professors. They saw us together and made assumptions. I wasn't talking about my personal life.

I talked to the commission on women who told me, "You don't have any legal protection anyway." They said in the past that they had tried to force the college to adopt a nondiscrimination policy. The faculty passed it, but the Board of Regents and president shot it down. I tried to set up an appointment with the president, who the parents had already talked to. The president refused to meet with me. I was left with no power on campus.

The other coaches were pretty supportive. The baseball coach felt bad, but he didn't think he could do anything. The swim coach [male] was a nice guy, but . . . The football coach, who was also the men's athletic director [AD], went to the president and had me stripped of the women's AD position. He wanted to be head of both. He said he didn't think I was appropriate as AD. The president agreed. The volleyball coach, who was a closeted lesbian, would see me in social settings but wouldn't be seen on campus with me. The straight woman track coach was supportive but wanted to know what they were saying about her.

The basketball team was awful. The athletes were negative. After one game, one of the fathers came up and bumped me, got right in my face, and said, "You are the worst coach I have seen. You are an awful person. I am going to have your job." After one game, parents' night, there was a gathering after the game, but none of the parents would speak to me. The team went out for dinner, and I was not invited. The team felt they didn't need to listen to me because they thought I was just a big dyke anyway. I was on my own with no support at school. No friends in the area. I thought, "If this doesn't kill me, it will definitely make me stronger." I contacted a lawyer, but he said I didn't have any recourse because the college could terminate me at any time for any reason. There was no nondiscrimination policy. No state law either.

I was petrified that I would wake up in the morning and have my tires slashed or other vandalism on my house. I would vacillate from anger to fear so quickly. I'd come home every night and cry. I know that they were keeping an eye on me. The players would drive past my house.

I had an assistant in mind for softball. She had great qualifications and experience both playing and coaching. The chair of the department thought she was qualified. The day before she was supposed to come in for an interview, the president denied her hiring. The parents protested against her, saying they did not want a friend of mine coaching. They implied that there was a sexual relationship between us, but there was not. The president finally allowed her to be hired, but they put her through hoops. She had a whole day of interviews with everyone. It was as rigorous as my interview for only a temporary, $1,500 position. None of the other assistant coaches had to go through any interview process.

I resigned in the beginning of April. The week before, I got a call from the women's basketball coach at a nearby college. She heard that I had been fired already, before I turned in my letter of resignation. She heard from her sports information director, who heard it from an AD at another college. I went to the chair about these rumors and asked, "What is going on?" She said, "Your contract will not be renewed." The provost confirmed this. I got a letter from a parent saying that he was glad I was fired. He told me I did a lot of harm. He was the one who bumped me at the basketball game.

I made a point of being out as soon as I got here [at her present school]. At the first faculty-staff gathering, I said, "My partner, Tammy . . ." I made a point of helping when we had a portion of the AIDS quilt here. It's not like I force it on people or talk about it all the time. It seems like people accept it as a part of my life, which is what I would hope they would do. This school has a nondiscrimination policy and domestic partner benefits as part of the state system.

My basketball players are great. The softball players are wonderful. They know I am a lesbian. Parents have been civil and supportive. The previous basketball coaches were lesbians too. Last year we had a JV [junior varsity] game, and one of the rookies said, "Coach, do you have a boyfriend?" All the veterans turned and stared at her. She is just one of those kids who doesn't have a clue. I'm sure the rest of them filled her in later. One of the former volleyball players came in and was talking about her girlfriend, so they know they can talk about these issues if they want to. Quite a few athletes have met my girlfriend. I helped with resident assistant training on homophobia, and some of my players are RAs. I am also one of the contacts on campus for people coming out. My athletes know this.

I haven't experienced negative recruiting here, but it was happening at the other school. A friendly coach told me it was happening. One of the parents of the kids I was recruiting said so too. His daughter ended up coming to my school. He said, "It isn't an issue with us; we don't agree with negative recruiting," and he thought the other coach was a fool for doing it.

As much as I want to say it isn't an issue, I think you have to first evaluate your environment before you come out. Are there other out people? Are there blatantly homophobic people? Are you going to have support? What I did is change my environment. I found a place where I can be out. I know they will listen if I have problems. It has to be up to the individual. If you are questioning yourself about being out, you can't change your mind. It is definitely something you need to be sure of. You don't see a lot of Division 1 coaches who are out. There just aren't a lot of role models out there.

My experience at my former school was horrible, terrifying. It was hurtful to me as a person. I've always considered myself to be a good person and to have people attack me for who I was, was frightening, and not to have any recourse, it was pretty terrifying.

When I was going through this, I could find no way to make contact with other coaches who have been through similar situations. I knew there are people who have had similar experiences. It would have really helped to talk to some-one. It is still happening, people going through this situation exactly.

It was hard for me to be out, but I knew I had to do it. As bad as that experience was, it has made me a stronger person. I am much more sure of myself. I would have thought that it might have rattled my self-esteem, but it didn't. It didn't pull me down. It is emotional for me to discuss it. If I forget it, I am forgetting a part of who I am. ▼

Jane is a white, 20-year-old, Canadian college basketball player. Jane is a pseudonym.

My experience has been very positive. I started coming out last year in Febru-ary. I told my sister over the phone, but I don't think it was the best way. She was shocked and cried about it, but she said she loved me no matter what. She's been very good about it. I didn't tell anyone else the rest of the summer. At the end of September, I was reading the school newspaper and saw they were starting a lesbian/gay/bisexual student group. I thought about joining it. I met with the counselor starting the lesbian/gay/bisexual group a few times before going to the group. The people in the support group are awesome.

I went to my ex-coach, who is now the AD, and I came out to her. She was 100 percent supportive. She has friends who are gay, and former players of hers are lesbians. I knew I could go to her because she is like a mother. I trust her, and I knew it would remain confidential.

At that point I thought I should go to my head coach. Some of my practices haven't been that great. This had been on my mind. I came out to her, and she was very supportive. We sat and talked in her office for two hours. She said that I should have come to her earlier. I don't think I would have gone through with it [coming out] if my coach and the AD had reacted differently.

Up to this point, my parents didn't know. My coach and I agreed I should tell my parents before I tell the team. I mailed letters to my parents. They got them Friday. We were away at a tournament. I wanted to give them time to process the whole thing. Mom had called five times and Dad zero times by the time we got back on Sunday. They took it hard. I expected more from them. I didn't think they were that naive and set against it. I sat and cried for two hours while my mom told me not to tell anyone else on the team. She told me, "All it takes is one person to have a problem with it, and the coach will kick you off the team."

Her biggest concern is my safety. Basically she wants me to keep my mouth shut, finish my degree, and become credible, then I can tell people. The biggest factor with my parents is giving them time to accept it. I sent some information home about being gay. We haven't really talked about it since then. My mother has more questions, and she has been to the library to get books. She said she might go to PFLAG [Parents, Families and Friends of Lesbians and Gays].

I didn't cry with my dad. I had to lead the conversation. He's a right-wing conservative. He doesn't believe in same-sex benefits. He said, "I don't agree with the lifestyle, but you will always be my daughter." I knew that would be my dad's reaction.

I came out to one teammate a week before I told my parents. We get along well, and she is very open-minded. She was surprised, but she said it wasn't going to change anything. I came out to her so that someone on the team would know. When we went on road trips I felt more comfortable staying with her.

I spent some time trying to decide if I wanted to tell the rest of the team and how to go about it. I didn't know how to tell them. A lot of them are from small towns and have never encountered this. Coach seemed to think it will be a good learning experience for them. She wanted to bring the counselor from the support group in to answer questions. I wasn't sure if the team really needed to know, but it is a big part of my life. I got tired of them saying things like, "Oh, we've got to get Jane a guy."

We had a lesbian/gay/bisexual group meeting one day, and when the school paper announced the meeting, the team said things like, "Oh my God, we should go to see who is there." There was a lesbian on the team before, and she was quite open about it. They still talk about her. I didn't want to be the topic of their little gossip sessions, and I didn't want to be treated differently because I'm gay.

I thought the team would be shocked initially, but I didn't think I would be ostracized in any way. I tried to think about sitting in a room with all 12 of them. How do I bring it up? That scared me. I had never come out to a big group before. I had only come out to one person at a time, and I had chosen the people wisely. My biggest fear was I didn't want the whole campus to find out. I didn't know if I could trust them [teammates] with this.

The decision to come out to the team was somewhat spontaneous. I told them one day before practice. Prior to that I had talked with my coach a lot about it, and she said anytime I was ready would be fine with her. Two of my teammates knew now, and we talked about what would be the best way to tell the rest of the team. My coach suggested that the four of us should meet and discuss the options. At this point I was still not sure I wanted the team to know or if they needed to know. It is a big part of my life, but at the same time it isn't. I didn't want to make it into something bigger than it actually is. How do you bring something like this up in conversation and how do you end it?

I don't know what really prompted me to tell them. I thought to myself, "This is nothing to be ashamed of and at some point in my life, I've got to start being me." The four of us never did meet, and we really did not come up with any "plan." One day before practice my coach was taping me, and I told her that this was the day. She really wasn't surprised. She just asked me what I wanted her to do. We agreed that after our prepractice chat, she would ask if anyone had anything to say. I told my two teammates about my plans, and they thought it was a good time. So, with the two of them at my side, I came out to the team.

There was that initial moment when nobody said anything. I wish I had a camera. My coach stepped in and said if anyone had any questions, they could come to me or her. She also asked them to keep it within the team because I did not want the rest of the campus to know. After that, practice began, and that was really awkward. Later that day I tried to talk with everyone individually to see how they were doing with things. All of them were shocked but said it would change nothing. One teammate asked me, How do you know you are gay and when did I know? Another told me she has a relative who is gay and it wasn't a big deal to her. Another teammate gave me a big hug and said she was proud of me for having the courage to come out to the team.

I wasn't sure if coming out to the team would be a positive thing, but I was wrong. I now have a support network of 14 amazing people who are there, willingly, if I need to talk. Since I've told them, my relationship with them has not changed. I don't feel left out in any way because I am gay. Initially they asked me about it, but now they seem to have dealt with it, and the shock has worn off. It is a relief for me to talk about it. I'm more confident, and I have finally accepted who I am. ▼

Beth Emery is 39 and crew coach at Wesleyan University in Connecticut. She is white. She was a scholarship rower at Northeastern University in Boston.

About four years ago student members of the campus queer alliance invited Dave Pallone, a gay professional baseball umpire, to come and speak on campus. The athletic department was asked to cosponsor Pallone since he was involved in athletics and intended to speak about homophobia in sports. The athletic director and members of the athletic department did not want to sponsor the event. I don't remember all of the rationale for not wanting to sponsor him, but I do remember that, from my perspective, the athletic department was in denial about their own homophobia. One stated reason for not wanting to sponsor this talk was that they did not want be associated with a topic that might make anyone feel uncomfortable or offend anyone.

I came out officially to the athletic department in response to the discussions about the Dave Pallone talk. If I was going to talk about why I thought the department should sponsor this speaker, I thought the impact would be greater if I was direct about being gay. First, I told the athletic director that I was a lesbian and talked about my concerns and the implied homophobic message in choosing not to sponsor this speaker. Next, I told the whole department at the next meeting. I was nervous and a bit scared about what I was going to say publicly. There was only one other lesbian professor on campus who was out at the time. I had never completely hidden my sexuality, but I had also never been outspoken about being a lesbian. I remember being concerned about how to come out and how it would be received. I prepared with notes and an outline. I talked for what seemed like 15 minutes, but it was only about 7. It is very liberating to not worry anymore about who might know or not know. I am free to talk about my life with anyone and include my partner with a name rather than talking about a vague "we."

The aftereffects of my coming out were interesting. I heard from one woman who is in the closet that she thought it was great that I came out and she respected me for it. A couple of other department members nodded their heads and said it took guts to speak out. One guy said he disagreed with me but respected my ability to stand up for what I thought.

Over time the athletic department and the university community have treated my partner and me like a couple. A few people are uncomfortable, but no one has shown any hostility. We attend athletic department social events together, once or twice a year. It really is OK for the most part. I think my partner and I are enjoyable and interesting people to be with socially. We are nice to folks, gay and straight. We have no chips on our shoulders or anger at the way life has treated us. The more we are out, the more comfortable we are in going to "straight" events as a couple. The truth is, though, that I just don't share that much with many members of the department. Most of my social life is with gay and straight friends outside of the athletic department.

I never say anything to the team at the beginning of the season about being a lesbian, but my partner is often around, and I bring her up in conversations. I guess I do not say it because most married women do not announce that they are married at the beginning of the season either. All of my athletes know my partner, Julie. There is nothing I have done to keep my lesbianism a secret. The team is great with Julie, and she is great to them. She is one of our biggest fans. Win or lose, she is there to support the team. She is also a mentor to some of them and invites athletes to visit and watch her work in her medical practice. Julie and I had a commitment ceremony, and three athletes who I believe are straight attended. When they found out about our plans for a commitment ceremony, they insisted on coming, so we sent them an invitation. Former rowers always ask how Julie is and ask that I remember them to her. Many parents have also come to know her through their daughters' stories or at races, and they ask about her if she misses a race or when they call or write to me. Whenever I am interviewing an assistant coach, I do come out to them directly. I don't want to be working closely with someone in a shared office and have them find out later that I am in a lesbian relationship. I don't want anything weird to happen like they leave the job, undermine me, or just be uncomfortable sharing an office with me. Only once have I felt like someone may have quit my team because they realized I am a lesbian.

I've had lesbian rowers. Some choose to be out to me, and some choose not to be. There are also some openly gay men on the men's crew team. Most of the men's and women's teams are very gay-friendly. I hope that my being out has helped the athletes at the boathouse to feel safe about being out. A woman who graduated last year was out early in college or maybe in high school. At first her parents had some difficulty accepting this. Before she graduated, Julie and I got to know her parents, and they liked us. I think by being a role model for this athlete and her parents, I made it easier for her parents to deal with her sexuality.

I have also noticed that being out helps athletes come to terms with having gay or lesbian parents. I have had a few athletes with gay fathers and lesbian mothers, and it is clear to me that athletes find it very important to introduce me to their parents. A few years back I recall an athlete introducing me to her divorced father. He came to races by himself at first. Then he started to bring his male partner. Slowly this athlete started to introduce her father and then his partner to her teammates. At first she was uncomfortable, but I think it helped that she had a queer coach. By her senior year everyone knew her father and his partner and loved all of the wonderful photos they had taken of the team. Because I was out, I had nothing to fear in befriending her father and his friend and making sure they were both introduced to the team. I think the relationship between this athlete and her father changed over the time I knew her in some ways because I am gay, out, proud, and accepting of myself.

When Julie and I first got together we had separate households. We kept my apartment for about eight months so we could pretend that we did not live together. I was really nervous about my athletes' response and afraid that it would affect how they interacted with me as a coach. I had one of our annual get-togethers in the apartment I continued to rent for these special occasions. It was so ridiculous and silly. I felt like I was living a lie and that lying affected how I interacted with the team more than being an out lesbian. Now Julie and I invite the team to our home two or three times a year. They are interested to see how we live and tour the one bedroom home just "checking it out." Some athletes will ask how we met; some never ask any personal questions. Team members have also house-sat for us in the summer or during winter breaks when we are out of town. It is a lot easier to be out than being in. I feel like I can be a whole person. When I am in the closet, I feel like I'm not quite being myself. I love being able to be the person I want to be. Being so private, being in the closet, you are just not whole unless you are with other lesbian friends, and that is like living half a life. Every person who is out in a big way makes it easier for others. It is freeing to be out. I can't imagine going back.

Angee Phong is a Division 2 lacrosse player. She is Chinese-American and 20 years old.

If I walked into a bookstore wearing jeans and a white T-shirt, people would see me as just another customer. I do not look stereotypically gay—for example, the short hair, baseball caps all the time, and the masculine stride. I am just the opposite actually. I have shoulder-length hair, usually wear my hair down or in a ponytail, and my stride is far from masculine. It isn't that I consciously carry myself this way to avoid looking like or being called a lesbian, it is just me being myself.

My friends tell me I am flaming because of the things I wear. I have a variety of [gay-themed] T-shirts that I wear around campus and to lacrosse practice. I feel secure enough with myself that I can be more visible around campus so that other gay students will know they are not alone. I don't hear a lot of negative remarks around campus because our campus doesn't condemn us, but they don't support us either.

Everyone on the team and the coaching staff knows I am gay. My freshman year I had a long discussion with my head coach about the whole gay issue. She wanted to know if I saw any problems on the team with me being so out. She said she admired me for being so out. She asked me if I felt like I pushed it on people since I wear my gay T-shirts all the time. I don't feel as if I push it on people because what I wear is part of who I am. It's a form of self-expression. I have fun wearing my gay T-shirts. They all have different kinds of sayings like, "Gay Games," "Dykes Rule," and "Strong Enough for a Man, But Made for a Woman." I wear my rainbow socks for all my games as good luck. So far, so good this season. My most recent purchase was a rainbow crocheted bikini, which was icing on the cake for spring break.

I am vice president of the campus lesbian/gay/bisexual organization, and I also serve on the lesbian/gay/bisexual task force. I am the only athlete in both organizations. There are others on the team who are gay, but only one of them is out. The players who are gay or bisexual on my team are very close. There are so many cliques on our team—the blond heteros, the rich and snobby, and the gay players—the whole team is broken up. Once we walk out on the field we are one, off the field we are separate. Some of my teammates walk past me on campus and look right through me. They make comments about other teams, like how a player's hair is cut, how she looks, whether she is aggressive or not. They usually call the aggressive players dykes. When I hear them make comments I don't like, I let them know by telling them I don't appreciate it. Sometimes they talk about gay characters on TV or in the movies, and it is so disgusting. I think it is harder for the people from small towns to deal with it, because for a lot of the girls on the team, I am their first gay friend or teammate.

My girlfriend and I are very committed. We even bought rings for our one-year anniversary. I've had teammates who were together, and a lot of people knew but didn't really care. I never get involved with teammates [sexually].

It's more obvious that I am Chinese than gay. My opponents [on the lacrosse field] call me "chink" sometimes. I don't have many Chinese friends; there are like five Asians here, and four are related. There isn't a big Asian community around here. I guess the closest is Philadelphia. There are African-American and Hispanic groups on campus, and they are trying to start an Asian group. I never notice racism from my gay friends.

I came out to my sister a year ago. My oldest brother used to be very homophobic, especially to men, but he has become more open and understanding. He has come a long way. We've gone out together with my girlfriend and his friends, and that was a big step for all of us. I'm really proud of him. I used to be very close to my other brother because he is only two years older than me. We talked about two years ago, and I tried so hard to come out to him, but it seemed like he was trying to push me back in the closet. I haven't come out to him, but my sister told me that he knows and that he is probably having a hard time dealing with it because we are so close.

I believe it's important to be secure with who you are and never forget where you come from. Be honest with yourself and learn from all your struggles. It is hard for a lot of my friends to be out at school, but not at home. That's how it is for one of my friends. Her mother said, "If I find out you are gay, you are out of the house."

I am lucky because my parents accept me and my girlfriend for who we are. I've had a lot of support from my friends and past teachers. My middle school gym teacher was very supportive. I admire her, and she is one of my role models. I also keep in touch with my basketball coach from high school. She has also been someone special to me. I am grateful for her support and knowledge. She was very supportive and wanted to know how she could be more supportive to other lesbian/gay/bisexual students. She has been there for me through all of my ups and downs. My best friend, Susan, has been great. She was so accepting when I came out and has been there for me ever since.

I'm very open to the future. I hope to be with my girlfriend for a very long time, and we plan for our future together. I believe in the sexual continuum. Some people are heterosexual now, and maybe they will be for the rest of their lives, but there is also the chance that they will move along the continuum and have an experience with someone of the same sex. You just never know what will happen in the future because it is just that, the future. I believe that people should fall in love with a wonderful person who makes them laugh and is special. It just happens that the person I fell in love with is a womyn [Angee's preferred spelling]. I'm proud to be out, and I hope others will come out also. ▼

K.L. is a 24-year-old, African-American woman. She played basketball at a Division 1 school. She is now a graduate student in psychology.

I knew I was a lesbian in high school, but I was not out. High school was difficult. When I started to realize who I was, I tried to be straight, hiding from the team, joining in homosexual jokes.

In college I didn't know what to expect. I came out in the locker room to the team. A teammate thought I was flirting with her boyfriend. There was a big argument. That's when I came out. There were lots of lesbians on the team my freshman year. My senior year half the team was gay.

The team was open about it. We talked about our lovers in the locker room. Some of the straight players went out to women's bars with us. Lesbians on other teams were not out. They made up boyfriends and were afraid of everything. My coach was lesbian too, but she did not come out to me until after graduation. Our academic advisor was, too. We used to have conversations about being gay.

My freshman year I was dating a senior. My coach asked me to be more discreet about the relationship. She heard the rumors that I was staying in my lover's room a lot, in an athlete dorm. I said, "You know, Coach, this is me. I am not a great liar." I was trying to tell her I was not going to pretend I was someone else to make it easier for everyone. From then on we had a better relationship. I think she had respect for me.

At a Division 1 school there is pressure, and people are in your business. People are talking behind your back. A woman on the track team started rumors about me, saying I had been caught in bed with a woman or was downtown holding hands with a woman. I confronted her. I told her, "What is your problem? If you want to know something about my life, ask me."

In the beginning I was seen as rough, dykey. I fit that stereotype. It was harder for me because of that. Another more femmy dyke could fit in. It got easier though. I knew who I was and got more comfortable. When I first got to college, I was so happy to be with other gay women. I wore it on my sleeve. I was a lesbian chauvinist, in your face. A senior told me to calm down. She was not out. She said I was drawing attention to the team and the team would get a reputation. I thought she was kind of out, but she was not out on campus.

I was out on campus, but there weren't any campus groups. This was a Catholic school. No lesbian/gay/bisexual groups were allowed. We had a mixed black and white lesbian community. I don't remember any racism among the lesbians. There was a lot of interracial dating among lesbians. With my team, only two African Americans were dating other African Americans. My lover now is black, my first. I've always had white lovers. We had parties, but we didn't call them lesbian parties. Others just knew when the basketball team gave a party, it was lesbians.

It's hard to separate racism from homophobia. I remember one incident with a white player a year behind me in school. By my junior year we didn't get along. I didn't know whether it was racism or homophobia. We were roommates on a European tour. We got into a fight. I was getting this hostility from her, but she was unable to own up to it. She was very defensive.

It's especially important for African Americans to know there are some of us (black lesbians and gay men) out there. At my graduate school [black university] lesbianism is taboo. The black community here just doesn't embrace lesbians. The environment on campus is hostile to lesbians. If I went here as an undergrad, I wouldn't be out. My undergrad experience was an exception. I didn't know how lucky I was. I understand why some people are in the closet. All the gay bashing, even not physical or directed at you, just knowing about it.

Sometimes I feel I must make a choice. It's like I can't be both lesbian and black. It's like I have three strikes against me: black, woman, lesbian. All three parts of me are intermingled. A lot of people want me to be just one part me. I'm a whole, not my parts. I think being a black lesbian gives me more depth. You have to understand who you are as a whole. You can't be black on one day, a lesbian on another, and an athlete on another.

A few grad students were having coffee and talking about the oppression of women. They were saying that racism and sexism are separate issues. I told them they can't talk about it as separate issues. If I'm being discriminated against, I don't know why. Is it because I'm black, a woman, a lesbian, or all three?

I'm from a huge family. I'm out to them. My family let me be who I wanted to be. They accepted me even before I knew I was a lesbian. They are extremely supportive. I think you have to be true to yourself. You don't have to slice yourself into sections. ▼

 Chase is a former Division 1 basketball player. She is white. Chase is a pseudonym.

I always knew on some level that I was a lesbian. I was about 14 or 15 when I first heard the word *lesbian* used. In high school I had friends in a lesbian relationship. That was the first time I let myself think that I might be a lesbian. When I got to college and was on campus about a week, I met lesbians and said, yes, these are my people.

My first year on the basketball team was difficult. I spent that year dealing with suicidal thoughts, drinking, and going to bars. I was not out to my family. My best friend on the team was a lesbian, and I was hanging out with her. Everyone assumed because of who I was associating with that I was a lesbian. I told one other person, and she outed me to the rest of the team. It was pretty uncomfortable. I wasn't ready. The coaching staff were gay but were not a resource. They were very closeted. They did not talk about it at all. The head coach and the assistant coach were together. They never talked about their relationship. They invited the team to their home but had two bedrooms set up with two beds. They created an atmosphere that said, "Do not talk about this. It is too scary to talk about." If anything, they encouraged me to be closeted, not talk, or get help.

At the beginning of my sophomore year I was playing about 20 to 25 minutes a game. Once we went on a road trip and got killed by the other team. In the airport I was talking with a lesbian teammate. She had a bad game, and I hugged her to comfort her. A minute after I did that, the assistant coach ran over and told me to sit down and shut up. In the next couple of weeks the assistant coach came and told me the head coach was all upset and my behavior [at the airport] was unacceptable. She wanted an apology to the head coach. I refused. I didn't play at all for the next two weeks of games. The assistant coach kept at me. Finally, I apologized because I wanted to play. I went to the coach and said I didn't think it [hugging a teammate] was inappropriate, but I apologized.

In my freshman and sophomore years, some of the team were supportive in that they didn't say anything negative about lesbians or me personally. They weren't too keen on hearing anything about my life though. Some people bordered on hostile. One teammate said it would hurt the team with me being so out and I should think about the team. I thought I had something to be ashamed of. I had this team who were supposed to be a source of support, but I had to look outside the team to find support. My team was supposed to be my family, so I felt like I was losing my family again and again.

I looked to lesbians who had been in sports, former athletes or current athletes on other teams. There were several from different sports that hooked up from spotting each other at sports events. I spent a lot of time at games. That's where I met lots of other lesbian athletes. Our lesbian athlete community started out fairly closed. We talked about what we were going through. We were all going through the same things. We were all pretty scared. I believed I should be in the closet and that I shouldn't rock the boat. They also believed that and were ashamed about who we were. It wasn't very helpful.

Until I came out to my parents at the end of my sophomore year, I went through a horrible time. I had a secret affair with my best friend's girlfriend. There was all kinds of lesbian drama, lying to everyone in my life. This is not something I thought I would do. I was punching holes in walls and feeling suicidal. I drank a lot through sophomore year. When I drank, it was to excess. I can remember going out three or four nights a week to clubs.

My coaches were worried about me. The head coach asked me if I was OK after I came to practice with a cut on my hand from hitting a wall. I said I was OK and she went away. It was showing on the basketball floor too. The trainer called my parents and asked what was going on in my relationship. My parents knew nothing, so I thought the trainer and coaches were trying to out me. My parents asked me if I was a lesbian. They were immediately supportive of me. I felt like I had my family back. Coming out to my parents was definitely a turning point for me. Finally I went into therapy, and that was helpful.

Half of the team wanted to get rid of the coach because we weren't having a good year. Some of the team used the coach's lesbianism against her in this. One of the leaders claimed that the head coach showed favoritism to lesbians on the team. I was embarrassed and scared. I didn't want to be a part of tearing her down. I did not want her to think I was a part of this. It had nothing to do with her coaching. I thought it was cruel. She has such a strong public persona. Outwardly she was strong and brushed it off, but it must have been horrible at home.

As I went through my coming-out process, I opened up to other groups on campus. I started associating with people doing homophobia education and outreach. There were many lesbians of color in the Multicultural Bisexual, Lesbian, Gay Student Alliance: Asian women, Latina women. For me, initially, I was totally unaware of my own prejudices and participation in racism, then I became more aware. I struggled with how do I as a white woman be friends with all these people and understand how they want their own space? The lesbians of color in our campus group felt pulled between two communities: lesbians and African-Americans, Chicanas, or Asians. I had heard from several of my friends that the black student union didn't address lesbian or gay issues. You can have your culture, or you can have your sexual orientation. I saw that a lot with my friends.

I think it is important to make sure you have a support network built in, friends or family, so you have a place to go and regarner your strength. I really believe in the strength of being out to combat the homophobia on my team. I was with them so much. I couldn't imagine not being out. I used to think there were no gay youth because in our culture we are taught that gay youth don't exist and that identifying yourself as lesbian, gay, or bisexual comes later in life. More and more people are coming out sooner. I think they need to find out what kind of a team they are going to. There are coaches who will use that information [knowing a player is gay] against you to revoke scholarships.

Unfortunately the coaches that I knew were lesbian taught me to be quiet. But they were great people and good athletes. I admire anyone in the public eye who has integrity about this. Melissa Etheridge, for example. She is being so honest. She has no shame. "This is who I am, and let's get on with it." It gives people no room because they have the problem. If we are ashamed, we are targets. ▼

Marla Weiss is white. She teaches math and science and coaches girls' and boys' high school volleyball.

I'm pretty out. I was getting tired of the burden of hiding myself. A year ago I was teaching a health class where I do a unit on diversity and include lesbian/gay/bisexual issues. Job security came up, and I brought up that in California, lesbian, gay, and bisexual teachers are protected. I told them I am a lesbian and cannot be fired for being gay. Nothing happened. I asked if they had questions, and the only questions I got were why we wear shirts and symbols and stuff. It was at the end of the period. I had a PFLAG [Parents, Families and Friends of Lesbians and Gays] group come in later. It was a non-event, like talking about the weather.

The next spring there was a newspaper article on gay and lesbian teachers with a huge picture of me. It was posted at school for three months on a bulletin board. The men had a reaction that was not to my face. There was quite a bit of discussion I heard from the women like, "I'm straight, and I haven't had a newspaper article written about me; this isn't news."

I don't deny or cover. I'm pretty vocal if there is cause to be. I say I am personally offended if someone says something I think is homophobic. There are quite a few gay or lesbian teachers older than me who are not out. One of the biggest reasons I felt comfortable coming out is I am a well-respected teacher and I have tenure. It isn't the way it should be, but I think lots of teachers wait to come out until they are respected.

I think my job performance speaks for itself. It is hard for people to pass judgment on someone after they like them and respect them. I have a good rapport with my students. I am a nurturing teacher. I am in contact with a lot of teachers in my daily routine. I'm not in their face. I stand up for what I think is right, but I am not aggressive. I don't have my own personal agenda. I don't stand up at the beginning of the year and say I am gay. I think teachers appropriately bring their personal life into the classroom. I do that, but I don't bring it in just for the sake of discussing it. I've been put in the position of being the expert on gay and lesbian issues, but I have no horror stories.

All of my athletes know, and I have no problems. I was a little concerned with my boys' team, but it has been uneventful. I am sometimes wary, but nothing has happened. It's been a non-issue. No comments from parents. Each year I don't know who has heard or anything. I don't know if they know I am a lesbian. I've had no problems with girls or parents. I had a couple of boys on my team in my class when I came out. I thought they might not listen to me after that. If you know your sport and do a good job, it should be a non-issue.

I have one girl on the team who is struggling with her sexuality and comes to Gay-Straight Alliance meetings. I think it has helped her. She and another girl put up a huge display in school on gay and lesbian books. Her mom saw it, and she mentioned that she didn't think that belonged in the school. Her mom doesn't know her daughter put up the display. The daughter thinks her mom would go ballistic if she knew, so she can't come to the meetings anymore because she is afraid her mother will find out. I've had very open discussions with her and let her know she can talk with me. I've given her a couple of news articles I use in class. All those typical concerns we have about lesbian and gay youth, she has: not many friends, suicidal, athletics is her only outlet, erratic academic record, can't wait to graduate. She could play college basketball or volleyball in Division 2 or 3.

I had a few athletes come back and visit me after they graduated. I told them I came out. They said, "We all knew, but we didn't care. How are the kids responding?"

I don't know about how other coaches feel. I think they know. I'm not sure. I've never heard anything to my face. I end up meeting more teachers who are closeted through GLSTN [Gay, Lesbian, Straight Teacher's Network], not through my coaching. A lot of the gay teachers I know are out to faculty but not to students. The girls' basketball coach at this school is out to most of the faculty and had a commitment ceremony. She told her team she was marrying, and they asked who the man was. She told them it was a woman. The team knows her lover because she comes to games; there is no problem.

I think you have to have done a little homework about your school so that you are prepared for any problems. Unfortunately, the situation is that you need to have established yourself as a teacher or be very confident in your administration. I was already an established and respected teacher. There was nothing to criticize about me. If all of a sudden things got bad for me, you knew it was because I came out. For someone who already has problems, the fact that you are gay can be used against you. I came out to be a role model. We all talk about how we should be proud of who we are, but we [coaches and teachers] are all in the closet. They know lesbian and gay coaches and teachers are there and that we are afraid to come out. It's worth any stress to be a role model for young people, especially in athletics. ▼

THE TRUTH WILL SET US FREE

These profiles describe the experiences of some lesbian athletes and coaches who have chosen to disclose their identities in athletics. I believe these women represent a growing number of coaches and athletes who will insist on their right to live as openly as they choose. They are women who refuse to lie about their lives and will not suffer discrimination and prejudice in silence.

Every group needs high-profile people who help to educate and change values. Celebrity lesbians such as Martina Navratilova, Muffin Spencer-Devlin, Ellen DeGeneres, Melissa Etheridge, and kd lang all provide this kind of role model for lesbians working their way out of their own closets. I believe, however, that "ordinary" women who are not famous choosing to live openly is also a powerful and perhaps more persuasive part of the social change process. When people learn that family members, teammates, coaches, friends, or others with whom they have personal relationships are lesbians, it becomes more difficult to justify prejudice and discrimination. Lesbians stop being mysterious aliens and are recognized as part of the diverse tapestry masked by the bland phrase, "women in sport."

At a press conference in Chicago during the Virginia Slims Legends Tour in April 1997, Billie Jean King summed up her feelings about coming out:

> I've struggled with my sexuality for years. But times have certainly changed. It's much better now. In fact, if you want to talk about your sexual orientation, the acceptance level is way up. I can tell you that in the 70s, there was this huge fear about coming out. The whole environment has changed. But it takes individuals coming out to help personalize it. I think families are much more willing to accept it—our chosen families—so it's possible to have a close nucleus of support. . . . I think it is really important to come out because the truth does set you free, there's no question.

Some of the women profiled in this chapter talked about the role that the lesbian athlete community played in their lives. Others talked about falling in love with other athletes or coaches. Both the community and love they find in sport have long played an important role in the lives of lesbian athletes and coaches. Chapter 10 focuses on these two issues.

10

Love and Community in the Locker Room:

Double Trouble or Double Standards?

Love and community are important parts of all of our lives. If we are fortunate, most of us develop love relationships in communities that nurture us and help us to grow. We find people who love us for the talents and loving qualities we have and forgive us for our shortcomings. Most of us seek love and community among people whose values and interests we share. Therefore it should be no surprise that lesbian athletes and coaches often find love and community among other women who share a love of sport. Especially if the families we are born into reject or abandon us, the families we choose—our lesbian and gay communities—often take on immense importance. This chapter will explore community and love among lesbians in sport.

COMMUNITY AMONG LESBIANS IN SPORT

Sport has played a historic role in the development of community among lesbian athletes (Rogers 1994; Zipter 1988a, 1988b). Industrial sport leagues, professional touring teams, community recreation teams, college teams, and other sport events have provided a place where lesbian athletes could share their common passion for sports and women in a community that shared their need for secrecy and discretion in a hostile society (Cahn 1994). From the 1930s through the 1960s, with few exceptions, women's sports attracted little attention from the mainstream culture or media. Because being an athlete was still outside the boundaries of acceptable feminine heterosexuality during this period, women athletes, who had already stepped out of bounds, found a safe haven in which to nurture lesbian identity and community in the relative obscurity of women's sports.

Players in the short-lived International Professional Women's Softball Association (1976-1979) recalled the joy of summers spent competing, traveling, and socializing with teammates. Going to private parties or local women's bars after games was a regular part of the softball experience for many lesbian players.

> When we were on the road we would always look forward to the social time with players from the other teams. We would pack up the vans after a game and go to a gay bar to dance, talk, and tell stories. A lot of those friendships were the start of some long-lasting connections. They also were a network for coaching jobs later. At home games our headquarters was in a motel, and after games we would go there and eat sandwiches and continue our socializing with the other team. We were all friends with players from the

other teams, and our bench jockeying was fun because we knew each other. It was more teasing than mean or cruel.

—*Former Connecticut Falcon player*

Players on the early LPGA and WTA tours also recalled a similar sense of camaraderie among players, and the socializing among women athletes was an integral part of the tour experience.

> *We had a lot of fun on the road in those days [the 70s]. . . . From the first time I was allowed out of Czechoslovakia, I sensed the freedom and camaraderie of the women players. . . . They hung out together more than we do today, and they had a good time together. . . . We played together, we traveled together, we partied together, we worried about money together (Navratilova and Vecsey 1985, 141, 145).*

College women's sports teams of the 60s and 70s provided a similar haven for lesbians. At a time when there was little public interest in women's sport and less acceptance of women as athletes, lesbian athletes developed a social network among teammates and competitors that sustained them in the face of social hostility.

As women's sport has moved from the margins toward the mainstream and as Title IX has increased opportunities to play, lesbian community in sport continues to thrive, despite increased media attention and participation by heterosexual women. Closeted lesbian friendship networks within and among college teams are commonplace at many schools. In the absence of support from coaches who are closeted lesbians or antilesbian heterosexuals, these invisible communities serve an important social and psychological role for lesbian athletes. For some lesbian athletes this community is their only source of support in the face of parental, coach, and campus hostility. When traditional support systems designed to serve the needs of young people fail to address the needs of young lesbians and bisexual women, the community of lesbian athletes often fills this need. This community enables young lesbian athletes to come out into a social network that provides role models, love relationships, and friendships among other women who share a love of sport.

Many of the college athletes I talked with described how their association with other lesbian athletes at their school was a primary source of support, guidance, and community. For some women, these lesbian athlete social groups provide a place to talk about their experiences and develop a sense of pride and empowerment. For others, membership in a lesbian athletic community provides a group who parties together.

> The softball team is a community. We do things together. Every two months we do a dinner, 14 to 16 of us, all couples. We go to the lesbian bar every

once in a while. We go off in twos or fours and do things together, like play golf. We are really open with each other in that group.

    —Division 2 softball and basketball player

There was an informal social group [of lesbian athletes]. It was a big "drive to the city to a bar, drink, and dance" gang. I was not a big social person. We [she and her partner] were "Betty and Susie homemaker," and they were sowing their wild oats. People tended to stay with their teams. So if people wanted to go out, they went with their teams.

    —Former track athlete

In the absence of adults who will acknowledge or affirm the presence of lesbians in sport or provide guidance in negotiating lesbian identity in athletics, older lesbian athletes often become role models and confidants to younger women. Lesbian teammates support and counsel each other.

I wasn't really out [to the campus] as an undergrad. I found the community of athletes in school. Most of the friends I was hanging out with started coming out, and then I figured out I was [a lesbian] too. It was a religious school, but I found a really strong community where I could be who I was. They were older, mostly softball, soccer, and basketball players. I was invited to parties a lot on campus, and a couple of women had us over to their house. They would come and pick us up. They kind of adopted us freshmen. They were role models athletically, and then I found out they were gay too. It was kind of like a family. They helped me with school and sports. It was a really close community. We did our fair share of drinking, but not in excess. We got our work done and trained hard. Most of us are still friends 12 years later.

    —Former Division 1 volleyball player

This lesbian college-athlete community serves a heroic role on campuses where there are no institutional or personal supports for lesbian, gay, and bisexual students. According to a Department of Health and Human Services study, lesbian and gay young people are two to three times more likely to attempt suicide than are other young people (Gibson 1989). Without any source of support or guidance for making sense of their confusion and fear about having sexual attractions to other women and in a climate of silence and hostility, young athletes must be included in this at-risk group. One basketball player I spoke with described how she and her teammates stood a "suicide watch" for one of the younger members of the team who was deeply depressed and confused about her identity. Her fear of being cut from the team prevented her from talking with her coach, who had made it clear that lesbians were not allowed on the team. Fear of being judged and cut off from family kept her from talking with her parents. She also felt bound by a loyalty to protect the team image and a distrust of campus therapists that prevented her from seeking counseling. Her lesbian teammates took turns staying with her 24 hours a day until they realized that she needed more help than they could provide. At that point they called her parents and, without revealing any details, let them know their daughter was in trouble. She left school, and when her parents discovered the reason for her depression, they forbade any contact with the team. They blamed the women who may have saved their daughter's life for her distress. The coaching staff, by their hostility to lesbian athletes, cut off the most logical sources of help, leaving these young women to cope on their own, as best they could, with a life-threatening situation.

As noted in chapter 9, the intersection of other social identities can complicate this search for community. For lesbian athletes of color or lesbians of any racial group who come from poor and working-class families, finding a community of lesbian athletes where they can feel safe and welcomed sometimes depends on their abilities to "fit in" by overlooking the racism of white athletes or the classism of middle-class teammates. This need to compromise one's sense of self in order to belong to a primarily white, middle-class, lesbian athletic community can be intensified when either support services for students of color do not exist on campus or these services do not welcome lesbians and gay men of color.

The reality of lesbian athletic communities on many college campuses is that young women create whatever support they can for themselves. This support is often in the shadow of hostile coaches and teammates or the silence and fear of closeted lesbian coaches who distance themselves from their lesbian athletes to protect their professional reputations. It should be a matter of professional shame among coaches and sport administrators that these young athletes are left on their own to cope with discrimination, harassment, and the internalized self-hatred that is a commonplace experience among many lesbian college athletes (Krane 1996a). Many lesbian athletes, faced with the consuming time demands of athletics and the pressure to hide their identities or risk dismissal or ostracism from the team, find the lesbian athletic community in college the only safe place to be themselves.

This lesbian athletic community is sometimes extended to include athletes from opposing teams, who get to know each other at tournaments, through mutual friends from other schools, and from playing against each other over the course of a four-year college career.

I hang out with the rugby team. That is where I started to feel comfortable. I think I know every gay person in town now. We met other teams from up and down the east coast. You go through so much with each other: practice, games, parties.

—*Division 2 rugby player*

My coaches and straight friends provided some support, but I have to say it was more comfort in numbers than anything. We [the lesbians on the team] had a lot of camaraderie because we knew about each other. When our team traveled, I was able to make friends with other lesbians. Somehow we always "knew" who we were and enjoyed seeing each other whenever we were scheduled to play. It was comfortable, like coming home to family.

—*Division 1 volleyball player*

Not all lesbian athletes rely solely on a community of other lesbian athletes. Some women who are more open about their lesbian identity include the broader community of lesbian, gay, and bisexual people on campus as part of their support and friendship network.

I have lots of lesbian friends at school who support me. When I was coming out last spring, there were a number of women, and we got together every week and talked about being gay, and I met a lot of women through them. There is more of a community developing now, but I get support from my crew teammates too.

—*Division 1 rower*

Lesbian athletes are less isolated than we were in college. They are more out, more involved in coed intramurals, campus activities. They have more support from heterosexual men and women. It's OK to be completely out on campus. Some of them don't know what they will do when they graduate because they are used to being out.

—*Division 3 athletic director*

Lesbian Sports Fans

Lesbians are among the most loyal women's sports fans. The NCAA women's basketball Final Four, ABL or WNBA games, the professional golf and tennis tours, and local college basketball or softball games are great favorites among lesbian fans. In fact, the annual Nabisco Dinah Shore LPGA tournament in Southern California is well known in the lesbian community as "lesbian spring break," attracting 20,000 lesbians for a week of parties, sports, and other social events along with a little golf spectating on the side (C. Hall 1996; Mansfield 1997). Lesbian fans are especially appreciative of athletes or coaches who they suspect are lesbians (Lurie 1994).

I remember playing away matches, and I'd look up into the stands, and there would be many lesbians sitting together. They would specifically cheer for me whenever I touched the ball. It was really fun. It was very important to feel welcomed and accepted. I had lots of fan mail, mostly from young lesbians who wanted to know what it was like to be a "sports star." I didn't go out in the local community to anything that was lesbian identified until I was a senior. It seemed like the whole lesbian community was waiting for me to show up. The first dance I went to, people kept coming up and making comments. It was exhilarating and a bit overwhelming too.

—Division 1 volleyball player

Lesbian fan clubs—such as Husky Hoops, who support the University of Washington women's basketball team—are loyal and visible women's sport supporters (*Fans of Women's Sports* 1995; M. King and O'Neil 1993). Husky Hoops is unique in that this group integrates a love of women's basketball with a decidedly political edge. They insist on the visibility of lesbian sports fans at games and encourage the University of Washington to address homophobia in women's sports. Husky Hoops also is an annual, visible lesbian presence at the Final Four, displaying a booth in the exhibition hall and speaking out in conference sessions.

Unfortunately, lesbian fans are not always appreciated by the sport organizations or the athletes they support. If the coach or the team is self-conscious about visible and boisterous lesbian fans, their enthusiasm can be a source of embarrassment and discomfort for players and athletes concerned about "image problems." Drawing attention to lesbian participation in sport or discrimination against lesbians in sport lifts a curtain of silence around these issues that many coaches and many athletes would prefer not to disturb. At a University of Washington women's basketball game in 1992 a group of lesbian fans held up a 10-foot banner during pregame warm-ups and at every time out. The banner read, "Support Lesbians in Sports." The group also passed out informational flyers protesting discrimination against lesbians in sport. One of the women in the group was quoted in the local paper, "Those of us in the [lesbian] community realize that sports are a big part of the lesbian culture and we want to be recognized and treated seriously." This event caused quite a stir in the media and in a nervous athletic department. A university administrator described the public perception of lesbian involvement in the women's basketball program as "a powder keg that could explode the program apart" (Wright 1992, C1).

Other athletes also described the discomfort that university officials feel with an openly lesbian fan presence:

The university basketball team is the center of social life for the dyke community here. The coach seems a little uncomfortable about it though.

—Former Olympic rower

During my last home game some friends in the stands put up a sign that said, "Three cheers for the queer three pointer," signed the Fairy Godmothers.

They held it up for the whole game. It was great. Some of the team thought it was great, and some thought it should have been taken down. The coach didn't say anything about getting it down. An administrator tried to get them to put it down, but it stayed up for the whole game.

—Former Division 1 basketball player

The LPGA and Nabisco maintain a nervous, neutral public stance toward the increasing popularity of and public attention paid to the lesbian social events surrounding the Dinah Shore tournament. They appreciate the money lesbians spend but do not like the association of the golf tournament with the lesbians who come to party. An April 1997 story about these lesbian social events at the Dinah Shore tournament in a *Sports Illustrated Golf Plus* supplement prompted Titleist and Foot Joy, two long-time *Sports Illustrated* advertisers, to cancel $1.5 million of advertising (Mansfield 1997; Uihlein 1997). Titleist and Foot Joy chief Wally Uihlein called the article "way out of bounds" and "symptomatic of a condescending mindset toward women in golf in general." Uihlein also criticized a *Sports Illustrated* article of the previous year in which golfer Muffin Spencer-Devlin came out as another example of *Sports Illustrated*'s demeaning treatment of women athletes. Though Uihlein objects to the association of women's golf with lesbians, he apparently does not consider the annual swimsuit issue out of bounds or demeaning to women, though these features aren't even remotely related to sport and present women solely as sex objects for male readers' enjoyment.

Sports Events for Lesbians

In addition to enjoying sports from the stands, many lesbians are sport participants in privately sponsored or community-sponsored sport events for lesbians and gay men. Many of these participants are former collegiate athletes who are enjoying sport participation for the first time as openly lesbian athletes. Among the increasing number of openly lesbian and gay sport options are national associations promoting competition in events as diverse and varied as softball, volleyball, and rodeo (Pitts 1994).

Local and regional lesbian and gay leagues also thrive. The largely rural Northampton-Amherst, Massachusetts, area (two hours from Boston) has supported 14 to 16 lesbian softball teams in an independent league for 20 years. With team names such as "Common Womon" and "Hot Flashes," these softball teams and games form the core of social events and friendships for many lesbians during the spring and summer. Special sport events organized for lesbian participants and their friends also provide opportunities to compete and socialize. The Betty Hicks Classic is an annual golf tournament organized and run by Betty Hicks, the former amateur national champion and one of the founding mothers of the LPGA. This event attracts 100 to 150 women each sum-mer for an 18-hole scramble competition and dinner dance near San Jose, California. Other local, privately organized golf tournaments with names such as The Tilted Tee (for women who can't tee it up straight) also take over golf courses and clubhouses for an afternoon and evening of fun and competition for lesbians of all ages and abilities.

The Festival of the Babes is an annual soccer tournament in the San Francisco area for lesbians and "heterosexual women who don't mind if people think they are lesbians." Another event in the Bay area, The Lesbian Mixed Doubles tennis tournament, was an annual fund-raiser for Lyon-Martin Women's Health Services from 1991 to 1995. The 150 competitors were advised that a "sense of humor is mandatory," as each doubles team was required to dress as a "butch and femme" couple or be docked points during the competition. The tournament took place on or around Halloween to encourage players to get into the costume spirit. According to founder and organizer Nanette Gartrell, the tournament raised over $100,000 and was Lyon-Martin's biggest fund-raiser.

Probably the largest and best-known lesbian and gay athletic event is the Gay Games (Coe 1986; Forzley and Hughes 1990; Labrecque 1994; Lipsyte 1994; Patton 1990). First organized in 1982 by former Olympic

Opening Ceremonies at the 1994 Gay Games in New York City.

decathlete Tom Waddell, this international athletic and cultural event takes place every four years. Waddell's vision was to gather lesbian, gay, bisexual, transgender, and supportive heterosexual athletes in an international athletic competition in which athletes could openly celebrate both their athletic and sexual identities in ways not currently possible in most mainstream sporting events. In 1994 in New York City, Gay Games IV attracted more participants than the 1992 Barcelona Olympics. Gay Games V will be held in August 1998 in Amsterdam.

The association of lesbians with sports is not just a stereotype used to control and intimidate women athletes. Many lesbians do find community among lesbian teammates and other lesbian athletes and coaches. Many lesbians in and out of sport describe the network of friends and ex-lovers whom they feel safe with and affirmed by as *families of choice*. These families of choice for many lesbians serve the functions that their birth families fail to provide: love, care, acceptance, stability. They also create an opportunity for lesbians in sport to meet and fall in love.

LOVE IN THE LOCKER ROOM: DOUBLE TROUBLE OR DOUBLE STANDARDS?

Women athletes who share a common passion for sport spend huge amounts of time together practicing, competing, and traveling. Some of these women also share a passion for other women. Given these facts, it should not be surprising to find that sexual attractions and relationships occur among women in sport. Moreover, the infinite variety that these attractions and relationships take defy any single stereotype of "lesbian lifestyle."

Part of the problem with addressing lesbian relationships in athletics is the double standard that is applied to lesbian and heterosexual relationships. Lesbian and heterosexual relationships are viewed through the twin distorting lenses of homophobia and heterosexism. These distortions cut off rational discussion about how to fairly respond to lesbian relationships in athletics and short-circuit any discussion about problems posed by dysfunctional and coercive heterosexual relationships in athletics.

Sexual Harassment and Sexual Coercion

Unwanted sexual attention or attempts at sexual coercion are wrong, regardless of the sex or sexual identities of the people involved. When lesbians are guilty of exerting sexual coercion or sexually harassing other women, this behavior is no more acceptable than when the sexual aggressor is a heterosexual man. Unfortunately, in athletics we often have a double standard in how we respond to these situations, depending on the sexual orientations and sex of the people involved. Because of the sexual predator image attributed to lesbians, many parents, young athletes, and heterosexual coaches believe that women athletes are safer with heterosexual male or female coaches or on teams where lesbian athletes are not allowed. The irony is that, given recent reports of sexual misconduct by male coaches and male athletes and the statistics on sexual harassment in general, young women athletes are at far greater risk of being sexually harassed, hit on, or raped by their heterosexual male coaches or by heterosexual male athletes than by lesbian coaches or teammates (Bondy 1993; Crosset, Benedict, and McDonald 1995; Deford 1993a; Moore 1991; Nack and Munson 1995; Neimark 1991; *USA Today* 1991; Witherspoon 1995). In fact, recent reports on sexual harassment in athletics indicate that alarmingly high numbers of young women athletes are sexually abused by or involved with male coaches (Deford 1993b; Howard 1997; Lackey 1990; Latimer 1996; Lenskyj 1992).

In addition, women athletes report that some male athletes use women's fear of the lesbian label to coerce them into sex as a way to "prove" their heterosexuality. Women athletes who are already defensive about their heterosexuality are reluctant to reject unwanted sexual attention from male athletes out of fear of being perceived as not sexually interested in men. This is an especially volatile issue for women athletes who are either questioning their sexuality or who are ashamed of their sexual attractions to women (Lenskyj 1992). They are particularly vulnerable targets for sexually aggressive male coaches or athletes.

> Guys on the men's [basketball] team would hit on us and say things like, "We hear you all are dykes. Is it true?" This really made some girls on the team mad, and for some of them, the only way to show that they weren't lesbians was to have sex with these guys. Even some women who were lesbians did it to cover things up.
>
> —*Division 1 basketball player*

The instances of male athletes sexually assaulting women reflect the antiwoman and antigay environment present in some men's team sports (Curry 1991). This environment affects women athletes directly or indirectly in at least three ways. First, sexually aggressive behavior among male athletes contributes to the generally hostile environment toward women in athletics. Second, female and male athletes are often friends and sometimes date each other. Third, male athletes sometimes become coaches for women's sports.

"She's Staring at Me," "She's Hitting on Me," and Other Homophobia-Induced Perceptions

Looking through a lens clouded by stereotypes, heterosexual coaches and other team members have few guidelines about what to expect from or how to react to lesbians and their relationships. In this climate of mixed hostility, fear, defensiveness, ignorance, secrecy, and deception, is it really a surprise that sexual attractions and relationships among women in sport provoke such strong reactions?

In this climate numerous misinterpretations abound. Some young women are unsure of their own sexual identities and, as a result, are alternately repelled by and curious about their attractions to women. To avoid taking responsibility for a sexual encounter with another woman, they may blame the lesbian they are attracted to, peer pressure, or alcohol for their feelings and actions. By portraying themselves as innocent victims of aggressive lesbians or as losing control of their actions because of alcohol, these young women feed the lesbian stereotypes of their parents, coaches, and heterosexual friends while avoiding personal responsibility for actions and feelings they cannot accept in themselves.

Similarly, some young athletes talk about being stared at or hit on in the locker room by lesbian teammates. While one cannot deny the possibility that lesbians might look at another woman's body in the locker room, in many instances these perceptions are projections born out of fear and curiosity. I remember my college basketball team's fascination with a woman on another team that we played at least twice during the season. She was an excellent player who projected a strong and androgynous appearance. We were sure that she tried to touch us inappropriately while on defense, and we made jokes about how she looked like a man. Yet the sense of anticipation we all shared before games with her team was revealing. We started retelling stories about her from the last game and professing fear about what would happen in the upcoming game. By the time we arrived at the gym, the stories had evolved into descriptions of full-blown sexual assaults on the basketball court. Looking back, we had no reason to think this woman was interested in anything more than winning the basketball game. We interpreted her aggressive play as sexual out of our own fears about and fascinations with lesbians. I am also ashamed to say that part of my participation in making fun of this player was to camouflage my own lesbianism from my teammates. My participation in ridiculing this woman also reassured me that, though I was in love with one of my teammates, we were different from the "real" sexually predatory lesbians we had heard about.

Romantic Interest or Sexual Assault: Can We Tell the Difference?

What if a lesbian does express a romantic or sexual interest in a woman who does not return these feelings? Even adult women can be thrown into a crisis by the possibility of attracting the sexual interest of a lesbian. Conditioned by our culture to interpret such an event as a moral crisis, even the most well intentioned heterosexual women can be knocked off balance: What about me makes her think I'm a lesbian? Is this sexual harassment? What do I do now? I had a conversation with a retired heterosexual professional golfer whom I counted as an ally because she was working to develop an understanding of homophobia in women's sports. We were at a women's sports dinner when she asked me what is the "appropriate" way to turn down a lesbian asking for a date. First, I asked her how she knew it was a request for a date, and then I asked her what she would say to an invitation from a man she was not interested in dating. She smiled and laughed as she realized the point I was making: We need to question our assumptions that lesbians are always on the prowl with sexual intent. An appropriate response to any invitation that we are not interested in, whether from a man or a woman, can be a simple "thanks, but no thanks." If someone turned down in this way persists, whether male or female, then it might be sexual harassment warranting more serious action, but some women overreact at even the possibility of attracting a lesbian's romantic interest.

Some heterosexual women, especially those who are afraid of lesbians or those who are upset if someone assumes they are lesbians, are predisposed to interpret an expression of potential romantic interest by a lesbian as a full-scale sexual assault or a sexual insult (How dare you assume I might be a lesbian!). Dot Richardson, the shortstop on the 1996 Olympic gold medal softball team, described such an experience during her college days (Richardson 1997). Richardson described how she was hurt and disappointed throughout her athletic career by people's presumption that any athletic woman is a lesbian. She was "crushed" when a friend called her a lesbian during an argument and "freaked" when a teammate came out to her in the 10th grade. She then described her successful efforts to ignore the topic of homosexuality, even though she had lesbian teammates:

> It worked, because no one bothered me. No teammate said anything to make me uncomfortable. I got over my anxieties and became close friends with my gay teammates. They didn't give me grief about my choices. I didn't give them grief about theirs. (Richardson 1997, 41)

Richardson's conditional tolerance was based on her lesbian team-mates' willingness to maintain total invisibility and silence so that she would not be "bothered" or "uncomfortable." She goes on to describe "one of the most *disappointing* moments in my life" in which her gay roommate, who was one of her best friends, asked if Richardson would "consider her sexual views." Richardson interpreted this question as a sexual advance. Her response to this fairly straightforward question was to completely freak out:

> I rushed out of my room. I was so hurt. I looked at my dorm neighbors who were in the hall and blurted, "If you have a daughter, don't let her compete in sports, because it is not worth it!" That's when I hit my low point. I was sobbing as I ran to my car. . . . As I drove away from the dorm in a torrential downpour, I was crying so hard I could hardly see. I was so hurt that I actually thought about getting into an accident that night and killing myself. (Richardson 1997, 41)

I couldn't have created a better example of how homophobia affects women in sport who do not identify themselves as lesbians. Dot Richardson is telling us that she contemplated suicide because her best friend *asked* her if she would consider her sexual views. It is testament to how far we are from a sports world in which women of different sexualities can compete together respectfully, that a world-class, presumably sophisticated athlete such as Dot Richardson comes apart at the seams at the possibility of being perceived as a lesbian.

We need to move on to the next step beyond the necessity for lesbian athletes to keep their identities and attractions locked tightly in the closet and the interpretation of any open expression of lesbian identity or interest as sexual assault, harassment, or insult. Richardson's story demonstrates how we need practice in navigating a new social terrain in which lesbian, bisexual, and heterosexual women compete together and respect each other with more than a fragile tolerance that can be threatened by a simple question.

Sexual Relationships Between Women Athletes

Two athletes on the same team becoming sexually involved with each other is probably a far more common occurrence than coaches of either sex becoming involved with an athlete. Many lesbians in sport develop and nurture mutual loving relationships with teammates despite the pressures of the closet and hostility from coaches, families, and other teammates. Nurturing and sustaining any relationship—whether heterosexual, gay, or lesbian—is difficult. In addition to the typical challenges facing any intimate relationship, problems in lesbian athletes' relationships can develop because these relationships often develop in isolation, with few relationship role models, and in an atmosphere of constant fear of discovery and rejection by hostile coaches, teammates, and families. Perhaps the surprise is not so much that relationships between women in sport develop, but how many of them flourish and are healthy despite the obstacles created by homophobia and heterosexism in athletics.

Sexual relationships between women teammates can affect team relationship dynamics in the same way that a heterosexual relationship in any workplace can affect relationships among the work unit. Even when these relationships are mutual and consenting, the rest of the team must adjust to the dynamics of having intimate partners participate together. Add discomfort with lesbians to these dynamics and the potential for relationship and communication problems among teammates increases. In fact, some coaches call attention to these potential problems as reasons for prohibiting lesbians on teams or discouraging or forbidding sexual relationships between teammates under threat of dismissal from the team. In addition to the difficulty of monitoring athletes' personal lives and encouraging dishonesty among lesbian athletes in relationships with teammates, this "solution" places the blame on and discriminates against lesbians for complicating team dynamics. Blaming lesbians does not call on anyone to confront the homophobia and heterosexism that is the foundation for much of the reaction to lesbian relationships among teammates.

Rather than blaming or discriminating against lesbians to avoid the possibility of disrupting team dynamics, coaches who reflect on these issues can identify ways that homophobia and heterosexism encourage a double standard when addressing relationship issues for lesbian and heterosexual athletes. They can then engage in some creative problem solving to identify more equitable ways to accommodate and respect all athletes on the team regardless of sexual identity.

Two examples illustrate how a double standard affects the ways coaches respond to heterosexual and lesbian relationships among athletes. Some coaches express concern that relationships between teammates disrupt team dynamics, yet two heterosexual teammates dating the same male football player can create similar friction within the team. Why doesn't this potential disruption to team dynamics receive more attention? As another example, worries about team image often focus on the presence or perception of the presence of lesbians on a team. What about perceptions that team members are heterosexually promiscuous as a legitimate team image problem? Rather than assuming that only lesbian athletes create potential communication problems on teams or image problems for teams, a more productive approach would be to identify ways to address all these relationship issues fairly and effectively.

Locker Rooms

Several unique issues are raised by the presence of lesbians on women's athletic teams that are different from double-standard issues raised by heterosexual women athletes' involvement with men who are not on the team. Many of these issues center around the locker room and the hotel room and the fears that some women have about sharing these intimate spaces with lesbians or women they suspect are lesbians. Lesbian and heterosexual athletes share the locker room and see each other's bodies in the showers. For athletes who are concerned about being the object of lesbian locker room lust, this is no small matter. This concern is, in part, a result of the over-sexualization of lesbians. Some heterosexual women assume that lesbians are sexual predators whose obsession with sex overrides other more mundane locker room activities such as rehashing a game, getting dressed, treating injuries, or bantering and listening to music with teammates.

Assuming that all lesbians are leering at other women's bodies with sexual intent or that no heterosexual women are checking out other women's bodies creates a false dichotomy based on lesbian stereotypes. I remember a conversation with my swim team that occurred in the van on the way home from a meet. The conversation began with a few women expressing discomfort with the muscularity of their arms, backs, and shoulders, the visible results of weight training and hard practice sessions. As we talked more, however, it became clear that they were secretly very proud of their hard-earned muscles and strong appearance. They liked looking at themselves and each other, but they were uncomfortable acknowledging their pride in their own bodies or noticing other women's bodies. The conversation opened up more as women expressed appreciation for each other's strong appearance and the muscularity of other swimmers and women athletes in other sports. This group of mostly heterosexual women did notice other women's bodies, not necessarily in a sexual way, but they noticed and appreciated nonetheless. As a result of this conversation, team members felt freer to express not only pride in their own bodies, but also admiration for the strong-looking bodies of other women. Perhaps there was a sexual component of this admiration for some women. Our conversation did not broach this, but it was clear that both lesbian and heterosexual women were noticing each other's bodies and that this was not the kind of leering or objectifying gaze usually attributed to lesbians.

The physicality of the locker room, the whirlpool, the weight room, and the competitive arena itself can be erotic, especially in the context of the intensity of team bonding and the emotional and physical highs and lows of athletic competition. This eroticism is not, however, the sole province of lesbians. The sexual energy in a locker room or on a playing field is available for all women, even women who are committed to expressing their sexuality only with men. The problem is that awareness of this natural erotic component of women's sports has been so stigmatized and associated with "deviant" sexual behavior that women are afraid to acknowledge its presence or it is expressed only as fear of the lesbian boogeywoman.

Hotel Rooms

Heterosexism and homophobia also can distort and exaggerate the "dangers" of sharing a hotel room with a teammate who might be a lesbian. Coaches have many different methods of assigning athletes to hotel rooms on the road. Room assignments for some teams are up to the athletes. These coaches assume that athletes know with whom they are comfortable and that they will make choices based on their comfort. Some coaches assign athletes to rooms and rotate these assignments throughout the season so that every athlete rooms with every other athlete at some point during the season. For one team, three athletes were assigned to each double room: A senior got a bed to herself, and two underclasswomen shared the other bed. Team or individual performance determines other arrangements: On some softball teams, pitchers always get their own beds. One coach told me that her ace pitcher got extremely nervous the night before a game, and the shortstop, who was her lover, was always assigned to be her roommate on the road because she knew how to calm down her nervous partner and help her prepare to perform well the next day. As an issue of gender equity, I wonder how many male athletes are asked to sleep in the same bed with a teammate.

Some of these room-assignment strategies revolve around concerns about teammates being sexual with each other. Some coaches intentionally separate teammates who they suspect are lovers. When athletes or their parents raise objections about hotel arrangements, coaches respond differently. Some coaches avoid room assignments that individual players object to, regardless of the reason. Others believe that athletes need to learn to get to know each other and work out their problems. These coaches do not take personal preferences into account at all. A heterosexual coach described a conversation she had with parents of one of her players:

> I had parents call me because they were upset that their daughter was assigned to share a room with a lesbian on the team. I asked them if something had happened, did this girl do anything to make their daughter uncomfortable? They said no, but they just didn't want her in the same room with this lesbian. I asked them if they would make the same request for their daughter, who is white, if she was sharing a room with a black

teammate. They said, "No, of course not. That would be racist." I didn't hear from them again.

—*Division 3 softball coach*

How Can I Pass Her the Ball When She Broke My Heart Last Night?

As with heterosexual relationships in the workplace, things may be fine as long as relationships between lesbian teammates are stable. However, just as in heterosexual relationships, painful transitions and dishonorable partners can affect individual and team play as well as team dynamics. When teammates break up, triangles among teammates emerge, love is unrequited, or someone cheats on someone else, the ensuing dyke drama is no less traumatic than in a troubled heterosexual relationship in the workplace (Zipter 1988b). It may be more traumatic for lesbians because of the pressure for secrecy and the isolation that homophobia and heterosexism in sport encourage.

Some coaches see any romantic involvement, whether gay or straight, as a potential distraction from athletic performance.

> I must be really stupid because I know there are players who have been together. I don't know if it has been a problem for the team. What does become a problem is if two players break up and they can't deal with each other. That's more of an issue. If they can't function with each other, that creates huge problems for the team. If they can't leave it outside the fence, then they can't be on the team, either one of them. It can't be. If you feel uncomfortable on the field, you can't perform, and if other people on the field are uncomfortable, they can't perform. It's a vicious cycle. When they walk through the gate to the field, they have to leave it. They have to find a way to survive it.... I hope I don't treat gay and straight athletes differently. They don't talk to me about their personal lives unless it is affecting their performance. I've talked to heterosexual and homosexual athletes about things that go on in their relationships that affect their performance. If it affects their performance, then we have to talk about it. But the farther I keep from their social lives, the fairer I can be to deal with everybody.
>
> —*Division 1 field hockey coach*

Creative thinking can identify equitable and humane ways to deal with relationship troubles among athletes on a team. Whether love relationships are heterosexual or lesbian and whether they are within the team or between an athlete and someone not on the team, team policies can be fair and reasonable for all. Team policies about public displays of affection can apply to any romantic relationship. If it isn't acceptable for lesbian partners to hold hands in public, then heterosexual partners should refrain from this display of affection too. Heterosexual or lesbian athletes having relationship problems can be referred to counseling, and equitable expectations for team participation can be set. When team dynamics are affected because of conflicts or upsets related to either heterosexual or lesbian relationships, expectations for team communication and performance can apply equitably to both lesbian and heterosexual athletes. A basic tenet of all team policies about relationship issues should be that all athletes are treated equitably and that all athletes are expected to treat each other with respect. The goal is to create fair policies that apply to all athletes regardless of their sexual orientation.

Sexual Relationships Between Coaches and Athletes

I want to emphasize that I believe that sexual relationships between coaches and athletes are unacceptable, regardless of the sex or sexual orientations of the participants in the relationship. Coaching ethics should include a prohibition against coaches becoming sexually involved with their athletes, period. The American Swimming Coaches Association's and the American Volleyball Coaches Association's codes of ethics include sections on relationships between coaches and athletes. These codes unambiguously prohibit sexual relationships between coaches and athletes. More coaching associations and sports governing bodies need to adopt similar regulations to protect athletes.

Coaches must understand the power and control they have over young athletes' lives and careers. Even if an athlete consents to a sexual relationship, coach-athlete relationships are based on huge differences in power that make the ability of a young athlete to give "consent" questionable. Athletes often revere and trust their coaches in a way that makes it both flattering to receive sexual attention from them and difficult to reject this attention. In addition, high school and college athletes are usually young adult women who are not financially independent from their parents or not experienced in negotiating the complexities of a sexual relationship with a peer, let alone an adult who has control over a significant part of their lives.

In addition to all these individual issues, team factors also must be considered. When a coach is sexually involved with one or, even worse, more members of a team, serious intrateam repercussions are inevitable. Team chemistry often depends on a delicate balance of relationships that rely on the coach's ability to be fair and equally accessible to all team members while maintaining a clear professional distance from all athletes. When other athletes find out about sexual relationships between a coach and a teammate, they often feel betrayed and angry and also have their sense of propriety violated.

After I graduated, some women still on the team knocked on my door and told me they wanted me to talk to one of their teammates because they thought she was seeing the assistant coach. The teammate they were talking about had come out to me before. The rest of the team thought it was unprofessional and believed the assistant coach was paying too much attention to and only coaching her lover since they had this little thing going. I let it slide because it felt too weird to talk to the teammate about it. A few weeks later she came to me and told me, "I wish you had told me everyone was talking behind my back." She told me she and the assistant coach were not having a relationship, it was all rumors. I knew she was lying. They hold hands and sit on the back of the bus together. I had to believe the others. I knew she was just scared. I told her, "Even if you are not having a relationship, try to cool it off until the end of the year; it's only a month. Lay off so everyone stops talking." It's one thing if you are in a relationship with another athlete, it's another thing if you are in a relationship with a coach. The assistant coach resigned at the end of the year, and they are seeing each other now. The team didn't care if she was a lesbian or straight, they just didn't like one of the coaches dating someone on the team.

—*Former track athlete*

Lesbian coaches I have talked to who have been sexually involved with an athlete agree that relationships between coaches and athletes are unacceptable and that they could not have defended their behavior if they had been challenged. One former college coach who is now coaching in high school told me, "As a college coach I did some stupid things. I dated a student. I don't care if it is gay or straight, it was stupid."

Sometimes young coaches, both male and female, who are only a few years older than the athletes on their team have a difficult time drawing clear lines between their athletes and themselves. All coaches, regardless of sexual orientation or sex, need preparation for managing their feelings in these situations. This information should be included in coaching certification courses, coaching ethics statements, and new coach orientation programs.

Several recent articles indicate that male coaches' sexual involvement with female athletes is a problem that has only recently come to light (Deford 1993b; Feinstein 1992; Howard 1997; Hudson 1995b; Latimer 1996; Lenskyj 1992; Mewshaw 1993; Nelson 1994). Similarly, many of the people Mariah Burton Nelson (1994) interviewed agreed that knowledge about sexual relationships between male coaches and female athletes was widespread among other coaches and athletes. A former Olympic cross-country skier I interviewed said that while she was competing, it was commonly accepted that male coaches were sleeping with their female skiers and that before she came out, she had slept with her male coach. This perception was confirmed by a lesbian coach I interviewed, who said:

I have six or seven friends who have slept with their male coaches. I had one friend who had a three-year relationship with her track coach in high school …and he was married. It was the first person she had ever slept with, and he kept promising he was going to leave his wife and marry her. He got really jealous when other guys were around. It screwed her all up. I get really mad. All these men are taking advantage, and as a lesbian, I have to always be so careful because all the parents are thinking I am trying to convert them [her athletes, to lesbianism].

—*Division 3 basketball coach*

Moreover, many male coaches whom Nelson (1994) interviewed did not see the problem with becoming sexually involved with athletes as long as the relationship was "serious" or the coach married the athlete. Only in the last few years, as sexual harassment has begun to be taken more seriously in the larger culture, have relationships between male coaches and female athletes begun to be treated as a serious problem.

Parents of young athletes and the athletes themselves do not assume that a heterosexual male coach will sexually harass their daughter, nor should they. In contrast, however, many parents and their daughters, as well as other coaches, assume that lesbian coaches are a sexual threat to young women on their teams, usually without any information to justify these fears. Sportswriter Frank Deford (1993b) summed up this inconsistency well:

Curiously, the scandal of coach-player or even father-player sex and/or violence has been obscured through the years by the far greater fascination with homosexuality in women's sports. That's more titillating. Ergo, the heterosexual abuses have been ignored while all the cunning investigative reporters have searched about for older gay female athletes and players seducing the young innocents.

This double standard of expectation often extends to the treatment given to lesbian and heterosexual male coaches who do become sexually involved with an athlete on their team. In 1982 *Sports Illustrated* (in one of the few stories about women's sports they chose to cover that year) did a story about University of South Carolina women's basketball coach Pam Parsons (Lieber and Kirshenbaum 1982). Parsons was accused of being sexually involved with one of her players, Tina Buck, and was fired as a result. Parsons sued the university over the *Sports Illustrated* article in an attempt to save her reputation and coaching career. During the trial, Parsons and Buck denied that they were lesbians under oath. Subsequently, both women were sentenced to 109 days in jail for perjury when a disc jockey from a gay bar testified that Parsons and Buck were in the bar together numerous times. Since then both women, who are still in a relationship, have endured poverty, ridicule, and rejection by their families. Pam Parsons is a pariah in college women's basketball. Buck never finished college.

The *Charlotte Observer* did an extensive follow-up story on Pam Parsons in conjunction with the NCAA women's basketball Final Four in 1996 (L. Chandler 1996). The full-page story with several photographs of Parsons and Buck competed for space with the semifinal game results, engendering rage from many of the coaches and players at the championships. The story's placement and timing emphasized a link between lesbians and women's basketball in a negative way that enraged coaches and players and drives lesbian players and coaches deeper into the closet. The story also enflamed fears about lesbian coaches as sexual predators by validating parents' worst nightmares for their daughters' college athletic experiences. Unfortunately, Pam Parsons is the only publicly identified lesbian associated with women's college basketball. No other coaches, particularly in Division 1, have publicly identified themselves. Without other models, and given the persistence of the lesbian sexual predator stereotype, the media attention paid to Parsons and her relationship with Buck reinforces the perception that lesbian coaches are a dangerous sexual threat to their players, despite the hundreds of lesbian coaches who would never think of becoming sexually involved with a team member.

Compare the reaction to Pam Parsons's sexual involvement with an athlete with what happened at Oregon State University in 1991. A member of the women's volleyball team borrowed a teammate's car. In the glove compartment she found love letters from their coach, Guy Enriques, addressed to her teammate. Several members of the team had long suspected that the two were sexually involved. They had previously confronted Enriques, who was married with a child, with their suspicions, but he managed to deflect their concerns and made them feel bad for having these suspicions. With the letters as proof, the team went to the athletic director expecting Enriques to be fired. Instead, the athletic director told them nothing could be done since the letters were stolen. The players then confronted Enriques and asked him to resign. He protested, saying that this was a "real relationship" and that he and the player "really cared for each other." When the players threatened to go public with their demands, Enriques resigned for "personal reasons."

The athletic director, Dutch Baughman, accepted his resignation saying, "Please understand that this is a very delicate issue. He tendered the resignation for personal reasons, and I accepted it." Baughman told the team to keep the incident quiet and not to talk with the media about it. According to some of the players, Baughman told them, "Be smart about this. Some things are private. It is a small affair, don't blow it out of proportion. What is personal, should remain personal." If the players had not chosen to talk about it, the incident would never have been made public (Nelson 1994). No *Sports Illustrated*. No front-page story at the NCAA Volleyball Final Four. When a heterosexual male coach is caught, it is a delicate, private matter, not to be blown out of proportion. When a lesbian coach is caught it is an event worthy of national news coverage, and the coach must be punished and banished from the sport.

Mitch Ivey, a two-time Olympic swimmer and several-times coach of the women's Olympic swim team is another example of this double standard. Despite repeated relationships with several of his swimmers and a reputation for sexually harassing his swimmers, Ivey was respected in swimming circles and even hired as the women's swim coach at the University of Florida. He was offered this position despite their knowledge of his having been fired from a private swim club coaching position for being sexually involved with women swimmers on his teams. In 1991 and 1992 he was named Coach of the Year in the Southeastern Conference.

Not until after a 1993 ESPN program on coach-athlete abuse, which featured several of his former swimmers describing his abuse and harassment, did the University of Florida fire Ivey. For legal reasons, according to the Florida athletic director, Ivey was fired "without cause." As a result, he was paid for the two remaining years on his contract (Nelson 1994). Due to the testimony of his swimmers at the University of Florida, Ivey was finally fired. Yet these same swimmers issued a statement following his firing "completely" supporting Ivey "no matter what has been said." They went on to say, "He is one of the best swimming coaches in the world, and he is the reason we have developed into a team that is vying for a national title. We are stunned by this decision and feel very sorry that Mitch will be denied the opportunity to use his talents to better ours" (Brennan 1993, D5). This quote, from the women he sexually harassed, demonstrates the power that coaches have and the desire for excellence that motivates athletes to endure abuses of all kinds at the hands (sometimes literally) of an influential and domineering coach.

Compare the reactions to Parsons and Ivey: Parsons was ostracized by other coaches and effectively banned for life from coaching for her misuse of coaching power. No one in women's basketball spoke up in her behalf. Though it was well known in swimming circles that Ivey was sexually harassing his women athletes, he was hired and defended by university administrators, parents, and swimmers after his abuses became known until it became politically impractical to continue to support him. Even then he was defended by the women he harassed.

Reactions to and treatment of coaches who become sexually involved with athletes that differ based on the coaches' sex and sexuality reflect the assumption that men should have sexual access to women and that these relationships are "normal," even if inappropriate. Lesbian

relationships between coaches and athletes, on the other hand, are perceived as inherently exploitative and abnormal. Sexual relationships
between coaches and athletes are serious professional and ethical
breaches that need to be addressed regardless of the sex or sexual orientation of the people involved.

Sexual Relationships Between Coaches

The double standard for lesbians and heterosexuals extends to relationships between coaches. During the 1995-96 basketball season, much
media attention was focused on the married co-coaches of the University of San Francisco women's basketball team. The heterosexual married relationship between co-coaches Bill Nepfel and Mary Hile-Nepfel
was highlighted in several stories in the national and local press (Colino
1996; Curtis 1996; Gustkey 1995; Patrick 1996). In these news items, readers learned how the coaches met, how well they work together, and even
how they eat breakfast together. Originally, USF wanted to hire Mary as
the women's basketball coach. She had been an all-American player with
the USF team. When university officials found out that Mary was married to another basketball coach, they offered the job to both of them.
The Hile-Nepfels then decided to be co-coaches. In one news article the
co-coaches talked about how their heterosexual married status gave
them a "big edge in the recruiting area" (Gustkey 1995, C1):

> *"We fit into parents' comfort zones, when they are worried about sending
> their 17-year-old off someplace," Bill said, "They like the idea of their daughter
> playing for a married couple."*

Having a heterosexual married couple coaching a women's team was
probably perceived as a major public relations and recruiting bonanza
by the USF athletic department as well. What better way to reassure
parents and young athletes who worry about predatory lesbians in sport
than having coaches who create a "normal" family environment. Many
heterosexual married coaches highlight their married status in college
team media guides by including pictures of themselves with their heterosexual spouses and children. In contrast, heterosexual married
women coaches who choose not to use their marital status as a recruiting tool run the risk of having prospective athletes and their families
assume that they are lesbian.

At one university, where the marital status of the women coaches
(but not the men) was indicated on the athletic department phone list,
any coach without a Mrs. preceding her name was assumed to be a lesbian. An attempt to delete the marital status of women coaches resulted
in an offer to list all coaches, male and female, with their spouses' names

instead. Lesbian coaches pointed out that this would in effect require all of them to come out and possibly subject them and their programs to antilesbian discrimination. Including the partnered or marital status of any coach in a professional directory or media guide is extraneous information that serves no professional purpose other than to mark heterosexual, privileged status. In a heterosexist society, when the marital status of women is indicated, single women are often marked as potential lesbians in the eyes of parents and prospective athletes concerned about lesbian coaches.

Contrast the positive attention focused on Bill Nepfel and Mary Hile-Nepfel to the suspicions often raised about all-women coaching staffs. Innuendos and fears about lesbian relationships among an all-women coaching staff are often threats to recruiting. When lesbian partners are coaching a team together as head and assistant coach, this fact is hidden from the media and parents out of the fear of negative publicity that could jeopardize recruiting.

> At a big basketball tournament, we were in the hotel restaurant. The head coach and her assistant coach for the state university team were eating there too. Everyone knows they are a couple. It was so sad because, when they finished, one got up and left the table. The other one waited for a few minutes, then she got up and left too. I couldn't help thinking they were leaving separately so no one would see them leave the restaurant together and go to the same room.
> —*Division 2 basketball coach*

Coaches who are also partners sometimes maintain separate homes and studiously avoid being seen together in social settings or giving any public appearance of being more than professional associates. Some women head coaches, including some lesbian coaches, also prefer male assistant coaches to counteract any lesbian aura that might be associated with an all-women coaching staff.

The issue is not whether coaches are in relationships with each other or whether the coaches are lesbian or heterosexual. What is at issue is the contrast in the experiences of heterosexual married coaches and lesbian coaches who are partners. Bill Nepfel and Mary Hile-Nepfel use their heterosexual privilege very publicly as a positive recruiting tool and a way to attract favorable media attention to their program. Partnered lesbian coaches carefully hide their relationships to avoid media attention and the possibility of losing potential high school recruits. This double standard has nothing to do with the talent or character of the particular coaches involved. Instead, heterosexism and homophobia benefit heterosexual married coaches and punish lesbian partners who are coaching together.

Love and community are important to all of us regardless of our sexual identity. Sport has always played a special role in the lives of lesbian athletes in creating community and finding love. Despite the stigma attached to both lesbian community and love in sport, women have found ways to sustain themselves and each other in the face of prejudice and injustice. Lesbians have sustained themselves while making enormous contributions to the development of women's sport. It is to the discredit of athletic departments and sport organizations everywhere that lesbians are not acknowledged for their continuing contributions to women's sport but instead are pressured to hide their identities and relationships to protect their right to participate in sport. It is long past time to question the assumptions made about lesbians in sport and to take on the challenge to create a new vision of sport in which women athletes and coaches are judged on the basis of their competence and character rather than their sex or the sex of the people they love. How can we transform women's sport so that this vision can become reality? This is the subject of the next chapter.

11

Opening Minds, Opening Closet Doors:

Transforming Women's Sport

O ver the last 10 years, much has changed for lesbian, gay, and bisexual people in the United States. In 1987 only one state, Wisconsin, had a law prohibiting discrimination based on sexual orientation. As of fall 1997, there were 11 (California, Connecticut, Hawaii, Maine, Massachusetts, Minnesota, New Hampshire, New Jersey, Rhode Island, Vermont, and Wisconsin). In 1996 the Supreme Court ruled that it is unconstitutional to place lesbian, gay, and bisexual people outside the protection of the constitution as Colorado's Amendment 2 tried to do in 1992. Over 100 colleges and universities have included sexual orientation in their nondiscrimination policies. A Massachusetts State Department of Education program assists educators in making schools safe for lesbian, gay, and bisexual students. Increasing numbers of large private businesses, municipalities, and colleges and universities provide domestic partner benefits to same-sex couples. In California and Massachusetts the custody and adoption rights of lesbian and gay parents have been upheld. Hawaii might become the first state to recognize same-sex marriage. Iceland, Norway, Greenland, Denmark, and Sweden already recognize same-sex unions.

Ten years ago, it was surprising to see a single gay character on television or read about any gay-related topic in the newspaper. Now there are so many gay and lesbian characters on so many television shows, I can't keep up with them. There are so many news stories about lesbian and gay topics, I have given up reading them all.

To be sure, some groups, primarily those affiliated with right wing religious groups, strongly and vocally oppose these social changes. The opposition faced by President Clinton's original plan to drop the military ban against lesbian and gay service members and more recently the flurry of state and federal legislation reaffirming marriage as a heterosexual-only institution indicate that we have not reached anything close to a societal consensus on the rights of lesbian, gay, and bisexual people and families in the United States.

Nonetheless, most major institutions in the United States are grappling with lesbian and gay issues in some way: the military, the government, the legal system, health care, education, religion, and the media. Lesbian, bisexual, and gay people and the issues they raise for families, friends, and professional organizations are not going to go away. How can we think that athletics is exempt from this growing demand that we come to grips with integrating openly lesbian, bisexual, and gay people into U.S. culture? How can we think that athletics will evade the call to address the broad gap between our professional ideals of fairness and justice and our treatment of lesbian, gay, and bisexual athletes and coaches?

FROM CONDEMNATION TO AFFIRMATION

I think of transforming sport as a journey with several different stages. I believe it is important to "keep our eyes on the prize" as we move from stage to stage toward the goal of fully including women and men of all sexualities in sport. It is easy to be grateful for tolerance when we live with condemnation, but tolerance is not our ultimate goal. Institutional protection against discrimination is better than relying on individual tolerance, but recognizing lesbian participation in sport as a positive presence is even better. However, when we live with condemnation, it is difficult to envision the affirmation we deserve.

Tolerance

For the most part, lesbians in athletics participate in an atmosphere of conditional tolerance. This tolerance is based on our willingness to be invisible. Though preferable to condemnation, tolerance implies "putting up with" someone or some value without actual acceptance. Tolerance creates a power dynamic in which those tolerating can withdraw that tolerance at any time. Tolerance encourages a dependent relationship in which the tolerated feel pressure to conform to the expectations of and to be grateful to the tolerant. Tolerance of lesbian, gay, and bisexual athletes and coaches might be a transitional stop on our journey out of condemnation and hostility, but it is not the final destination. Without institutional policy and legal protection against discrimination, tolerance provides lesbians in sport with only a tenuous foothold on a slippery cliff.

Nondiscrimination

The next step toward transformation is to develop and enforce institutional policies that protect lesbian, gay, and bisexual people in athletics from discrimination and harassment. Over the last few years right wing religious and political forces in the United States have promoted the notion that only certain groups have a legitimate claim to civil rights protection (Herman 1997). According to their criteria, lesbian, gay, and bisexual people are not among the so-called legitimate minority groups who deserve civil rights. Nonetheless, national surveys consistently reveal that most Americans are opposed to discrimination against lesbian, gay, and bisexual people, even though they may not be comfortable with homosexuality (Turque 1992). These polls reflect a widespread belief that discrimination based on social-group membership rather than individual conduct and character is wrong. While nondiscrimination policies do not address underlying hostile or prejudiced beliefs about lesbians, they do provide lesbian athletes and coaches with institutional leverage for challenging discrimination based on this prejudice.

Nondiscrimination policies require that coaches who have antilesbian beliefs separate these values from their professional responsibility to provide safety and fair treatment to all athletes and colleagues. Nondiscrimination policies and laws formalize legal protections that are not present in an atmosphere where tolerance depends on individual goodwill. This institutional protection is important, and the adoption of antidiscrimination and antiharassment policies in all aspects of athletics will go a long way toward changing the lives of lesbian athletes and coaches, but this should not be our ultimate goal. As long as lesbians are tolerated only on the condition of invisibility, using antidiscrimination policies to protest unfair treatment will be risky because protesting discrimination requires that lesbians come out publicly.

Full Inclusion

Lesbian, gay, and bisexual people in athletics deserve full inclusion as equal partners in sport, not mere tolerance protected by nondiscrimination policies. By full inclusion I mean the expectation that lesbians will be safe and treated fairly. Nondiscrimination policies will be available if needed, but people's belief in the importance of respect for diversity and social justice will guide interactions and institutional decisions. Full inclusion does not necessarily mean approval. In a society with so many conflicting values and beliefs, it is both unrealistic and unnecessary to win approval in order to achieve full inclusion. In an inclusive atmosphere lesbians will be respected for their individual competence and character, even by those whose personal convictions lead them to disapprove of lesbians' life choices and identities.

Affirmation

We are so far from affirming lesbian presence in sport that it is difficult to imagine, but I believe lesbians must be affirmed for our unique contributions to sport. Lesbians in sport have much to be proud of, and these accomplishments need to be publicly honored. Our commitment and dedication to creating and sustaining sport opportunities for girls and women form a strong foundation of support for all we have achieved in women's sports.

Our affirmation should not be based on our ability to present ourselves as "just like" heterosexuals. One of the important roles that lesbi-

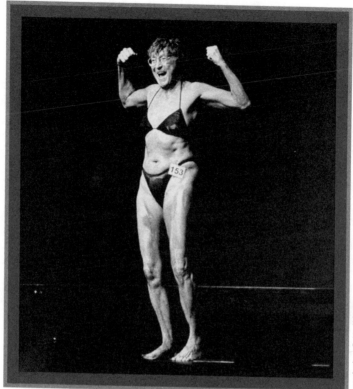

Photo by Joan Bobkoff © 1994

1994 Gay Games in New York City. Physique competition.

ans and gay men have played in the 20th century is to challenge norma-
tive conceptions of gender and sexuality. We have always lived on or
outside the margins of what is acceptable for women. Our very existence challenges the "naturalness" of femininity for women, masculinity
for men, and heterosexuality for all. As these boundaries are challenged,
other women and men are freer to express their gender and sexuality in
more varied and personally congruent ways rather than accept without
question what society dictates. The open participation of lesbian, gay,
bisexual, and transgender coaches and athletes will ultimately transform sport as artificial barriers based on confining expectations and
privileges of gender and sexuality fall.

Affirmation also invites us to understand the interconnections and
complexities of all aspects of who we are, not only our gender and sexuality, but also our race, religion, ability, age, and social class. The more
we can consciously live in our multiple identities, the more opportunities we have for finding common ground with others, and the more likely
we are to understand the social injustices that limit some of us and

Photo by Joan Bobkoff © 1994

Cyclist competing in the 1994 Gay Games in New York City.

advantage others. Recognizing how complex and varied our individual identity profiles are enables us to build better bridges of understanding to others who are different in some ways and similar in others.

Affirmation means a change in how lesbians in sport think about themselves. We have internalized so much shame living in a lesbian-hating culture that many of us cannot imagine life outside the closet, much less that we deserve to live as out and visibly as we choose to. We have little belief in our right to live openly nor do we have much faith in our heterosexual colleagues' sense of justice to support a sustained attack on our own closet doors. Simply put, more lesbians in sport need to come out publicly. Several research studies support the belief that one of the most effective ways to open minds is to open closet doors (Grack and Richman 1996; Herek 1994; Herek and Capitanio 1996). There is every reason to believe that this relationship between coming out and changing negative perceptions about lesbians will hold true in sport as well.

OBSTACLES TO TRANSFORMATION

I want to reintroduce a phrase from chapter 9, "unplayable lies," to describe several beliefs that present obstacles to transforming sport. These unplayable lies are assumptions that must be challenged as part of our journey toward transformation.

Unplayable Lie 1: Women in sport must present a public image that is feminine and heterosexual.

Women's sport advocates have spent 100 years defensively promoting an image of women athletes as feminine and heterosexual to gain some modest degree of public acceptance. We have always been on the defensive about our sport participation as we have responded to suspicions about our "normality" (femininity and heterosexuality). Though social expectations of women have changed over the years as more women take advantage of the increased opportunities to be athletes, we are not all heterosexual and we are not all feminine. Let's stop pretending and being defensive about the diversity of who we are.

Unplayable Lie 2: No one knows there are lesbians in sport (the hypocrisy of the glass closet).

A dance between lesbians and nonlesbians is required to avoid acknowledging the presence of lesbians in sport. The paradox is that everyone knows or suspects that there are lesbians in sport. People also know that many of us are pretending to be straight or at least trying to avoid being identified as gay. As long as we stay in the closet, however, a tentative bargain is struck. The glass-closet bargain requires a delicate equilibrium that allows lesbians to participate in sport and heterosexuals to ignore lesbian presence and their own prejudices against lesbians. The theory is that as long as we all keep the bargain, we can play or work together. The glass closet requires a bond of hypocrisy between the lesbians in the closet and everyone else outside of it. The problem is that the glass closet is a bad bargain for all women in sport. Suspicions about women athletes never go away. Women in sport are still fighting for equality. Lesbian baiting is still used to control all women in sport.

Unplayable Lie 3: The glass closet provides protection from discrimination.

Hiding one's lesbian identity seems to provide some illusion of protection. There are real dangers for some lesbians in being publicly identified: physical danger and danger of harassment and discrimination. Because we have no legal protection against discrimination in most states, lesbians are vulnerable to accusations and suspicions. Many people are willing to tolerate a lesbian presence in sport as long as lesbians remain closeted and do not ask for legal or policy protections and privileges that heterosexuals take for granted, such as nondiscrimination and antiharassment laws, health care benefits for partners, and freedom to talk about one's family and partner. Because we depend so heavily on this fragile silence of the closet for protection, we are reluctant to publicly fight even the most blatant discrimination.

It is difficult to challenge discrimination or harassment from the closet. Lesbians in the closet can always be silenced with the threat of exposure. If someone chooses to reach into our closet or threaten to wrench the door off its hinges, many closeted lesbians see no response other than to find another closet in another school or even another profession. Anyone can use our silence against us for any reason: a short haircut, a losing season, not enough playing time, being cut from the team.

Unplayable Lie 4: Lesbians are to blame for image problems in women's sports.

Lesbians are frequently blamed for the general public's slow acceptance of women's sports or for giving a particular program, team, or professional tour a bad image.

The truth is that, despite the confinement of the closet, lesbians in sport have made, and continue to make, vital contributions to our fields. We have been among the brave pioneers and relentless advocates for women's sports. We are revered champions, insightful leaders, and beloved mentors and role models. It is impossible to talk about all of the accomplishments of women in sport without talking about lesbians. As lesbian newspaper columnist, Deb Price (1995), said in encouraging lesbians on the LPGA tour to come out, "It is not easy to swing a club in the closet," but lesbians in sport have done that and more for years.

The truth is that what hampers women's sport is our collective willingness to accept, and even embrace, the sexist boundaries of what is acceptable for women by acting as if the femininity or heterosexuality of women in sport is important. Our defensiveness about whether or not we fit into these prescribed gender and sexuality roles restricts our sport experiences and limits our ability to accept the truth of our diversity. I long for the day when spokespeople for women's sports stop acting as if lesbian athletes and coaches are dirty or scary secrets that threaten to ruin women's sport and instead proudly acknowledge and affirm our diversity.

Unplayable Lie 5: The interest of lesbians and heterosexual women in sport are at odds.

Blaming lesbians for creating a bad image for sport deepens divisions between lesbian and heterosexual women. Potential political alliances among women that could benefit women's sport are weakened, and individual relationships among women athletes and coaches are stigmatized. When heterosexual women condemn lesbians or insist on lesbian invisibility in sport, they give power to anyone who would use the lesbian label to control or contain women's sport.

We must understand the interconnections among sexism, homophobia, and heterosexism and how the intersection of these systems of injustice disadvantage all women in sport before we will stand together united against them.

Unplayable Lie 6: A woman's sexual orientation is a private issue.

Perhaps in a world where sexual diversity is welcomed, lesbian identity would be only a private matter, but we are a long way from that world today. By claiming that a coach's sexual orientation is a personal or private matter, we justify the expectation that lesbians in sport should remain silent and invisible. If this really were merely a private matter, it might make sense to keep a separation between our personal and professional lives. However, charges of lesbianism are used against women in sport in very public ways. Discrimination and harassment are not private issues. They are professional issues, which should be a concern to all fair-minded people.

Insisting that lesbian identity is solely a private matter effectively takes any discussion about heterosexism and homophobia in sport off of the professional table. The belief that discrimination and harassment of lesbians in sport are inappropriate professional topics is justified on the basis that sexual identity is a personal and private issue. Even some lesbian coaches claim that being gay has nothing to do with their professional lives, yet in the next sentence they describe horrendous tales of bigotry and prejudice directed at them in the workplace despite their silence and supposed invisibility. Lesbians are entitled to as much privacy as anyone else, but secrecy and invisibility should not be misinterpreted as voluntarily chosen privacy. If we are to address discrimination against lesbians in sport and if we are to expose the ways that antilesbian prejudice supports sexism in sport, we need to stop claiming that sexual orientation is merely a personal issue. These are policy issues and social justice issues, similar to racism or sexism.

There is also a double standard related to the appropriateness of talking about sexual identity in sport. While lesbians are pressured into silence, heterosexuals won't shut up. Lesbians who are open about their sexual identity or who insist that their civil rights be protected are often said to be inappropriately "flaunting" their "lifestyle" or are called "activists," as if this was an insulting epithet. Meanwhile heterosexual colleagues who wear wedding rings, display family pictures on desks or in team media guides, and talk about their families and relationships are not seen as activists flaunting their "lifestyle," they are just sharing. We must see the importance of lesbians in sport choosing to live openly as one way to counter stereotypes and to escape the spirit-crushing effects of living a secret life.

Unplayable Lie 7: Lesbians in sport are a non-issue.

When LPGA officials and players claim that lesbianism on the tour is a non-issue, this is wishful thinking. This so-called non-issue was reported and analyzed in the sports and general news for several days, and follow-up stories appeared in the mainstream and sports press for a month after the first Ben Wright article appeared. If lesbian golfers really are a non-issue, the LPGA wouldn't be so concerned about the tour's image, more lesbian golfers would be publicly out, and no one would worry about the effects of publicly out lesbian golfers on corporate sponsors or attendance at tour events. If this was a non-issue, more Olympians, college coaches and athletes, and professional players in basketball and other sports would be out.

Unplayable Lie 8: Talking about lesbians in sport is talking about sex.

When the topic of homosexuality is raised, many people immediately think of sex. Our professional dialogue about heterosexism and lesbians in sport is not about sex. When the full, rich lives of lesbians are reduced to sex, we are dehumanized, and privacy issues are confused with social justice issues. Professional discussions about lesbians in sport are about prejudice, discrimination, stereotypes, bigotry, fear, and hatred. These discussions are also about safety, fair treatment, equal access, and education. All of these issues are of vital concern to a profession that aspires, as we do in sport, to treat people with dignity and fairness.

Unplayable Lie 9: Talking about lesbians and heterosexism in sport is "promoting a lifestyle."

Fundamentalist Christian political groups have successfully defined and divided the debate about gay rights in the United States into two polarized perspectives: condemning "special rights" for gay people versus "promoting a gay lifestyle." Any positive or even neutral discussion of homosexuality in this debate is framed as promoting homosexuality. Either you condemn gay rights or you are promoting a lifestyle. In this either/or frame, there are no other alternatives. The fear of being perceived as "promoting a gay lifestyle" intimidates corporate sponsors, athletic directors, coaches, and anyone else who attempts to address lesbian and gay issues in any way other than the strictest condemnatory terms. We need another, more humane and realistic frame for this discussion. When we talk about protecting lesbian athletes and coaches from discrimination, we are not talking about special rights—we are talking about civil rights. We are not talking about promoting a lifestyle—we are talking about insisting on the right of lesbians in sport to safety, fair treatment, and equal access. This discussion is not about approval or condemnation; it is about nondiscrimination and recognition of our differences. We must create the intellectual space for people in athletics to break out of this win-lose, condemnation-promotion framework constructed by religious political extremists.

Unplayable Lie 10: Your daughter will/will not become a lesbian if she plays sports.

Sport does not cause lesbianism, but some young women do identify themselves as lesbians while they are playing sports. This is true, and we must stop supporting the lie that it isn't. My friend Jim Genasci once told a group of coaches that he wished that he had been better prepared to be the father of a gay son. He wished that, along with the other educational brochures for new parents available in the hospital waiting room, there had been one telling parents that your daughter or son might be lesbian, gay, or bisexual. Jim said that if he had had more information and if he hadn't been led to believe that having a gay son was a shameful tragedy, perhaps he wouldn't have wasted so much time before accepting his son just as he is.

One of the tragedies of living in a culture that teaches us to fear, judge, or hate lesbian, gay, or bisexual people is that losing parents' love is one of the deepest fears of many lesbian athletes and coaches. Unfortunately, lesbian and gay young people often feel like aliens in their own families and do not receive the love and support that parents and siblings can provide.

Much of the antilesbian discrimination in college sports is justified by appealing to the sensibilities of parents who do not want their daughters associating with lesbians or who are afraid their daughters will be lesbians. Parents need to learn that having a lesbian or bisexual daughter is not the tragedy they have learned that it is. Millions of parents around the world are learning that their lesbian, gay, and bisexual children are happy, productive people and the quality of a relationship is more important than the sex of the people involved. International organizations such as Parents, Families and Friends of Lesbians and Gays (PFLAG) provide support and education for parents who seek help answering their questions and facing their fears. Athletic departments need to begin taking a stronger role in condemning rather than silently condoning the discriminatory practices of some coaches who play on these parental fears and prejudices.

STRATEGIES FOR TRANSFORMING SPORT

What strategies will help to challenge these unplayable lies and transform the climate for lesbians in sport from condemnation or tolerance to affirmation? I have a few suggestions. There is nothing innovative about these strategies. Most have been used by other social change movements and in the broader lesbian, gay, and bisexual rights movement. Perhaps listing them and applying them specifically to sport will encourage others who share this vision for transforming sport to find a place where they can join in the journey.

Education

I strongly believe in the effectiveness of education about social justice issues. A number of different constituencies can benefit from education about heterosexism, sexism, homophobia, and other social justice and diversity issues in sport: coaches, athletic department administrators, other athletic staff, athletes and their parents. In addition, education can benefit sport advocacy organizations, athletic conference administrators, and coaches' association leadership. Sports reporters, TV commentators, and other media personnel can benefit from this education as well. Sport psychologists and mental health counselors who work with athletes also need to develop an understanding of these issues as they work with athletes or coaches.

- Educators can develop material about heterosexism, racism, sexism, sexual harassment, religious discrimination, and classism for athletes and their families.
- Athletic departments can provide educational workshops focused on social justice and diversity for athletes, coaches, and other athletic department personnel.
- Athletic administrators and coaches can identify campus and community resources for a range of social justice and diversity issues and provide a list to athletes and coaches.
- Administrators and coaches can identify social justice and diversity resources on the Internet (listservs, bulletin boards, Web sites).
- Administrators and coaches can collect a departmental resource library of books, videos, and magazines that address social justice and diversity issues in athletics.
- Faculty members can develop and teach courses on social justice and diversity issues in athletics for athletes and other students.
- Athletic conference leaders, coaches' associations, athletic administrators' organizations, and sport advocacy groups can sponsor

educational programs focused on social justice and diversity in athletics.

Information

Research focused on heterosexism, homophobia, and lesbians in sport is in its infancy. Partly due to fear of stigmatization and negative sanctions or lack of institutional support, sport researchers have only begun to develop a body of literature about these topics. We have much to learn, for example, about how heterosexism and homophobia affect women's sport participation and how educational programs about heterosexism and homophobia in athletics change individual perceptions and behavior or institutional policy. Developing a research-based body of knowledge about these topics will provide guidance for institutional decision making and education.

- Academic faculty can conduct and sponsor graduate student research on social justice and diversity issues in athletics.
- Athletic department administrators and coaches can invite researchers to use the athletic context to study social justice and diversity issues in sport (with athletes' consent, of course).
- Corporate sponsors interested in athletics can sponsor research on social justice and diversity issues in sport.
- Academic conferences can be organized to disseminate research on social justice and diversity issues in athletics.

Legislation

An important aspect of addressing heterosexism and homophobia in sport is recognizing that interventions are needed at both the individual level (education) and institutional level. Athletic departments can take the following actions:

- Adopt or amend nondiscrimination policies to specifically include sexual orientation.
- Develop specific procedures and guidelines for the implementation of already-existing university nondiscrimination policies.
- Develop antiharassment policies that address harassment based on sexual orientation, race, sex, and religion as well as specific procedures for implementing these policies.
- Adopt coaching ethics policies that address ethical violations by any coach, without regard to sexual identity or sex.
- Implement domestic partner benefits policies.

Institutionalization

In addition to developing policies, there are a number of other ways to institutionalize a concern for social justice in athletics.

- Create a standing committee of coaches and athletes that focuses on social justice and diversity issues in athletics (racism, sexual harassment, gender equity, heterosexism, and homophobia, for example).
- Organize or identify existing support groups for potentially marginalized athletes: lesbians and gays, students of color, students from religious minorities, students from poor or working-class families, students with disabilities.
- Develop an ongoing series of educational events focused on a variety of social justice issues in athletics.
- Conduct annual new athlete and coach orientation sessions to make new members of the department aware of nondiscrimination, antiharassment, and coaching ethics policies, as well as campus and community resources related to social justice and diversity issues.
- Review all department materials and procedures to identify changes needed to make athletics more welcoming and safer for all athletes and coaches.
- Develop procedures for reviewing all personnel decisions for bias, conscious or unconscious.
- Develop material for parents and prospective athletes about department philosophy and perspectives on social justice and diversity issues.
- Identify and develop relationships with campus and community resources for potentially marginalized athletes and coaches (lesbians, gay men, bisexuals, people of color, working class or poor, religious minorities, people with disabilities).

Connection

Developing relationships across differences is an important aspect of transforming sport and encouraging social justice.

- Identify ways for athletes and coaches to socialize and get to know others who are different from them.
- Identify ways for coaches and athletes to learn about the cultures and experiences of others who are different from them.

- Identify specific projects related to social justice and diversity that athletes or coaches can work on together.
- Organize intergroup dialogues among coaches and athletes (people of color and white people, gay and straight, men and women, for example).

Agitation

Sometimes it is necessary to apply pressure to encourage organizations or individuals to take social justice and diversity concerns more seriously.

- Form a political action group focused on monitoring social justice issues in athletics.
- Write letters, send faxes, and make phone calls to express your social justice concerns to athletic department leaders.
- Write letters to the editors of local newspapers about your concerns for social justice in athletics.
- Organize a demonstration at an athletic event.
- Distribute posters or flyers describing your concerns and identify ways people can help.
- Contact campus or community organizations that can assist you: Affirmative Action office, office of human relations, ombuds office, civil rights office, women's center, lesbian/gay/bisexual center, commission against discrimination.
- Work in coalition with other groups to address each other's social justice concerns (athletes of color and lesbian, gay, and bisexual athletes; women of color and white women, for instance).

Visibility

Two kinds of visibility are important. First, lesbian, gay, and bisexual athletes and coaches need to be more visible. Though every context is different and some are safer than others, there are many ways in which lesbian, gay, and bisexual athletes and coaches can increase their visibility and the visibility of issues related to heterosexism and homophobia: Come out; object to antigay jokes and comments; challenge discrimination and harassment; ask for heterosexism and homophobia seminars. Second, heterosexual women and men can act as allies by speaking out against antigay actions and policies in athletics. I cannot stress enough the importance of heterosexual coaches and athletes who speak out against antilesbian discrimination and prejudice. The visibility of heterosexual allies makes sport more welcoming for all women and disarms the power of the lesbian label to intimidate all women. Particularly in hostile situations where lesbian, gay, and bisexual people have no protection against discrimination, heterosexual allies have an important role to play in addressing heterosexism and homophobia in athletics.

- More lesbian, gay, and bisexual athletes and coaches must come out to friends, teammates, and colleagues.
- Everyone can object to antigay actions, slurs, or policies.
- Heterosexual allies must support lesbian, gay, and bisexual colleagues and teammates by learning more about heterosexism and homophobia.
- Everyone can make sure heterosexism and homophobia are addressed in any program about social justice and diversity in athletics.

AGENTS OF CHANGE

A number of people in athletics, sport studies, and education are already addressing heterosexism and homophobia in athletics. Though this list does not include all people who are addressing these issues, the women and men listed here are working toward changing the climate in athletics and increasing the attention paid to making athletics more welcoming to everyone regardless of sex or sexuality.

Helen Carroll: As an out lesbian and athletic director at Mills College in Oakland, California, Helen speaks out to athletic directors, coaches, and community groups about homophobia and heterosexism in sport. She developed an innovative educational program at Mills in which athletic teams identify a social justice issue and plan a seminar for all coaches and athletes on that topic. Topics addressed over the years include racism, eating disorders among athletes, and homophobia.

Kathy Henderson: Kathy is an out lesbian athletic director and coach at Phillips Andover Academy in Massachusetts. Kathy is the cofounder of GLSTN (Gay, Lesbian, Straight Teacher's Network), a national support, education, and advocacy organization addressing heterosexism in schools. Kathy is a powerful role model for lesbian, bisexual, and heterosexual athletes in her school. As an out high school coach, by her personal example Kathy counteracts lesbian stereotypes and provides leadership for other educators and coaches.

Mariah Burton Nelson: Mariah is a former professional basketball player and is now an openly lesbian, best-selling author who writes about women and sport. Her first two books, *Are We Winning Yet? How Women are Changing Sports and Sports are Changing Women* and *The Stronger Women Get, the More Men Love Football: Sexism and the American Culture of Sport,* have affected the lives of thousands of women and men in sport and their families. She is a role model for lesbians in sport and an insightful feminist critic of sexism and heterosexism in sport.

Jean and Jim Genasci: Jean is a former school librarian, and Jim is a retired professor of physical education at Springfield College in Massachusetts. They are also the parents of a gay son, which led to their involvement and leadership in Parents, Families and Friends of Lesbians and Gays (PFLAG). Jean and Jim are activists against heterosexism and homophobia and allies to lesbian, gay, bisexual, and transgender people. Jim and Jean have organized educational programs for addressing homophobia in sport for a number of years and speak all over the United States about heterosexism in education and sport. They started the first support group for lesbian, gay, and bisexual people at Springfield College and have helped hundreds of families learn to love and accept lesbian, gay, bisexual, and transgender children, parents, and spouses.

Judy Bourell-Miller and Bob Miller: Judy is an associate professor of physical education, and Bob is the former women's basketball coach at Eastern Connecticut State University. For a number of years they have been a visible source of support for lesbian and gay athletes on campus. Judy now conducts workshops on homophobia in sport for colleges and professional associations around the country. Judy and Bob are excellent models for the effectiveness of heterosexual allies in addressing homophobia and heterosexism.

Helen Lenskyj: Helen is a Canadian writer and researcher who has been one of the pioneers in speaking out against homophobia in women's sport. Her analysis of homophobia, heterosexism, and sexism in sport have provided guidance for other feminist researchers who follow.

Donna Lopiano: As the executive director of the Women's Sports Foundation, Donna has taken an active leadership role in speaking out about a number of social justice issues in women's sport. She is outspoken in her opposition to homophobia and heterosexism, and the WSF under her leadership has developed a resource manual for addressing homophobia in women's sport and is a model in this area for other sport organizations.

Dee Mosbacher: Dee is a producer of documentary films about lesbian and gay issues. She is also a former college athlete who, inspired by both a former coach's and her own experiences as a lesbian in athletics, produced an award-winning educational film on homophobia in women's sports entitled *Out for a Change: Addressing Homophobia in Women's Sports* (Mosbacher 1992). This video and accompanying discussion guide are used in college and high school classes and with athletes and coaches around the United States. Dee plans to make a future video on homophobia in men's sport.

Carole Oglesby: Carole was the first president of the Association of Intercollegiate Athletics for Women (AIAW) and is a feminist pioneer in women's sport. It is impossible to read about the development of women's sport without encountering Carole's work. She is currently a sport psychologist at Temple University. Carole was the chair of the committee that put together the Women's Sports Foundation resource manual on homophobia in women's sport and is now involved in a research project about lesbian moral exemplars in sport.

Molly O'Neil and Maggie King: Molly and Maggie are the founders and guiding force behind Husky Hoops, a lesbian fan club for the University of Washington women's basketball team. Husky Hoops presents a visible lesbian presence at UW games and initiated a dialogue with the coach of the women's team about homophobia and lesbian athletes. Molly and Maggie are also a visible presence at the Women's Basketball Final Four and Women's Basketball Coaches Association (WBCA) convention every year, pushing the WBCA to address homophobia and acknowledge lesbians in basketball. They sponsor a booth in the exhibit area called "Block Out Homophobia" and distribute educational information on homophobia in sport to coaches and athletes.

Sue Rankin: Sue is the former Penn State University softball coach. She is now a senior diversity planning analyst in the Office of the Vice Provost for Educational Equity at Penn State. Sue came out as a lesbian while she was coaching and was probably one of the very few, if not the only, openly lesbian Division 1 coaches at the time. Her courageous, pioneering visibility provided a role model for other coaches and athletes. She now continues her work in addressing heterosexism and homophobia in athletics by speaking to campus groups around the United States and writing on this topic for professional publications.

Roxxie: Roxxie is the editor of *Girljock,* an unapologetic, in-your-face magazine for young lesbian (and heterosexual ally) athletes. Each issue includes articles and information about and of interest to lesbian athletes. *Girljock* is irreverent and celebrates lesbians and their sport experiences. Roxxie is also one of the organizers of an annual soccer tournament in the San Francisco Bay Area, the Festival of the Babes, which is advertised as a tournament for lesbians and "heterosexual women who don't mind if people think they are lesbians."

Courtesy of Roxxie

Roxxie (in the front) and supporters of Girljock.

Don Sabo: Don's groundbreaking research and writing on masculinity and sport from a profeminist perspective has led the way for a number of other men interested in exploring these issues. He is a sociologist at D'Youville College in Buffalo, New York. Don has worked with the Women's Sports Foundation for a number of years and is an insightful heterosexual male ally on issues of sexism and heterosexism in sport.

THE IMPORTANCE OF VISION

Martin Luther King described the importance of having a dream about what the realization of our goals for social justice would look like. We need to hold out a similar vision of what social justice for lesbians in sport would be.

My vision includes many more lesbian athletes and coaches choosing to come out. Part of this vision means that lesbians in sport have a real choice to disclose their identities, just as heterosexuals do, rather than misinterpreting enforced invisibility and secrecy as privacy. In my vision our choices will not be predicated on avoiding discrimination or harassment. I envision a sense of unity and community among women athletes based on a common joy in and love of sport. This unity will not require agreement on all things, but will be based on respect and understanding across our differences (gender, race, sexuality, age, class, religion, ability) and our commitment to work together without needing to erase our differences in order to be unified. Social justice is a foundation of my vision of the transformation of women's sport. This means that we will not only respect differences, but also understand the historical and social context that privileges some social groups over others and the power dynamics that disadvantage women in relation to men, women of color in relation to white women, lesbian and bisexual women in relation to heterosexual women, poor and working-class women in relation to middle-class and wealthy women. With this recognition will come a commitment to address these inequities through institutional policy and individual interaction. Women in sport will understand that addressing multiple issues of social justice is necessary for real social change and that this benefits all women.

In my vision women will take pride in our athleticism without apology. Women will not be constrained by socially constructed notions of femininity or compulsory heterosexuality. There will be no need to apologize about muscularity, physical competence, or passion for and commitment to sport. We will brazenly celebrate our athleticism and the joy that we find in sport.

In my vision of sport, women will value our relationships with other women. We will not be self-conscious about loving teammates and competitors as friends or lovers. We will value our relationships across differences of sexuality, religion, race, and class. Women will have equal access to resources. It will be a given that all women have access to sport participation at whatever level they choose.

Several years ago I attended a talk by Virginia Apuzzo, a lesbian activist who was the executive director of the National Gay Task Force in the 1970s. She described a conference phone call she had with several leaders of the black civil rights movement who were planning a march on Washington to celebrate the 20th anniversary of the 1963 March on Washington at which Martin Luther King gave his "I have a dream" speech. The march organizers had invited a variety of people representing a number of oppressed groups to speak at the rally following the march, but they had not invited any openly lesbian or gay speakers.

The purpose of the conference call was for Apuzzo to make a case to the march organizers that it was important to include an openly lesbian or gay person of color as a rally speaker, which—after painful consideration—they decided to do. In describing this conference call, Apuzzo told how these leaders of a national civil rights movement struggled with this challenge: their gut-level homophobia competing with their intellectual commitment to social justice and their knowledge of the presence of lesbian, gay, and bisexual people in the African-American community. There was a long silence in the conversation. Apuzzo described this pause as "the silence of good people struggling to live up to their ideals." I was struck by this phrase then, and I think it applies to many of us in women's sport now.

I would like to pose a challenge to all of us who care about women's sport to engage in this struggle to live up to our ideal of creating athletic climates in which social justice is an essential foundation. Future generations of young girls and women in sport are depending on us.

I am thinking about a young girl I know who fell in love with basketball in the fourth grade. She soaks up any instruction about how to shoot and dribble and drive. We are in her backyard shooting hoops on the small asphalt "court" her mother had paved for her birthday. It is dusk now, and I can barely see the ball, but still she shoots and shoots, the ball ripping softly through the net. Perhaps in her mind she is in the Final Four, the final seconds, the score is tied. She drives, weaving around the defense, pump fakes, and gently lays the ball off the backboard into the basket. The crowd goes wild.

In the gathering dusk I see a little girl with big dreams standing at the foul line, her attention focused intently on the basket far above her head. As I watch her, I smile in recognition. I know a sister when I see one. Another young woman, another generation, whose heart is filled with a passion for sport. We play one on one for awhile in silence. Letting the love and joy in the game speak for us. We both know the language.

My wish for my young friend is that she will never have to apologize for her passion. That the legacy of fear and apology will not be passed on. That no matter whom she chooses to love, she will be welcomed into sport and affirmed for the strong woman she will be. That she will welcome other women who are different from her. For her and her generation of strong women, I wish no more closets, deep or shallow, glass or steel.

We play on until the darkness finally drives us, sweaty and content, inside for dinner. I gently hand her the ball as we leave our game and suddenly feel as if this simple act is a symbolic passing of sport experience on to the next generation. I want to tell her that I've done what I can to make it easier for her to be a strong, athletic woman than it was for my generation. I suddenly see a line of strong women, each in turn passing balls or bats or goggles or cleats to the next young woman in line. I know that if I told her my thoughts, she would think I am "weird," as she would say. So I smile to myself and breathe deep the crisp, New England autumn air.

References

Acosta, V., and L. Carpenter. 1985. Women in athletics: A status report. *Journal of Health, Physical Education, Recreation and Dance* 56 (6): 30-37.

Anderson, L., and L. Randlet. 1994. Self-monitoring, perceived control and satisfaction with self-disclosure of sexual orientation. *Journal of Social Behavior and Personality* 9 (4): 789-800.

Arguelles, L., and A. Rivero. 1996. Queer everyday life: Some religious and spiritual dynamics. In *The new lesbian studies,* ed. B. Zimmerman and T. McNaron. New York: Feminist Press.

Associated Press. 1990. Navratilova called poor role model: Homosexual lifestyle hit. *Chicago Tribune,* 12 July, 2C.

Associated Press. 1995a. LPGA calls charges "absurd and ugly." The News and Observer Publishing Co., 13 May.

Associated Press. 1995b. LPGA-lesbianism. 15 May. Available: LGB-sports listserv, http://www.kwic.net/lgb-sports/.

Athletes in Action. 1996. Home page [cited 21 October 1996, last update 9 October 1996]. Available: http://www.aiasports.org/aia/.

Axthelm, P. 1974. Sportsmanlike conduct. *Newsweek,* 3 June, 50-55.

———. 1981. The case of Billie Jean King. *Newsweek,* 18 May, 133.

Ballinger, W. 1932. Spinster factories. *Forum* 87 (5): 301-304.

Baughman, C. 1995. *Women on ice: Feminist essays on the Tonya Harding/Nancy Kerrigan spectacle.* New York: Routledge.

Beach, B. 1981. A disputed love match. *Time,* 11 May, 77.

Bell, A., M. Weinberg, and S. Hammersmith. 1981. *Sexual preference: Its development in men and women.* Bloomington: University of Indiana.

Bellant, R. 1995. Promise Keepers. In *Eyes right: Challenging the right wing backlash,* ed. C. Berlet. Boston: South End Press.

Bennett, R., G. Whitaker, N. Smith, and A. Sablove. 1987. Changing the rules of the game: Reflections toward a feminist analysis of sport. *Women's Studies International Forum* 10 (4): 369-380.

Berlet, C., ed. 1995. *Eyes right: Challenging the right wing backlash.* Boston: South End Press.

Berube, A. 1990. *Coming out under fire: The history of gay men and women in World War Two.* New York: Free Press.

Birrell, S., and C. Coles. 1994. *Women, sport and culture.* Champaign, IL: Human Kinetics.

Blinde, E., and D. Taub. 1992. Women athletes as falsely accused deviants: Managing the lesbian stigma. *Sociological Quarterly* 33(4): 521-534.

Blount, R. 1995. PR bomb becomes PR boon for LPGA. *Star Tribune* (Minneapolis), 9 June, 2C.

Blumenfeld, W., ed. 1992. *Homophobia: How we all pay the price.* Boston: Beacon.

Bohis, K., and M. Wangrin. 1993. Diversity creates dilemma for Lady Horns. *Austin American-Statesman,* 3 August, C1, C3.

Bondy, F. 1993. When coaches cross the line. *New York Times,* 2 March, Sports section, 1, 3.

Brady, E. 1997. Colleges score low on gender-equity test. *USA Today,* 3 March, C1, C4.

Brennan, C. 1993. An exercise in self-control. *Washington Post,* 25 December, D1, D5.

———. 1996. *Inside edge: A revealing journey into the secret world of figure skating.* New York: Scribner.

Browne, D. 1996. Sport extremist. *New York Times Magazine,* 19 May, 30-33.

Brownworth, V. 1994. The competitive closet. In *Sportsdykes,* ed. S.F. Rogers. New York: St. Martin's.

Bryson, L. 1990. Challenges to male hegemony in sport. In *Sport, men and the gender order: Critical feminist perspectives,* edited by D. Sabo and M. Messner. Champaign, IL: Human Kinetics.

Bull, C. 1991. Bias allegations make Pennsylvania students call foul on coach. *Advocate: The National Gay and Lesbian Newsmagazine,* 23 April, 37.

Burroughs, A., L. Ashburn, and L. Seebohm. 1995. "Add sex and stir": Homophobic coverage of women's cricket in Australia. *Journal of Sport and Social Issues* 19 (3): 266-284.

Cahn, S. 1994. *Coming on strong: Gender and sexuality in twentieth century women's sport.* Toronto: Free Press.

———. 1996. "So far back in the closet we can't even see the keyhole": Lesbianism, homophobia, and sexual politics in collegiate women's athletics. In *The new lesbian studies,* ed. B. Zimmerman and T. McNaron. New York: City University of New York, Feminist Press.

Cantor, D., ed. 1994. *The religious right: The assault on tolerance and pluralism in America.* New York: Anti-Defamation League.

Cart, J. 1992. Lesbian issue stirs discussion. *Los Angeles Times,* 6 April, C1, C12.

Cayleff, S. 1995. *Babe: The life and legend of Babe Didrikson Zaharias.* Champaign: University of Illinois Press.

Chandler, L. 1996. Spotlight to shadow: Parsons looks back. *Charlotte Observer,* 30 March, 1A, 12A.

Chandler, T., and A. Goldberg. 1990. The academic all-American as vaunted adolescent role-identity. *Sociology of Sport Journal* 7:287-293.

Coe, R. 1986. *A sense of pride: The story of Gay Games II.* San Francisco: Pride Publications.

Colino, S. 1996. Perfect courtship: San Francisco boasts the NCAA's only husband and wife coaching team. *Sports Illustrated,* 18 March, R2.

Connell, R. 1992. A very straight gay: Masculinity, homosexual experience and the dynamics of gender. *American Sociological Review* 57 (6): 735-751.

Cowan, J. 1919. *The science of a new life.* New York: Ogilvie.

Cronin, D. 1996. Fine for fighting. *USA Today,* 22 November, C1.

Crosset, T. 1995. *Outsiders in the clubhouse: The world of the women's professional golf.* Albany: State University of New York Press.

Crosset, T., J. Benedict, and M. McDonald. 1995. Male-student-athletes reported for sexual assault: A survey of campus police departments and judicial affairs offices. *Journal of Sport and Social Issues* 19 (2): 127-140.

Cuniberti, B. 1978. Rookie Lopez cries at night. *Washington Post,* 12 June, D1, D8.

Curry, T. 1991. Fraternal bonding in the locker room: A pro-feminist analysis of talk about competition and women. *Sociology of Sport Journal* 8:119-135.

Curtis, J. 1996. Final Four is no longer a stretch for Lady Dons. *San Francisco Chronicle,* 25 March, E8.

Daily Hampshire Gazette. 1995. Golf analyst enrages players. 13 May, C1.

Davis, S. 1996. Religion and sports. *Philadelphia Tribune,* 3 December, PG.

Deford, F. 1993a. Do team sports culture encourage prospect of rape? *Morning Edition.* National Public Radio, 24 March. Available (by subscription): Electric Library, http://www.elibrary.com/getdoc.cgi?id=643...RL&pubname= Morning_Edition_(NPR)&puburl=0.

———. 1993b. Frank Deford reflects on coaches and girl athletes. *Morning Edition.* National Public Radio, 5 May. Available (by subscription): Electric Library, http://www3.elibrary.com/getdoc.cgi?id=64...RL&pubname= Morning_Edition_(NPR)&puburl=0.

de Mers, T. 1992. McCartney airs views on homosexuality at university press conference Monday. *Silver and Gold Record* (Boulder: University of Colorado.), 13 February, 1.

D'Emilio, J. 1983. *Sexual politics, sexual communities: The making of a homosexual minority in the United States 1940-1970.* Chicago: University of Chicago Press.

D'Emilio, J., and E. Freedman. 1988. *Intimate matters: A history of sexuality in America.* New York: Harper and Row.

Denney, M. 1992. Some attitudes haven't changed. *Fort Wayne News Sentinel* (Indiana), 15 July, 1S, 5S.

Diamond, S. 1989. *Spiritual warfare: The politics of the Christian right.* Boston: South End Press.

———. 1996. *Facing the wrath: Confronting the right in dangerous times.* Monroe, ME: Common Courage Press.

Diaz, J. 1989. Find the golf here? *Sports Illustrated,* 13 February, 58-64.

Dozier, W. 1995. Lesbian athletes fight against stereotyping. *Tampa Tribune,* 16 December, Bay Life section, 1, 3.

Duncan, M. 1997. Section III: Sociological dimension. In *The President's Council on Physical Fitness and Sports report: Physical activity in the lives of girls.* Minneapolis: University of Minnesota, Center for Research on Girls and Women in Sport.

Eliason, M. 1996. An inclusive model of lesbian identity assumption. *Journal of Gay, Lesbian and Bisexual Identity* 1 (1): 3-19.

Ellis, A., and E. Riggle. 1996. The relationship of job satisfaction and degree of openness about one's sexual orientation for lesbians and gay men. *Journal of Homosexuality* 30 (2): 75-85.

Engelmann, G. 1900. The American girl of today. *American Journal of Obstetrics,* December, 759.

Evert, C. (as told to C. Kirkpatrick). 1989. Tennis was my showcase. *Sports Illustrated,* 28 August, 72-79.

Exodus International. 1996. Overcoming lesbianism—Women and femininity. [August 14]. Available: http://www.messiah.edu/hpages/facstaff/chase/h/exodus/tapes/h3.htm.

Extracts, abstracts and notices of magazine articles. 1925. *American Physical Education Review* 30: 523-528.

Faderman, L. 1981. *Surpassing the love of men: Romantic friendship and love between women from the renaissance to the present.* New York: Morrow.

———. 1991. *Odd girls and twilight lovers: A history of lesbian life in twentieth century America.* New York: Columbia University Press.

Fans of Women's Sports. 1995. Fans in the stands. February/March, 7.

Feinstein, J. 1992. *Hard courts: Real life on the professional tennis tours.* New York: Villard.

Fellowship of Christian Athletes. 1996a. Fellowship of Christian Athletes' mission. [21 October]. Available: http://www.fca.org/mission.html.

Fellowship of Christian Athletes. 1996b. A heart yielded to God's game plan. [October 21]. Available: http://www.fca.org/stv-mar/mccartney.html.

Fellowship of Christian Athletes. 1996c. Locker room Q & A's. [October 21]. Available: http://www.fca.org/q6.html#homo.

Fellowship of Christian Athletes. 1996d. Up close with Tom Osborne. [October 21]. Available: http://www.fca.org/osborne.html.

Felshin, J. 1974. The triple option . . . for women in sport. *Quest* 21:36-40.

Festle, M.J. 1996. *Playing nice: Politics and apologies in women's sports.* New York: Columbia University Press.

Figel, B. 1986. Lesbians in the world of athletics. *Chicago Sun-Times,* 16 June, 119.

Forzley, R., and D. Hughes, eds. 1990. *The spirit captured: The official photojournal of Celebration 90: Gay Games III and cultural festival.* Vancouver, BC: For Eyes Only Press.

Frank, B. 1993. Straight/strait jackets for masculinity: Educating for "real" men. *Atlantis* 18 (1-2), 47-59.

Galindo, R. 1997. *Icebreaker.* New York: Pocketbooks.

Gallagher, J. 1992. Colorado coach's antigay comments spark dispute. *Advocate: The National Gay and Lesbian Newsmagazine,* 24 March, 28.

Garrity, J., and A. Nutt. 1996. No more disguises. *Sports Illustrated,* 18 March, 70-77.

Gay Community News. 1990. Girl soccer player's gender questioned. 11 November, 2.

Gerber, E., J. Felshin, P. Berlin, and W. Wyrick. 1974. *The American woman in sport.* Reading, MA: Addison-Wesley.

Gibson, P. 1989. Gay male and lesbian youth suicide. *Report of the Secretary's Task Force on Youth Suicide: Vol. 3. Prevention and interventions in youth suicide.* Washington, DC: Department of Health and Human Services.

Gilbert, B., and N. Williamson. 1973. Women in sport: Part 2. Are you being two-faced? *Sports Illustrated,* 4 June, 47.

Golf Illustrated. 1987. Gallery shots: The image lady. July, 9.

Gomes, P. 1996. *The good book: Discovering the Bible's place in our lives.* New York: Morrow.

Gornick, V. 1971. Ladies of the links. *Look* 35 (10): 69-76.

Grack, C., and C. Richman. 1996. Reducing general and specific heterosexism through cooperative contact. *Journal of Psychology and Human Sexuality* 8 (4): 59-68.

Griffin, P. 1988. How to identify homophobia in women's sports. In *National Coaching Institute applied research papers,* ed. M. Adrian. Reston, VA: American Alliance for Health, Physical Education, Recreation and Dance.

———. 1992a. Changing the game: Homophobia, sexism and lesbians in sport. *Quest* 44 (2): 251-265.

———. 1992b. From hiding out to coming out: Empowering lesbian and gay educators. In *Coming out of the classroom closet: Gay and lesbian students, teachers and curricula,* ed. K. Harbeck. New York: Haworth.

———. 1994. Homophobia in sport: Addressing the needs of lesbian and gay high school athletes. In *The gay teen,* ed. G. Unks. New York: Routledge.

———. 1996. The lesbian experience in sport: The good, the bad and the ugly. In *The new our right to love: A lesbian resource book,* ed. G. Vida. New York: Touchstone.

———. 1997. The lesbian athlete: Unlearning the culture of the closet. In *A queer world: The Center for Lesbian and Gay Studies reader,* ed. M. Duberman. New York: New York University.

Gustkey, E. 1995. Married . . . with players: USF co-coaches Bill and Mary Nepfel share life (and a bench) in a successful program. *Los Angeles Times,* 23 February, Sports section, 1.

Guthrie, S. 1982. Homophobia: Its impact on women in sport and physical education. Master's thesis, California State University, Long Beach.

Hall, C. 1996. Dinah Shore week: It's ultimate girls' night out. *Los Angeles Times,* 31 March, home edition, A3.

Hall, M.A., ed. 1987. The gendering of sport, leisure and physical education. *Women's Studies International Forum* 10 (4).

———. 1996. *Feminism and sporting bodies.* Champaign, IL: Human Kinetics.

Hastings, J. 1918. Are we giving the child a square deal? *Women's Century,* special issue, 152.

Heath, B. 1996. Spencer-Devlin aftermath. Gannett News Service, 13 March. Available (by subscription): Electric Library, http://www.elibrary.com/getdoc.cgi?id=643...=RL&pubname=Gannett_News_Service&puburl=0.

Herek, G. 1994. Assessing heterosexuals' attitudes toward lesbians and gay men: A review of the empirical research with the ATLG scale. In *Lesbian and gay psychology: Theory, research and clinical applications,* edited by B. Greene and G. Herek. Thousand Oaks, CA: Sage.

Herek, G., and J. Capitanio. 1996. "Some of my best friends": Intergroup contact, concealable stigma and heterosexuals' attitudes toward gay men and lesbians. *Personality and Social Psychology Bulletin* 22 (4): 412-424.

Herman, D. 1997. *The anti-gay agenda: Orthodox vision and the Christian right.* Chicago: University of Chicago.

Hicks, B. 1979. Lesbian athletes. *Christopher Street,* October, 42-49.

———. 1981. The Billie Jean King affair. *Christopher Street,* July, 12-17.

Hill, J., and R. Cheadle. 1996. *The Bible tells me so: Uses and abuses of the holy scripture.* New York: Anchor Books/Doubleday.

Hodges, M. 1995. The lesbian presence, both among players and fans. Gannett News Service, 12 May. Available (by subscription): Electric Library, http://www2.elibrary.com/getdoc.cgi?id=54343505x0y688&OIDs=0Q003D027&Form=RL.

Howard, J. 1997. Betrayal of trust. *Sports Illustrated Women/Sport,* spring, 66-77.

Hudson, M. 1995a. CBS keeps Wright after he denies remarks on LPGA. *Los Angeles Times,* 13 May, C1.

———. 1995b. When a coach crosses the line: America's gymnastics federation is leading a tough campaign to reduce the potential for sex abuse in a sport that often involves close contact. *Los Angeles Times,* 20 May, home edition, A1.

Huntington, A. 1997. Interview with Terry Gross. *Fresh Air.* National Public Radio, 18 March.

Kane, M.J., and L. Disch. 1993. Sexual violence and the reproduction of male power in the locker room: The "Lisa Olsen incident." *Sociology of Sport Journal* 10 (4): 331-352.

Katz, J. 1983. *Gay/lesbian almanac.* New York: Harper and Row.

———. 1995. *The invention of heterosexuality.* New York: Dutton.

Kaufman, M. 1993. The last bastion: Homosexuality remains a taboo subject in sports. *Detroit Free Press,* 23 April, C1, C6.

Kavanagh, K. 1995. Don't ask, don't tell: Deception required, disclosure denied. *Psychology, Public Policy and the Law* 1 (1): 142-160.

Kenealy, A. 1899. Woman as athlete. *Living Age* 3:368-369.

Kidd, F. 1935. Is basketball a girl's game? *Hygeia* 13:834.

King, B.J., and F. Deford. 1982. *Billie Jean.* New York: Viking.

King, M., and M. O'Neil. 1993. Lesbianism, women's sports and wearing dresses. *Seattle Gay News,* 12 March, 12-13.

Kinsey, A., W. Pomeroy, and C. Martin. 1948. *Sexual behavior in the human male.* Philadelphia: Saunders.

———. 1953. *Sexual behavior in the human female.* Philadelphia: Saunders.

Kirshenbaum, J. 1981. Facing up to Billie Jean's revelations. *Sports Illustrated,* 11 May, 13.

Kitzinger, C. 1987. *The social construction of lesbianism.* London: Sage.

———. 1996. Speaking of oppression: Psychology, politics, and the language of power. In *Preventing heterosexism and homophobia,* ed. E. Rothblum and L. Bond. Thousand Oaks, CA: Sage.

Knapp, G. 1995. Homophobia still par for the course. *San Francisco Examiner,* 30 November, D1.

———. 1997. Another case of don't ask, don't tell. *San Francisco Examiner,* 30 March, B1.

Krane, V. 1996a. Lesbians in sport: Toward acknowledgment, understanding and theory. *Journal of Sport and Exercise Psychology* 18:237-246.

———. 1996b. Performance related outcomes experienced by lesbian athletes. Paper presented at the Association for the Advancement of Applied Sport Psychology, 29 September, New Orleans.

Kupelian, V. 1995. Ben Wright wouldn't be the first person to . . . Gannett News Service, 13 May. Available (by subscription): Electric Library, http://www2.elibrary.com/getdoc.cgi?id=5434505x0y688&OIDS=0Q001D008&Form=RL.

Lackey, D. 1990. Sexual harassment in sports. *Physical Educator* 47 (2): 18-25.

Latimer, J. 1996. Athletes admit abuse. *Herizons* 10:12.

Labrecque, L. 1994. *Unity: A celebration of Gay Games IV and Stonewall.* San Francisco: Lebrecque Publishing.

Lederman, D. 1991. Penn State coach's comments about lesbian athletes may be used to test university's new policy on bias. *Chronicle of Higher Education,* 5 June, A27-A28.

Lenskyj, H. 1986. *Out of bounds: Women, sport and sexuality.* Toronto: Women's Press.

———. 1990. Power and play: Gender and sexuality issues in sport and physical activity. *International Review for the Sociology of Sport* 25 (3): 235-245.

———. 1991. Combating homophobia in sport and physical education. *Sociology of Sport Journal* 8 (1): 61-69.

———. 1992. Unsafe at home base: Women's experiences of sexual harassment in university sport and physical education. *Women's Sport and Physical Activity Journal* 1 (1): 19-33.

Lieber, J., and J. Kirshenbaum. 1982. Stormy weather at South Carolina. *Sports Illustrated,* 8 February, 30-37.

Lieberman-Cline, N. (with N. Jennings). 1992. *Lady magic.* Champaign, IL: Sagamore.

Lipsyte, R. 1991. Gay bias moves off the sidelines. *New York Times,* 24 May, B1.

———. 1994. Relaxed in a game of their own. *New York Times,* 26 June, 15.

Longman, J. 1991. Lions women's basketball coach is used to fighting and winning. *Philadelphia Inquirer,* 10 March, 1G, 6G.

Lorde, A. 1984. *Sister outsider.* Freedom, CA: Crossing Press.

Louganis, G., and E. Marcus. 1995. *Breaking the surface.* New York: Random House.

Lurie, R. 1994. Martina and me: A trilogy. In *Sportsdykes,* edited by S.F. Rogers. New York: St. Martin's.

Manasso, J. 1994. Athletes may feel pressured. Gannett News Service, 2 January. Available (by subscription): Electric Library, http://www3.elibrary.com/getdoc.cgi?id=64...=RL&pubname=Gannett_News_Service&puburl=0.

Mansfield, S. 1997. Major party women go to the Dinah for the golf and for the scene that has grown up around the tournament. *Sports Illustrated,* 7 April, G6.

McCall, C. 1981a. The Billie Jean King case: A friend's outrage. *Ms.,* July, 100.

McCall, C. 1981b. Larry and Billie Jean King work to renew their marriage and put her affair behind them. *People,* 25 May, 73-79.

Mechem, C. 1995. LPGA column is cruelty disguised as commentary. *USA Today,* 23 May, C3. Available: LGB-sports listserv, http://www.kwic.net/lgb-sports/.

Messner, M. 1992. *Power at play: Sports and the problem of masculinity.* Boston: Beacon.

Messner, M., and D. Sabo. 1994. *Sex, violence and power in sport: Rethinking masculinity.* Freedom, CA: Crossing Press.

Mewshaw, M. 1993. *Ladies of the court: Grace and disgrace on the women's tennis tour.* New York: Crown.

Monaghan, P. 1992. U. of Colorado football coach accused of using his position to promote his religious views. *Chronicle of Higher Education,* 11 November, A37(2).

Moore, D. 1991. Athletes and rape: Alarming link. *USA Today,* 27 August, C1-C2.

Mosbacher, D. 1992. *Out for a change: Addressing homophobia in women's sports.* Produced and directed by Dee Mosbacher and Woman Vision Educational Media Productions. Videocassette and study guide. San Francisco: University of California Extension Center for Media and Independent Learning.

Nack, W., and L. Munson. 1995. Special report: Sports' dirty secret: When scarcely a week passes without an athlete being accused of domestic violence it is no longer possible to look the other way. *Sports Illustrated,* 31 July, 62-74.

Navratilova, M., and G. Vecsey. 1985. *Martina.* New York: Knopf.

Neimark, J. 1991. Out of bounds: The truth about athletes and rape. *Mademoiselle,* May, 196-199, 244.

Nelson, M.B. 1991. *Are we winning yet? How women are changing sports and sports are changing women.* New York: Random House.

———. 1994. *The stronger women get, the more men love football: Sexism and the American culture of sport.* New York: Harcourt Brace.

Newton, E. 1989. The mythic mannish lesbian: Radclyffe Hall and the new woman. In *Hidden from history: Reclaiming the gay and lesbian past,* ed. M. Duberman. New York: New American Library.

New York Times. 1995. Questions at LPGA not about game. 13 May, 29.

Novosad, N. 1996. God squad. *Progressive* 60 (8): 25-27.

Palzkill, B. 1990. Between gymshoes and high heels: The development of a lesbian identity and existence in top class sport. *International Review for the Sociology of Sport* 25 (3): 221-234.

Parry, A. 1912. The relation of athletics to the reproductive life of woman. *American Journal of Obstetrics* 66:348-349.

Patrick, D. 1996. San Francisco's success forces marital teamwork. *USA Today,* 21 March, C5.

Patton, C. 1990. Gay Games III. *Z Magazine* 3 (11): 98-102.

Peper, K. 1994. Female athlete = lesbian: A myth constructed from gender role expectations and lesbiphobia. In *Queer words, queer images,* edited by J. Ringer. New York: New York University.

Pharr, S. 1986. *Homophobia: A weapon of sexism.* Inverness, CA: Chardon Press.

———. 1996. *In the time of the right: Reflections on liberation.* Berkeley, CA: Chardon Press.

Phelan, S. 1994. *Getting specific: Postmodern lesbian politics.* Minneapolis: University of Minnesota.

Phillips, J. 1995. Intolerable. *Women's Sports and Fitness* 18:23.

Pitts, B. 1994. Leagues of their own: Growth and development of lesbian and gay sport in America. Presented at the First Gay Games Congress of Athletics, 17 June, Arts & Sciences, Baruch College, New York.

Plowman, E. 1972. Campus crusade: Into all the world. *Christianity Today,* 9 June, 38.

Potter, J. 1996. Controversy resurrects old theme. *USA Today,* 15 May, C1-C2.

Pratt, M. 1993. The all-American girls' professional baseball league. In *Women in sport: Issues and controversies,* ed. G. Cohen. Newbury Park, CA: Sage.

President's Council on Physical Fitness and Sports. 1997. *The President's Council on Physical Fitness and Sports report: Physical activity in the lives of girls.* Minneapolis: University of Minnesota, Center for Research on Girls and Women in Sport.

Price, D. 1995. LPGA lesbians should just come out swinging. *USA Today,* 19 May, C3.

Pronger, B. 1990. *The arena of masculinity: Sports, homosexuality, and the meaning of sex.* Toronto: University of Toronto Press.

Rankin, S. 1995. The perceptions of heterosexual faculty and administrators toward gay men and lesbians. PhD diss., Pennsylvania State University, 1994. Abstract in *Dissertation Abstracts International* A 56/03:841 (Order # AAC9518849).

———. In press. The lesbian label in women's intercollegiate athletics. In *Working with lesbian, gay, and bisexual college students: A guide for administrators and faculty,* edited by R. Sanlo. Westport, CT: Greenwood.

Rentzel, L. 1987. *Emotional dependency: A threat to close friendships.* San Raphael, CA: Exodus International.

Richardson, D. 1997. Sex, lies and softball. *Sports Illustrated Women/Sport,* spring, 40-44.

Riley, L., W. Anderson, and G. Garber. 1992. Stereotyping builds a barrier for women. *Hartford Courant,* 25 May, B1, B6.

Roberts, S. 1981. Bad form, Billie Jean. *Newsweek,* 25 May, 19.

Rogers, S.F. 1994. *Sportsdykes.* New York: St. Martin's.

Rotello, G. 1995. Lesbians in golf's locker room closet. *New York Newsday,* 18 May. Available: LGB-sports listserv, http://www.kwic.net/lgb-sports/.

Rutkoski, R. 1996. Religion: Jocks and God, together on the field. Gannett News Service, 7 October. Available (by subscription): Electric Library, http://www3.elibrary.com/getdoc.cgi?id=64...=RL&pubname=Gannett_News_Service&puburl=0.

Ryan, J. 1995. *Little girls in pretty boxes: The making and breaking of elite gymnasts and figure skaters.* New York: Doubleday.

Sabo, D., and M. Messner, eds. 1990. *Sport, men and the gender order: Critical feminist perspectives.* Champaign, IL: Human Kinetics.

San Francisco Chronicle [Associated Press]. 1995. Golf analyst in trouble for remarks on lesbians. 13 May, A1, A13.

Scanzoni, L., and V. Mollenkott. 1994. *Is the homosexual my neighbor? A positive Christian response.* San Francisco: Harper Collins.

Scarton, D. 1992. Coming to terms with women, sports. *Seattle Times/Seattle Post-Intelligencer,* 27 December, F7.

Schwartz, H. 1997. Out of bounds. *Advocate: The National Gay and Lesbian Newsmagazine,* 18 March, 56-59.

Sedgewick, E. 1990. *The epistemology of the closet.* Berkeley: University of California Press.

Shapiro, L. 1997. Using the gridiron as a pulpit, many players publicly display their religious convictions. *Washington Post,* 19 January, D1, D6.

Solomons, A. 1991. Passing game: How lesbians are being purged from women's college hoops. *Village Voice,* 20 March, 92.

South, J., M. Glynn, J. Rodack, and R. Cappettini. 1990. New gay sex scandal rocks tennis. *National Enquirer,* 30 July, 20-21.

Spander, D. 1991. It's a question of acceptability: Homosexuality in sport is still a delicate topic. *Sacramento Bee,* 1 September, D1, D14, D15.

Spong, J. 1992. *Rescuing the Bible from fundamentalism.* San Francisco: Harper.

Sykes, H. 1996. Constr(i)(u)cting lesbian identities in physical education: Feminist and poststructural approaches to researching sexuality. *Quest* 48:459-469.

Szekely, P. 1996. LPGA tour player Spencer-Devlin declares she is gay. Reuters, 12 March. Available (by subscription): Electric Library, http://www2.elibrary.com/getdoc.cgi?id=54343505x0y688&OIDS=0Q007D000 &Form=RL.

Theberge, N. 1987. Sport and women's empowerment. *Women's Studies International Forum* 10 (4): 387-394.

Turque, B. 1992. Gays under fire. *Newsweek,* 14 September, 34-40.

Uihlein, W. 1997. My shot: Out of bounds. [Golf plus/news and notes]. *Sports Illustrated,* 28 April, G20.

USA Today. 1991. Sportsview: Athletes and rape. 27 August, C8.

Vaid, U. 1995. *Virtual equality: The mainstreaming of gay and lesbian liberation.* New York: Anchor.

Vecsey, G. 1981. Athlete as an idol—and human frailty. *New York Times,* 15 May.

Waddell, T., and D. Schaap. 1996. *Gay Olympian: The life and death of Dr. Tom Waddell.* New York: Random House.

White, B. 1995. Top 10 jobs Ben Wright can take . . . Gannett New Service, 12 May. Available (by subscription): Electric Library, http://www2.elibrary.com/getdoc.cgi?id=5434505x0y688&OIDS=0Q006D007&Form=RL.

Wilkinson, S., and C. Kitzinger, eds. 1993. *Heterosexuality.* London: Sage.

Wilson, N. 1995. *Our tribe: Queer folk, God, Jesus and the Bible.* San Francisco: Harper.

Wilstein, S. 1996. The gay emergence. *San Francisco Chronicle,* 21 June, E1, E7.

Witherspoon, W. 1995. Closer scrutiny: Recent cases of alleged sexual misconduct may prompt county coaches to polish up tarnished image. *Los Angeles Times,* 3 October, Orange County edition, special section 1.

Woog, D. 1995. *School's out: The impact of gay and lesbian issues on America's schools.* Boston: Alyson.

———. 1998. *Jocks: True tales of America's gay male athletes.* Los Angeles: Alyson.

Wright, B. 1992. Lesbians' banner makes UW game arena for cause. *News Tribune,* 3 March, C1.

Yelaja, P. 1995. Speaking of boobs . . . *Newsday,* 13 May, A5.

Young, P.D. 1994. *Lesbians and gays and sports: Issues in lesbian and gay life.* New York: Chelsea House.

Zipay, S. 1996. CBS drops Wright as golf analyst. *Newsday,* 10 January, A52.

Zipter, Y. 1988a. *Diamonds are a dyke's best friend.* Ithaca, NY: Firebrand.

———. 1988b. The double play or, love on the softball field. *Outlook* 1 (3): 32-35.

Zwerman, G. 1995. *Martina Navratilova: Lives of notable gay men and lesbians.* New York: Chelsea House.

Index